Showers and Raindrops

Showers and Raindrops

Fifty Years of Reflections on
Eritrea, Ethiopia and Sweden
(1970–2020)

By
Ezra Gebremedhin

THE RED SEA PRESS
TRENTON | LONDON | NEW DELHI | CAPE TOWN | NAIROBI | ADDIS ABABA | ASMARA | IBADAN

THE RED SEA PRESS
541 West Ingham Avenue | Suite B
Trenton, New Jersey 08638

Copyright © 2023 Ezra Gebremedhin

All rights reserved. No part of this publication may be reproduced, stored in a retrieval system or transmitted in any form or by any means electronic, mechanical, photocopying, recording or otherwise without the prior written permission of the publisher.

Book design: Dawid Kahts
Cover design: Martin Nilsson

Cataloging-in-Publication Data may be obtained from the Library of Congress.

ISBNs: 978-1-56902-813-1 (HB)
        978-1-56902-814-8 (PB)

Table of Contents

Dedication	xi
The Cover Photo	xiii
Preface	xv
Acknowledgments	xxi
Chapter 1. Discovering and Making Sweden Our Home (1973)	1
Chapter 2. Coffee Instead of Machine Guns (1975)	11
Chapter 3. A Letter to King Carl XVI Gustaf of Sweden on the Ethio-Eritrean Conflict (1975)	21
Chapter 4. Rain-Drops: Extracts from My Diary (1974–1994)	25
Chapter 5. Generators of Contact and Conflict among Swedes and Ethiopian and Eritrean Refugees (I) (1997, 2020)	37
Chapter 6. Generators of Contact and Conflict among Swedes and Ethiopian and Eritrean Refugees (II): Points of Contact (1997)	45
Chapter 7. Generators of Contact and Conflict among Swedes and Ethiopian and Eritrean Refugees (III): Possible Generators of Conflict (1997)	57

Chapter 8.
The Undying Call to Dialogue—
Some Parting Words (2001)   69

Chapter 9.
Salt (2001)   73

Chapter 10.
As We Move On (I):
Respect for Our Common Humanity (2002)   75

Chapter 11.
As We Move On (II):
Respect for the Integrity of the Individual (2002)   79

Chapter 12.
A Giver's Request:
Some Personal Words on asmarino.com (2002)   83

Chapter 13.
The Years in Sweden—
Have They Influenced My Theology? (2002)   87

Chapter 14.
Recurring Festivals and Memorials:
To What End? (2002)   95

Chapter 15.
On The Wings of New Year's Day (I):
Taught by Yesterday (2002)   101

Chapter 16.
On The Wings of New Year's Day (II):
Poised for Tomorrow (2002)   107

Chapter 17.
Where Is My Mother? (I) (2002)   111

Chapter 18.
Where Is My Mother? (II):
The Necessity of Reciprocity (2002)   115

Chapter 19.
Encounter or Confrontation? (2003)   121

Table of Contents

Chapter 20.
Bus Eritrea (2003, 2020) — 129

Chapter 21.
Roots Unlimited (2003) — 137

Chapter 22.
For Light and Life: Portraits of Four Women (2003) — 143

Chapter 23.
The Body and the Self: More Rain-Drops
(1973–1996) — 149

Chapter 24.
While We Wait (2003) — 155

Chapter 25.
Pentecostalism: Risk or Resource (I)—
Introduction (2019) — 159

Chapter 26.
Pentecostalism: Risk or Resource (II)—
A Resource in Several Senses (2004, 2019) — 169

Chapter 27.
Pentecostalism: Risk or Resource (III)—
Wheat Mixed with Tares. (2004, 2020) — 177

Chapter 28.
Some Comments on my Articles on Pentecostalism:
An Interview with Dr. Agne Nordlander (2019) — 189

Chapter 29.
On the Seasons around Uppsala (I): (2004–2005) — 197

Chapter 30.
On the Seasons around Uppsala (II): (2005, 2019) — 207

Chapter 31.
Glimpses from Eritrea's Battlefields (I):
Reflections on Nakfa—
The Town on the Rock (2005) — 215

Chapter 32.
Glimpses from Eritrea's Battlefields (II):
Nakfa and Nadew Commands as Remembered
by Ethiopian Generals (2005, 2019)   225

Chapter 33.
Glimpses from Eritrea's Battlefields (III):
Göran Assbring (1950–1983), a Swede Who Gave
His Life for Eritrea (2019)   235

Chapter 34.
Michela Wrong: A British Journalist's Narrative on
Eritrea's Struggles (2005)   247

Chapter 35.
Water (2005)   251

Chapter 36.
A Nordic Perspective on Ethiopia and Eritrea
(2005, 2019)   253

Chapter 37.
The Cough Which Was Permitted (2010)   257

Chapter 38.
Aboy Aregai Kibreab:
A Person Who Helped Me Discover
Eritrea in Sweden (2012)   259

Chapter 39.
Words Along the Way (2013)   271

Chapter 40.
Our Way to the Referendum on Eritrea
(April 17, 1993, Uppsala, Sweden) (1993, 2020)   275

Chapter 41.
Integration (I): Sweden's Growing Challenge (2019)   283

Chapter 42.
Integration (II):
Ethiopians and Eritreans Meet the Challenge (2019)   295

Chapter 43.
Integration (III):
An Ethio-Swedish Family
Makes Sweden Its Home (2019)   309

Chapter 44.
A Farewell to Cars! (2005)   313

Chapter 45.
Eritrea's Nevertheless! (2010)   317

Epilogue (2020)   325

This work is dedicated to the People of Eritrea, Ethiopia and Sweden, with gratitude.

The Cover Photo

The title of this book begins with the words *Showers and Rain-Drops*. And here, in the cover photo, we have two women making or mending *qoffos* (ቆፎታት, the Tigrinja word for storage-baskets for grain). I can imagine that the inquisitive reader would begin wondering about the connection between the word "rain" in our title and "grain-baskets" in the photo. My answer would be: These words belong to the same family. They are related in the way that cause is related to effect, a source to a product, or a parent to a child. Indeed, in the last analysis, "showers" and "rain-drops" are the reasons, the rationale behind the existence of *qoffos*.

Who then are these women? The woman standing to the left, in the picture, is my mother, Aster Woldemariam. At the time when the picture was taken, she was 22 years old. Her co-worker in the rustic skill of making *qoffos* was a close family friend by the name of Sema'itu Awalom. I remember that she had a brother by the name of Ezra Awalom in Addis Ababa. People called him *Hakim Ezra* (Doctor Ezra), although he was a dresser or a nurse in the field of optical care (and a skillful one at that), trained, at least partly, by Swedish missionaries.

Aster and Sema'itu would receive the benefits of a basic education at the Swedish Mission at Addi Ugri (ዓዲ ዉግሪ) or Mendefera (መንደፈራ) in Eritrea. They were taught not only to read and write but also to use their hands in the practice of various home and family skills. One of their teachers was Rosa Holmer, the wife of Pastor Mikael Holmer, a missionary who was so highly revered that he was nick-named *Qiddus Mikael* (St. Michael)!

In a deeper sense, these women became the receivers and mediators of the blessings that showers and rain-drops can bring. Without the likes of these women, rain and grain-baskets would have hardly any meaning. These women, representatives of mothers in Eritrea, Ethiopia, and Sweden, were gifts from above. They too were "Showers and Rain-Drops."

My mother was buried in Asmara on May 14, 2000, at the age of one hundred years (less a month!), after having spent her last ten years with a sister of mine, Naomi, and her husband, Bruce Reed, in Los Alamitos, California. Mother was laid to rest at the cemetery called *Tsetserat* (ጸጸራት), in Asmara, in the presence of all her children but far from our father's grave in Addis Ababa. What is more, she was buried on one of the first days of a reignited war between Ethiopia and Eritrea. In fact, I remember seeing a jet plane or two in the skies of Asmara on the day of her funeral.

I can't forget what fellow-mourners said to us, relatives, as they made their farewell bows after the funeral: "May she leave moisture (meaning 'rain'), after her!" (በሊ ይግደፋልና ።). I am sure that a similar wish was expressed at the funeral of her friend Sema'itu!

Is our book title something of an echo of this wish?

Preface

round the year 1966, my senior pastor in Addis Ababa, Qes Bademma Yalew, told me the following story:

> An Ethiopian Orthodox Christian came to his father-confessor for confession on Good Friday. The penitent said, Father, Absolve Me! I broke the fast (meaning Lent) just a week after its beginning and also just a week before its end (አባቴ ይፍቱኝ፨ ጾም በገባ በሳምንቱ ገደፍኩ፨ ጾም ሊወጣ ሳምንት ሲቀረው ደግሞ ገደፍኩ፨).
>
> The Father-Confessor said, What audacity! So you would neither let the fast come in, nor come out! I order you to do 100 prostrations (ምን ዓይነት ድፍረት ነው፨ ጾሙን ሲገባ አላስገባም ሲወጣ አላስወጣም ማለትህ ነው? በል መቶ ስገድ፨).

Beginnings and Ends! Openings and conclusions! They can be worrisome also in other areas of life...writing a book, for example! I found it difficult to get started with this book, which consists of a number of articles on different and often unrelated subjects. I am also finding it difficult to bring the book to an end by writing a fitting Preface. Like the penitent mentioned above, I have broken my "fast," my challenge to abstain from worrying both at the beginning and at the end of my work with this book. I am now prepared to do my penance. I have decided not to allow worrying to become "a breaking of the fast." I shall let my dream of writing this book—my "fast"—come in peacefully and run its course peacefully.

The articles were written over a long period of time, at different places and under a variety of circumstances, between 1970 and 2020 (a period of fifty years), in Sweden but also in other countries. I would like to add that the articles appear in chronological order, with some exceptions. Some specific topics, on which I have written in detail, appear in clusters of more than one chapter under the same basic title. These are the heavier "showers" in this collection of articles. Chronological annotations like "2005

(2020)" mean that the original article was written in 2005 but that it was subjected to some kind of minor adjustments or updating or comments in 2020. My basic scheme of presentation is chronological, but not rigidly so.

At times, my concern to keep articles that deal with a common theme together does result in a departure from the strictly chronological scheme.

Some articles are based on purposeful planning and the gathering of facts. They reminded me of *Showers*. Other articles are pieces of writing noted down in obedience to impulses and inner nudges. They are the Rain-Drops. They were recorded at home, in libraries, at seminars, at railway stations, on trains, in hotel-rooms, and at the monastery called *Östanbäcks Kloster*, near Sala, Sweden.

This is one of the very few monasteries and convents within the (Lutheran) Church of Sweden. The monastery follows the Rule of St. Benedict. I used to come to this monastery in search of a quiet milieu for studies, rest, and guidance in my spiritual life.

A good friend, Tekeste Negash, wrote, "I did not know many of your writings at www.asmarino.com and other websites which portray another Aboy Keshi—more militant than I ever imagined. Well, we are all like the proverbial five blind men trying to describe an elephant."

I am sure that there is a polemical element in my writing, but I hope that I won't be a total disappointment to my readers! Another friend, Dr. Redie Bereketeab, writes:

> One of the major contributions, in my view, is that it touches the heart of the problem Eritrea and Eritreans are currently facing. Some of the problems are: the absence of listening to one another, tolerance, compromising, negotiations, dialogue, respecting opinion of others, in a nutshell, lack of a culture of peace and peaceful debate. In societal issues, there is no one reality only, therefore acknowledgement of that fact will go a long way, on how we communicate with each other. The advice and words of wisdom you are offering are what Eritreans need at the moment. I hope they will heed it.

I appreciate such words of encouragement.

It took me a long time to find a title to my liking. At last my publisher and I settled for the formulation: *Showers and Rain-Drops: Fifty Years of Reflections on Eritrea, Ethiopia and Sweden(1970–2020)*. The title reflects the way the articles in the book came about. It is proper that I begin with reference to Sweden, the country that has become my present homeland and has provided me with my base of reflections for almost 50 years.

There is a statement that I have quoted in several connections in my different writings through the years in Sweden. The words of the Jewish philosopher Martin Buber, an Austrian: *All real living is meeting!* In other words, all genuine existence is an encounter of hearts. It is my sincere wish that the articles in this book may contribute, in some small measure, to the kind of meeting of minds and hearts that Buber had in mind.

The reader will meet my reflections on Ethiopia and Eritrea, basically from Sweden as a point of departure. And there is something that unites my reflections on these three countries. Their contacts go back to a period that covers over 150 years. What is more, Sweden has become a home for thousands of persons with roots in Ethiopia and Eritrea.

If I were to specify the underlying goal of this book, I would say the following: I want to share, inform, and challenge. First, I want to share my *experiences* in Sweden. Among other things I have taken the seasons of Sweden to my help. In the second place, I want to provide as much *information* on Swedish society as I possibly can in the limited space that is available to me. In the third place I want to challenge my readers to appreciate the admirable culture of *open and free dialogue* in Sweden, and to learn from it.

A Preponderance of Articles on Eritrea

The majority of the articles in this book are on Eritrea. Most of the reflections in this category belong to what I would call *Showers*, i.e., the longer and more detailed treatments of specific titles. One can of course ask why the majority of my reflections deal with Eritrea, in spite of the fact that I was born and brought up in Ethiopia and spent a good part of my adult life there. A friend who knows this fact reminded me that Eritrea was the "Mother" that I didn't know!

My answer would be: Ethiopia is indeed "My Mother." I was born, brought up, nurtured, and honoured on her soil. Love and honour to her! At the same time, I cherish my ancestry, true to biblical precedent. I would speak in the spirit of the Bible (see Matthew 1.1–16!) if I were to say that I am "Ezra, son of Gebremedhin," a person who loved and fought for Ethiopia and was a veteran of the battles of Maitchew and Amba Aradom, but never forgot his Eritrean roots.

As a person born of Eritrean parents, I knew much more about Eritrea than many of my Ethiopian friends believed. Furthermore, coming to Sweden in 1970 brought me to a land with thousands of Eritrean refugees and immigrants. As a pastor among them I found my way into contacts and relations that became literally schools for the development of my use of Tigrinja as a language. These contacts also led to the deepening of my knowledge of Eritrea's history, regions, languages, cultural traits, and the years of armed struggle for self-determination. My involvement in the activities of the Swedish branch of the *Eritrean War-Disabled Fighters Veterans Association* (EWDFA) [later E.N.W.D.V.A – Eritrean National War-Disabled Veterans Association] for over twenty years gave me opportunities to visit Eritrea on several occasions and to meet Eritreans at home. I can say that I met and came to know Eritrea in depth here in Sweden. That explains the reason for the abundance of reflections on Eritrea in this book.

Some friends have asked me, "What is your central theme? What is the main plot, the red-thread in your story?"

I have no answer to this question. I wish that this work were a one-bodied, organically united narrative. It is not. It is more of a *smörgåsbord*, to use a Swedish word, a table with dishes of different kinds, both soft and solid food. To my reader I would like to say: Please choose and help your self![1]

Notes

1 A longtime friend, Dr. Bereket Yebio writes, "In my previous communication with you I was more concerned with the format. In your Preface, you have now given a more structured presentation which gives the reader answers to the questions of what? why? and how? I like your style of communicating." Such words are a source of encouragement.

Acknowledgments

I have found myself more of a companion, a team-member, than a client, in the adventure that led to the shaping and publication of this book. In the person of Ato Kassahun Checole, The Head of Red Sea Press, I found not only a publisher but also an engaged and compassionate co-editor. This book took shape, in good measure, at Red Sea Press, even though the building blocks, articles written in the course of my almost fifty years in Sweden, had been shaped long before. I thank Brother Kassahun from the depth of my heart.

I met his younger co-worker, Girma Demeke, in person only once. It didn't take me long to conclude that he too was a quiet and alert giver of support, a faithful workman, whose presence I felt from a quiet, though invisible, background. Thank you, Girma!

Prior to the publication of the book, there were several friends who read either the whole book or sections of it and came with encouragement and suggestions. Among those who read sections or the entire text of the earliest version of the book and gave their considered comments are Dr. Bereket Yebio, Dr. Tekeste Negash, Engineers Karl-Erik Lundgren and Karl-Gustaf Lundgren, Pastor Paul Persson, Pastor Hans Lindholm, Dr. Agne Nordlander, Dr. Tomas Nygren, Dr. (Med.) Maria Nygren, Dr. Yoahnnes Zeiler, Dr. Marianne Wifstrand Schiebe, Engineer Naigzy Gebremedhin, Dr. Viveca Halldin Norberg, Academy Steward Per Ström, Ato Herui Tedla, and Patent Engineer Lisa Assbring. Dr. Redie Bereketeab and Dr. Mussie Msghina came in at a late stage in my editorial work. Their comments were both relevant and encouraging. I can say, in all honesty, that all of these friends have put heart and mind into the reading of parts or of the whole of the more or less complete draft of my book, and encouraged me, often in words that I don't feel that I deserve. I am particularly grateful to my brother, Naigzy Gebremedhin, and Pastor Paul Persson for reading through the first version of the text in great detail and for making well-considered and detailed comments. Ingvar Svanberg, who came to my aid generously in an earlier essay, written almost thirty years ago, gave me some newer titles related to integration into Swedish society.¹ I am sincerely grateful to him.

My ever-loyal and generous brother, Naigzy Gebremedhin, provided the funds needed to prepare a print-ready text of the book. He has followed and commented upon this book right up to the time of publication. I thank him from the bottom of my heart. Chapter 45, entitled "Eritrea's Nevertheless!" is dedicated to him.

Girum Fantaye, a family-friend and a highly effective "trouble shooter" who lives in Addis Ababa, has helped me in securing Amharic-language literature and pictures on the persons and Eritrea-related missions of Ethiopian generals like Brigadier General Tesfaye Hailemariam and Brigadier General Tariku Ayné, both of whom are regarded as outstanding military actors in the war-scene in Eritrea. Through Girum I want to thank these Ethiopian men of arms and their relatives. Biniam Yohannes did all the insertions of Tigrinja and Amarinja words and expressions into the text of this book. I thank him for his humility and diligence.

A number of the articles printed in the present book were originally published on *asmarino.com* or on *www.dehai.org*. Whenever possible I have pointed to this fact in connection with the publication of said articles in this book. I am deeply grateful to the two websites for the venues that they once provided me. It has been years since many of my articles were published. I plead for understanding in case I have failed to locate and mention further articles by way of appreciation.

My friend and former-coworker in two publications in Sweden, Martin Nilsson, was not with me at the outset of the present project. When he noted my sighs of need, known to him from previous publication projects, he did not hesitate to quietly glide in and place himself on our side. Step by step, his gift in giving form to my formless texts and his skill in giving form to and suggesting fitting text-locations for pictures has provided me with the encouragement and sense of confidence that I needed. He has been intensely engaged in the edition of this book. I am deeply grateful to him. I am happy that Ato Kassahun recognizes and appreciates Martin's contributions.

Asmeret Rezene, a granddaughter to Aboy Aregai Kibreab, has been a generous and successful bridge builder in making the article on Aboy Aregai Kibreab known among members of his extended family. In so doing she has encouraged me greatly. My dear friend Eyassu Tesfay was our ally in the launching of this task of establishing contacts. I thank both Asmeret and Eyassu sincerely.

Per Andén, to whom my Eritrean friends within The Eritrean War-Disabled Fighters Veteran Association have given the nickname Andiki´el (

ግንደኪኤል), deserves sincere thanks for scanning and copying a number of my texts.

My wife Gennet has not only encouraged me, as always, in her quiet way but also made available those family-related albums that she had built up over decades and from which we have been able to select some pictures.

The Swedes have a saying: *"Det är mänskligt att fela!"* Literally: *"It is human to err!"* It is very possible that I have failed to mention persons who deserve to be named in my acknowledgments. I plead for their understanding. The reader may have noticed that a clear majority of those persons whom I have contacted for comments are residents of Sweden. My choice was partly influenced by the fact that this book deals with Sweden as the context of my reflections on Ethiopia and Eritrea. Outside of Sweden, yes in the rest of Europe and in the USA, there are many renowned scholars who have written on Ethiopia and Eritrea. Many are close friends. God willing, I hope to come back to them, in some measure, in due time.

I end as I used to end my letters to the alumni of The Ethiopian Evangelical College in Debre-Zeit (Bishoftu), in Ethiopia (where I taught during the school year 1960–1961), with the words: *Peace and blessings!*

Ezra Gebremedhin
Uppsala, 2020

Notes

[1] I. Svanberg is a Researcher and Lecturer at the Institute for Russian and Eurasian Studies of Uppsala University.

Year 1973
Chapter 1

Discovering and Making Sweden Our Home:

Lövudden: A YMCA Center Near a Lake

My family and I came to Sweden in August 1970 (fifty years ago). I was a recipient of a Lutheran World Federation scholarship, to work on a doctoral thesis in Theology. The church in which I was ordained in Ethiopia, The Ethiopian Evangelical Church Mekane Yesus, traces its origins back to the missionary efforts of The Evangeliska Fosterlands-Stiftelsen (EFS), known internationally as The Swedish Evangelical Mission (SEM), whose first missionaries came to Massawa, in present day Eritrea, in March 1866. This independent mission organization operated within The Church of Sweden. I had many friends and close acquaintances among former Swedish missionaries to Eritrea and Ethiopia, many of whom were back in Sweden when my family and I arrived in the country in late August 1970. We were received by The Reverend Manfred Lundgren, once a member of the 14-member Swedish Red Cross Ambulance Team, which came to Ethiopia's aid when Italy invaded Ethiopia in 1935, and later a revered missionary in different capacities in the country. We spent our first night at the guest house of the Headquarters of the SEM in Stockholm and then left for Lövudden, a YMCA centre by a beautiful lake, out in the country, not far from the industrial city of Västerås. The first part of my narrative in this chapter is related to Lövudden.

The letter shown below was written on June 25, 1971, only nine months after the arrival of my family in Sweden. I am publishing it not as an act of boasting but as a testimony to the generosity with which I was received in Sweden from the very start of my stay in the country. The letter reads:

TESTIMONIUM

Ezra Gebremedhin has for me undergone a course in Greek intended to prepare him in his studies for the theological, doctoral degree in Systematic Theology at the University of Uppsala. By a repetition of classical and Hellenistic grammar as a starting point this course has subsequently been pointed particularly to language and style in New Testament, early Christian and patristic texts.

The course has covered one hundred and five lessons.

Ezra Gebremedhin has carried out this study single-mindedly and very successfully. Both personally and intellectually he has represented his country and his task in a way that is worthy of all commendations.

For me it has been an intellectual experience to teach him.

Västerås 25th June 1971
Gunnar Bäärnhielm
Senior High School Master at Rudbeckianska Skolan, Västerås, Sweden

To be very frank, I was surprised by the content and tone of the letter. I could hardly believe that I had ascended to such heights of linguistic excellence. And that in Greek, the language of the learned, in all its literary varieties! I did not excel in Swedish, the language of the land to which we had come. Swedish was indeed the language we needed to learn, and right away. But Greek, one of the vehicles needed for my coming doctoral studies in Theology, was given precedence. Swedish had to wait.

My teacher, Gunnar Bäärnhielm, was Senior High School Master at Rudbeckianska Skolan, the first ever secondary school in Sweden, established in 1621 by Bishop Johannes Rudbeckius (1581–1646).

When I now (in 2019) read the letter, with its Latin title *Testimonium* (which means "Witness"), I cannot, for the life of me, remember that I had attended 105 lessons in Greek for the good and capable Gunnar Bäärnhielm. What I do remember is that I was often taken up with other duties and didn't get enough time to do my homework. For some months I was the babysitter for our two children Emmanuel, three and half years old, and Mimmi (Mahlet), one year and ten months old. My teacher in Greek must have had a very generous heart. He was definitely out both to teach me

Greek and to encourage me under the tight circumstances in which I found myself at the small lakeside YMCA community in Lövudden. I wouldn't have managed to come successfully through my first year, had the Swedish system not come to our aid through the provision of so-called *dagmammor* (literally "day-mothers"). These mothers took care of Emmanuel and Mimmi for a good part of a working day.

Some Words on Language

Writing to the congregation in Corinth, St. Paul maintains, "So it is with you. Unless you speak intelligible words with your tongue, how will anyone know what you are saying? You will just be speaking into the air." (I Cor. 14:9).

He writes further: "I thank God that I speak in tongues more than all of you. But in the church I would rather speak five intelligible words to instruct others than ten thousand words in a tongue." (1 Cor. 14:18-19).

These words were spoken in a specific situation in which the gifts of the Spirit were up for discussion in the congregation in Corinth. And yet they have a lot to say to us on the subject of communication in any community. Understandable language, language that is not only words but a living medium of communication, is a vital tool in the accommodation of any outsider in Swedish life. Language is the door into the soul of a people.

At the YMCA centre at Lövudden, we were lucky enough to be among people who knew English. In fact, my wife, Gennet, who taught Amharic at the course centre for Swedish volunteers planning to serve in Ethiopia, had English as her language of communication. A number of the members of staff at the SIDA course centre were from Great Britain or spoke English. (SIDA stands for Swedish International Development Agency.)

The person who comes to Sweden as an adult without some knowledge of the Swedish language is suddenly reduced to the state of an almost illiterate person. This fact has its social, psychological, and spiritual consequences. Sweden, however, has language services that are good promoters of integration. An expression that is heard often among both Swedish teachers and newly arrived immigrants and refugees is the abbreviation *SFI* (*Svenska för Invandrare*, Swedish for Immigrants). SFI is the national programme of instruction in Swedish for immigrants. The course is free of charge and anyone with a Swedish identity number or card is entitled to take part in the course.

The sponsor for this extensive educational undertaking, the *Folkuniversitetet* (The Folk University), has a long history and engages teachers with experience and dedication. The courses offered by SFI are tailor-made in ways that take the needs of individuals into consideration. In some places, courses are given online. Considerations are made for persons with hearing impairment and similar handicaps.

Unfortunately, I was not in a position to take advantage of SFI when I first came to Sweden. I did take part in a beginners' course for about three months.

An Unexpected Attack from My Body

But back to the YMCA centre at Lövudden. The head of the centre was a tall, easy-going, and warm person by the name of Walter Magnusson. I remember his wife, Ulla, also a warm and friendly person. They were very considerate towards our family with two small children and our one-room flat! Soon we moved to a bigger flat. The Magnussons and other members of the YMCA staff gave us material that would prepare us for our first winter in Sweden.

The dining hall of the centre, where staff and participants in different courses took their meals, was open for us in an undefined but very welcoming way. Gennet, who was an employee of SIDA, was allowed to eat some of her meals at the dining hall. Extra food somehow found its way into our kitchen throughout our stay at Lövudden. The babysitters for our children (the *dagmammor*, the "day-mothers") loved our children and treated them as members of their own families. An excellent atmosphere for the beginning of life in a new country with many challenges!

I remember one evening at Lövudden. I was at home to put our children to bed. My wife, Gennet, was at the course center. I started feeling pain on the lower right-hand side of my intestines. The children had already dozed off. The pain increased slowly but steadily. In fact, it rose mercilessly. I started agonizing audibly. As I noticed that my voice was disturbing the children, I tried to rub and caress them to silence. The pain rose to a crescendo! I simply cannot describe how terrible the whole thing felt. And then the pain died down, slowly.

Just then my wife came in. She saw that I looked miserable. Some inner voice had told her to leave the course center and go home. She and a female colleague from Great Britain called the ambulance, which took me to the emergency section of the main hospital in Västerås. The diagnosis came without delay. I had a ruptured appendix and had to be operated on right away. After the operation, the doctor told me that I would have ended in serious trouble had I come two hours later!

There is one thing I remember from that evening when I experienced excruciating pain. My mind went back to rural Ethiopia. I said to myself:

"Here I suffered but I received help in time. Poor farmers and the children of farmers in rural Ethiopia would have suffered and died in their suffering."

Why think of farmers only? Even in a city like Addis Ababa, I could have died for lack of coming to the doctor in time. I thanked God for Sweden and its medical services.

The Birth of a Daughter

Our third child, Bisrat (Bisse), was born in Västerås on September 26, 1971. I was away on a preaching tour when she arrived at the Maternity Department of the main hospital of Västerås, the same hospital where I had been operated on for a ruptured appendix. I felt that it was unfair that I should be away on such an occasion!

Interestingly enough, my brother Naigzy, who happened to be in Sweden for a very short period, saw Bisse before I did.

Bisse had problems with her digestive system from the very start. But I had to move to our new flat at Väktargatan 46 C in Uppsala with our children Emmanuel and Mimmi, only days after Bisse's birth. A surprise awaited us when we opened the door to our flat at Väktargatan 46 C. Someone had supplied the flat with additional furniture. The kitchen was fully equipped and breathed a welcoming atmosphere. The Principal of Johannelund's Theological Institute, Kurt Åberg and his wife Maj, former missionaries to Ethiopia and the wonderful Matron of the institute, Anna Lisa Olsson, had been there with some students. We felt enormously welcome, even though we missed Gennet and Bisse, whom we had left at the hospital in Västerås.

Our First "Lucia"

On the morning of December 12, 1971, we experienced our first Lucia celebration. Once again people at Johannelund Theological Institute had taken the initiative. Early in the morning, a Lucia delegation consisting of a candle-crowned Lucia and her maids, as well as *stjärngossar* (Star Boys), all dressed in white and bearing candles, glided into our flat, singing the famous song about "Sankta Lucia" (Saint Lucia). They gave us a breakfast consisting of *bullar* (Swedish buns) and coffee or tea. Talk of hugging and laughing and chatting in a winter atmosphere full of gratitude!

The Church's Preservation of Christian Antiquity

In time we were to discover many new things in and around Uppsala. One aspect of Swedish church life that has impressed me is the church's preservation of many valuable features of Christian antiquity. And Uppsala, with its Cathedral, University, and Castle, is in a class of its own in this regard.

Few countries and churches are as good as Sweden and The Church of Sweden in taking care of their past. This is true not least with regard to ancient buildings and places of worship. Doctrine and Liturgy are a part of this heritage. The fact that the history and culture of Sweden and the history of its church are closely interwoven explains why even secularized Swedes observe the main holidays of the Church Year. The First Sunday of Advent, Christmas, Epiphany, Easter, and Pentecost are occasions that tie the people and the church together and maintain the marks of the spiritual world on everyday life. The fact that the majority of Swedes still want Baptism, Confirmation, Church weddings, and Church burials, is an indication of the hold that Christian tradition has on Swedish life. [Bear in mind that these words were written in the early 1970s. Interest in church life and Christian rituals (the sacraments) has now gone down considerably. Many of Sweden's citizens in our day were born abroad and are followers of other religions.]

In the Swedish Church Year, I, an Ethiopian of a low-church tradition, have discovered a steady and renewing rhythm—a rhythm that is beautifully intertwined into the seasons of the calendar year. I come from a young church, whose members have sometimes criticized a much older church— The Ethiopian Orthodox Church—for its alleged formalism and stiffness. I have seen that there is something durable and stable about that which is old. The writings of the Swedish Bishop Bo Giertz are a good illustration of the fact that an old church can in fact combine faithfulness to tradition and spiritual renewal. The old can in fact contain renewing power and need not be regarded as dead and empty.

The Church of Sweden has the stability that more emotionally excitable religious groups do not possess, even though this stability often runs the danger of being devoid of missionary fervour. The sacraments still occupy a central place in the life of the church, in spite of the debates that have arisen recently on the subject of Baptism. One is impressed by the number of young people that one sees at the Eucharist (Holy Communion).

Trying to Be Relevant in a Secularized Society

The Church of Sweden is a good example of a church trying to be relevant in a secularized and materially secure society. Many may wonder if the church is trying to be relevant at all. The one who takes a closer look can discover that the church is indeed grappling with a difficult assignment—that of making God relevant in a welfare state. The Church of Sweden no longer has the extensive diaconal opportunities that, to take one example, churches in America have. The Swedish state has taken over these diaconal services to which, in older days, the church could point as concrete fruits of its faith and love.[1]

The church must now show a society that has much "bread" that man also needs God's Word. The church has been placed in the situation in which Peter and John found themselves at the entrance of the temple in Jerusalem, according to the story that is narrated for us in Acts 4. "Silver and gold have I none; but such as I have give I thee; In the name of Jesus Christ of Nazareth rise up and walk" (Acts 4:6). The actualization of this rich message is a great challenge but not an easy task facing The Church of Sweden.

I have mentioned the Church of Sweden's quality as a good steward of an ancient heritage of teaching, ministry and church practice. The question of theological truth, in the sense of normative formulations or presentations of the faith, comes into the picture. In a society that questions much and is not afraid of changing patterns of thought and life, how much of the Church's heritage is to be regarded as normative and unchangeable? And how much is to be refashioned according to the needs and demands of the times? A highly controversial question!

Mission-Related Experiences That Came to Our Aid in Sweden

The EFS/SEM was a part of my background, both in Eritrea and Ethiopia. Missionaries knew my grandparents, parents, uncles, and aunts. When we came to Sweden, we met Swedes who knew these relatives or had heard about these relatives. We were privileged enough to get to know dedicated missionaries to both Ethiopia and Eritrea. They became both examples and friends. Among them were the Stjärnes (on both Per's and Håkan's sides), the Hylanders, the Perssons, the Aréns, the Lundgrens, the Rubensons, the Månsons, the Åbergs, the Nilssons, the Backlunds, the Forslunds, the Lundströms, the Svenssons, the Rönnbäcks, the Normarks, and many, many others. I have had the joy and benefit of meeting these friends at different times during my years here in Sweden.

Back in Ethiopia, the book *A Faithful Guide to Peace with God,* by Carl Olof Rosenius (1816–1868), the "Father" of The Swedish Evangelical Mission" had given me a liberating peace of conscience in 1955, after a period of great spiritual anguish.[2] The relief came through Romans 4:5, which reads (in The King James Version):

> But to him that worketh not but believeth on him that justifies the ungodly, his faith is counted for righteousness.

In Sweden, we found our place in the grace-based fellowship whose fathers were Carl Olof Rosenius and his coworkers.

The spirituality that the missionaries from the EFS/SEM mediated in Ethiopia and Eritrea was personal, without being loud and noisy. That was the kind of spirituality that we met, especially within the EFS here in Sweden.

Swedes, both missionaries and those who worked for aid organizations like SIDA, kept their love and dedication for Eritrea and Ethiopia, even after returning to their homeland. In short, when we came to Sweden we met Swedes who "were sold" on Eritrea and Ethiopia.

We found the written records of Swedish missionary efforts both in Eritrea and Ethiopia, now available in archives of different kinds, very impressive. The letters, diaries, yearly reports, sermons, articles, etc. were windows into a world that belonged to us but that we didn't know.

The climate, the tempo of life in Sweden, and the necessity of taking care of one's life in all details, were experiences that taxed our energy. At the same time, we have rejoiced over the help that the welfare system gave us, over the different seasons of the year, the celebrations around Christmas time, the wonderful summers at the diocesan retreat centre in Rättvik, in the province of Dalarna, and the different EFS-sponsored *"läger"* (camps) that our children attended and where they made life-long friends.

We did experience "culture clashes." Our fellow Eritreans and Ethiopians had their expectations as far as traditional social obligations were concerned. Providing time for these obligations in times of sickness, mourning, weddings, and similar occasions, in a Swedish context, often created stress. The positive aspect of this practice was that we too found ourselves at the receiving end when our times of need came. What is more, we experienced that our Swedish friends treated us with understanding and patience if we failed to pay attention to them speedily enough in their times of sickness, mourning, and similar experiences. They simply waited for us.

Our stay in Sweden has also shown us traces of God's hands in action. We became elders, "shepherds," models, comforters, and teachers for Ethiopians and Eritreans who had come here to study or had fled from war and political persecution. In a way, we can say that we met both Ethiopia and Eritrea here again. Perhaps some of our problems were due to the fact that we didn't fully embrace the new discovery and challenge. In this sphere of responsibility too, our Swedish friends became our allies and supporters. These friends made the challenge of discovering and making Sweden a home an exciting and rewarding experience.

Notes

1 Deacons are, traditionally, responsible for the fulfillment, on behalf of the Church, of the dictates of the teaching of Jesus as expressed in Matthew 25:35: "For I was hungry and you gave me something to eat, I was thirsty and you gave me something to drink, I was a stranger and you invited me in, I needed clothes an and you clothed me, I was sick and you looked after me, I was in prison and you came to visit me." The church in a modern, welfare-state like Sweden has of course its "modern" ways of carrying out these services.

2 Carl Olof Rosenius, *A Faithful Guide to Peace with God* (English translation of *Vägledning till frid*), Trans. by N. J. Laache (Whitefish, Montana: Kessinger Publications, 2010).

Year 1975
Chapter 2

Coffee Instead of Machine Guns:
A Parable on the Ethio-Eritrean Conflict

Introductory note by Lennart Linder, the publisher of the Swedish version of this article published in the November 6, 1975 issue of the periodical, Budbäraren (The Messenger). Linder writes:

> Also this week, which is dedicated to developing countries, the political situation in many parts of the world is marked by disturbances and conflicts. One of the turbulent corners of the world, a place of concern particularly for readers of this periodical (Budbäraren), is naturally Eritrea, in Ethiopia. Jesus himself said "Blessed are the peacemakers!" And it is the task of His church to stand in the service of reconciliation, obviously without compromising on the demands of justice. We have received an article from Pastor Ezra Gebremedhin, who is working on his doctoral thesis here in Sweden. He himself was born in Addis Ababa, of Eritrean parents, and the article breathes the deep worry that he feels because of the difficult problem with which Ethiopia and Eritrea are now struggling. His article takes the form of an imagined conversation between two Ethiopian students here in Sweden.

Here comes the article:

I have often thought about what people in Ethiopia and Eritrea do when a house begins to burn. They cry for help. To help each other by crying out for help is very Ethiopian, and very Eritrean. Under normal circumstances, no one would be criticized or held responsible for deviant behaviour for shouting," Fire!" On the country, failing to cry for help at such times would indeed be regarded as a sign of indifference, or as a sign of the enjoyment of a secret joy at the destruction of a house.

The conflict in Eritrea is a fire that is ravaging the whole of Ethiopia. It is devouring Ethiopia's and Eritrea's sons from all parts of these regions. The conflict is consuming resources that are severely needed for the building up of the country.

Within me I carry deep love for the soil where I was born and brought up. I love the simple, humble, and hospitable people of Ethiopia. At the same time, I am fully aware of my Eritrean roots. I also revere the norms by which my Eritrean parents brought me up. I am a seed of both Eritrean and Ethiopian origin, sown and cultivated on Ethiopian soil. I hope that those who read this article will be able to understand why I am worried about the present state of things in Ethiopia and Eritrea and about their futures. To write on such a subject is to engage in tight-rope walking. There is a risk that the storyteller can fall or be pushed towards the one or the other side of the rope. I sometimes wonder if I risk ending up only in drawing emotional and verbal cannonades from all sides. I do, however, regard this article as a way of crying out for help because I see a house on fire. Such a cry would be better than the kind of silence that reflects indifference.

My reader has by now surely noted that I use the terms *Ethiopia* and *Eritrea*, *Ethiopians* and *Eritreans*. Before anyone jumps on me and calls me a promoter of tribalism or a destroyer of Ethiopia's unity, I would like to say that I am using the terms mentioned above as a simple matter of convenience.

I shall use a story to express what worries me. I don't know if my plan is going to succeed. My choice of this device reflects something Ethiopian and something Eritrean. Both peoples are good storytellers.

I have chosen a Swedish café in a small Swedish town as the scene of my narrative. A café not far from a monastery near a small town known as Sala! Time: The beginning of October, 1975. Persons: two good friends, Solomon Kiflom, born and brought up in Addis Ababa in an Eritrean family, and Hailu Moges, also born and brought up in Addis Ababa, in an Amharic-speaking family. The names and the story are made up. The substance of the story is, however, basically factual.

It was autumn. The trees were adorned in the yellow, brownish and green of an early Swedish fall. From where they sat at their small table in the café, Solomon and Hailu could look out of the window at a field of wheat reaching in waves of green to the feet of some low mounds, a good kilometer away. A palish-yellow leaf floated down gently through the half-open window and landed on their table.

"Welcome!" said Solomon to the leaf, quite unaware that a Swedish waitress had come and stationed herself near the table, pen and pad in hand, ready to take their orders.

Chapter 2

"*Kaffe och bullar*," whispered Hailu who was the host of the day. Coffee and buns!

By now both of them knew quite a bit of Swedish. Of course, Solomon always got a kick out of the way his friend Hailu pronounced the difficult letter "u" in Swedish.

"Did you order *balls* for us?" asked Solomon teasingly.

"Shut up," blurted Hailu, "You and your Swedish!" It was the old game again. A lot of teasing in a good, brotherly spirit!

Solomon looked at the Swedish people sitting around them. Some of them were warming their fingers around the coffee-cups. The smell of coffee started him daydreaming. He was basically a daydreamer, this Solomon. He had done a lot of that this past year. His friends were in fact getting a little worried about the whole thing. It all started about a year ago when things got into high gear in Ethiopia and Eritrea.

"Coffee," thought Solomon, "the great uniter of people! Just look at these good old Swedes around you. They are gathered around cups of coffee. That is in fact their link. Just think of it. Coffee, the common drink of the people of Ethiopia and Eritrea! Why don't people in Ethiopia get together and drink coffee instead of shooting at each other?"

He felt that he was getting carried away again into one of his many curious and seemingly ridiculous dreams. But these dreams had an immense power of attraction. He dreamt of the time when Ethiopian soldiers and guerilla-fighters of the Eritrean underbrush would get together and drink coffee together. He dreamt of the day when thousands of Ethiopian soldiers, now far from home, would return to their parents, their wives, and their children, and drink good, strong Ethiopian coffee with their neighbours.

Hailu noticed that his friend was away, in a world of dreams.

"Wake up, you fool!" he snapped at his friend, giving him a nudge. "I am not here to talk to your ghost, you know."

"Sorry," said Solomon with a start, as he tried to compose himself. "I guess I got carried away again."

"What were you dreaming about anyway? ," asked Hailu.

"Well," began Solomon, "It looks as if the vibrations in Ethiopia and Eritrea are growing more and more ominous."

"There we go again," said Hailu, leaning back into his chair, with a sense of having been let down again. "Can't you people think or talk about anything else? And particularly you who were born and brought up in Addis Ababa and know hardly anything about Eritrea!"

Hailu was of course exaggerating when he stated that Solomon knew hardly anything about Eritrea. But without having realized what he was saying, Hailu had actually touched upon a very vital point. Eritrea was a subject about which many people knew very little. Of course, it had never occurred to Hailu that he was among these people. Like many other Ethiopians and non-Ethiopians, Hailu felt that he knew just about everything there was to know about Eritrea and had come to the conclusion that he also knew how Eritrea and the Eritreans should be dealt with. And in many ways Hailu was not to blame. He knew very much about certain types of Eritreans. He knew Solomon's Eritrean family far better than many of the families of his own relatives.

The parents of Solomon and Hailu were very good friends. They had known each other over a period of more than 40 years. Their fathers had met at the Battle of Amba Ar'adom (አምባ አርዓዶም), February 10 to 15, 1936, perhaps the most decisive battle between the Italians and the Ethiopians before the collapse of organized Ethiopian resistance. Two years of shared hardship had molded Ato Kiflom and Ato Moges into close friends. Hailu knew that among those who never returned from the battlefield there were many Eritreans—individuals who had literally walked from the villages of their birth to Ethiopia during the days when many an Eritrean opponent of Italian colonialism felt a thrill at the very mention of flag and emperor. Those were the days when many an Eritrean referred to the Ethiopian flag as banderana (ባንዴራና), our flag. Hailu knew these things and often became bitter at the tendency to portray Eritreans as *banda* (ባንዳ), mercenary soldiers paid by Italians, or traitors who sniffed after Arab oil-dollars. He was angry enough about the cessationist movement among Eritreans, aided, according to many an Ethiopian, by oil-rich Arabs. At times Hailu would become so furious with Solomon that he would shout, "You crooks deserve what you are getting." But he was not a victim of indiscriminate propaganda against Eritreans.

Hailu was fully aware of the fact that Ethiopian society had always been plagued by an unequal distribution of resources and opportunities. He and Solomon agreed that all Ethiopians—and that of course included the Eritreans who had settled in Ethiopia—were to blame, in some form or another, for this state of injustice. But Hailu, who had something of the sense of decency and fair play of his father Ato Moges, felt that to put the main blame for this state of injustice on Eritreans was to seek a scapegoat. He used to say, "Finding scapegoats may lighten one's sense of guilt but it does not solve problems. Finding scapegoats is postponing the solution of a problem."

Hailu and his family were absolutely sure of one thing. Ato Kiflom was no exploiter of the Ethiopian masses. If he was guilty of anything, it was the fact that, after over forty years in Addis Ababa, he still spoke a curious brand of Amharic. But, of course, had Ato Kiflom spoken better

Amharic, Hailu and his family would have been deprived of many occasions of hearty laughter.

Solomon knew Hailu's father, Ato Moges, very well. He was one of those sterling characters who grace every tribe or ethnic group. Solomon's Eritrean father, Ato Kiflom, used to call Ato Moges *käwHi!* (ካዉሕ), "A rock," a designation that spells durability and dependability. Ato Moges was the god-father of one of Solomon's brothers. For many a Christian in Ethiopia and Eritrea, that fact alone ould say enough.

Yes, there were strong and deep links of love between these two families. But both Solomon and Hailu were beginning to get worried. As they sat in a Swedish café, far from home, they felt that this tremendous store of love was beginning to leak. They did not dare to admit their fears to each other, but a sixth sense told them that something had gone terribly wrong. Reports from the war in Eritrea were threatening to cast a shadow on this beautiful relationship of long standing. The bitterness arising out of this war was poisoning everything in its way. How long should this poisoning of relationships among lifelong friends be allowed to continue?

Solomon knew what an increasing number of Eritreans were thinking and feeling about this issue. He also knew where the majority of Ethiopians stood on the matter. The records were not very encouraging.

"You know," continued Solomon, "I have a growing feeling that you don't quite have a full grasp of the Eritrean question."

"Of course I do!" said Hailu, with a sense of total certainty. "After all, you and I have known each other since childhood. You yourself know that there is hardly a secret that our parents have not shared. What is it that you don't know about me, or that I don't know about you? I sometimes feel that it is your typical Eritrean arrogance that shows itself in your complaint that people don't understand you. Are you Eritreans that much of an unexplored reality?"

Solomon took a deep breath, folded his hands and pressed his mouth against his folded hands. As usual he felt that there was some truth in what Hailu had just said. Perhaps the average Ethiopian did understand much more about the Eritrean than the Eritrean was aware of. But still, Solomon was sure of one thing: Hailu knew only a fraction of what there was to know about Eritrea. In spite of his Eritrean background, Solomon himself knew very little of the deep-seated sentiments that prevailed among Eritreans born and brought up on Eritrean soil.

"Let me use a parable to explain what I mean," continued Solomon. Hailu scratched his head and reluctantly settled back into his chair. He knew that his friend was a lover of examples and stories, not all of which he found edifying.

Solomon started:

> The story of Eritrea is the story of two sisters: an older sister who stayed at home with her large family and a younger sister who moved southwards with her few children. For the majority of commentators on Eritrea, the history and fate of the older sister is shrouded in mystery. These people know only the younger sister whom they have met in Ethiopia and in several places outside Eritrea. For these people, the history of Eritrea is the history of the younger sister. Most of their observations and conclusions are based on their observations of the younger sister and her children. It has hardly occurred to most of them that the history of the younger sister is only a fraction of the history of Eritrea. Much confusion and misunderstanding has resulted from this fact. The fact that the younger sister and her children often look prosperous and happy in Ethiopia, away from home, tends to make the whole Eritrea issue appear like an outrageous case of ingratitude.

Hailu was evidently becoming more and more interested in this parable, which sounded ridiculous but which was now becoming more and more intriguing. He nodded at his friend to continue.

Solomon continued:

> That is why I said earlier on that you, in fact, knew very little about Eritrea. Even I, numbered as I am among the many children of the younger sister, am almost as ignorant as you are on this issue. It is the older sister who stayed at home who appears to have been systematically reduced to rags. It is she who is undergoing devastation in the present conflict. Many say that she looks pale and thin. She eats her scanty bread with tears. Her villages have been battered to pieces. The smell of fire and smoke never seem to leave her nostrils. She has already buried thousands of her children. She has sent thousands of her kin into the bushes. Thousands of others have taken shelter in neighbouring countries. The common callings of farming, trading, studying, travelling, marrying, and feasting have been disrupted or are on hold among her people. She has even come to the point of suspecting that the water in some of her wells and rivers has been poisoned. Many are becoming to wonder whether the older sister is ever going to pull through this nightmare.

In spite of his grudging admiration of the smart turn that the parable had taken, Hailu was beginning to boil with rage. His eyes betrayed his wrath.

"Where in the world did you pick up such a bizarre story?" Hailu asked, "You begin by telling me that you are ignorant on the Eritrean issue and then pour out the sort of tale that gives one the impression that you have just returned from a fact-finding trip to Eritrea! Look here! It is months since any stupid journalist visited Eritrea. You yourself haven't been in Ethiopia or Eritrea for ages. Where in the world do you get these outrageous bits of fiction? Do you make them up?"

Solomon lowered his head like a child who had just received a sharp reprimand. He took a deep breath and started tapping gently on the table at which they sat.

"Well," he continued. No, I don't make them up. I don't even enjoy talking about them. Can one really be happy talking about these things? Can one who loves the soil and people of Ethiopia really have the sort of maliciousness that makes up such stories? No, I don't make them up. Making reasonable allowance for the obvious difficulties involved in getting any news from Eritrea nowadays, I would say that some of these things are pretty well documented. Some periodicals of considerable international renown have already mentioned them. The rest of the items have come to my attention the Ethiopian way. You know what I mean. Jungle telegraph!"

"There you are," Hailu interrupted. "That is exactly what I suspected. Rumours! Rumour mongering! I am really disappointed with you. I thought that you, by now, knew better than to go by rumours."

"I fully understand your concern," Solomon continued, "To speak with absolute certainty about something for which we have no first-hand evidence would be irresponsible. But not to raise questions, particularly on an issue on which there is a news blackout, would be equally irresponsible. I think of the severe famine in Wollo and Tigrai. A few years ago there were people who believed that news on the famine were exaggerations, lacking any first-hand evidence. And you and I know that many who minimized or denied the seriousness of the famine paid dearly for their response. Who knows? Some years from now you and I may be held responsible for not having raised questions on the Eritrea-issue."

Hailu had become somber. He began to see that this whole problem was far more complicated than he thought. Of course, he now remembered that the crime that was punished ruthlessly in Ethiopia in recent months was the crime of silence around the famine in the north. And now, like a returning tide, silence seemed to be coming back into the centre of Ethiopia's life.

"Look here," continued Solomon, "You and I seem to have a flare for exaggerating and dramatizing things. I guess that this is one of the things we have in common. Incidentally where is your older sister, Almaz, that lovely creature?"

"She is married and lives in the Ethiopian province of Balé with her family," replied Hailu.

"Lucky the man who got her," added Solomon. "May joy and blessings follow her and her family!"

He kept pondering for a while. In a flash, a train of thought started moving in his mind. He could not withstand the temptation to use Almaz and her family as a teaching aid in the clarification of the sensitive issue that he and Hailu had just touched upon.

"Excuse the thought, Hailu," said Solomon, "But I just couldn't withstand the temptation to return to our subject again. Suppose that you, who were living in Addis, were to receive news to the effect that Almaz and her family in Balé were being slowly battered to pieces, that all their property had gone up in flames and that she and her children had been driven to the woods. Would your emotions remain indifferent? Would you remain completely unmoved?"

"I get your point," continued Hailu, "But I can't quite justify Almaz and her children being actively involved in acts of treason against Ethiopia. Suppose now that Almaz and her family had become cessationists of some kind! Can such a stance be ignored?"

"Certainly not!" retorted Solomon, "But which of your reactions would come first—the logical or the emotional? Your reasoning or your worry and concern about Almaz and her family? I don't want any of your philosophizing now! I want to know how you would react as a being of flesh and blood. Would you, supposing that you still lived in Addis, say to yourself: 'Well, since I have prospered here in the capital city and since I am treated very well, I shall not show any special concern or sympathy for Almaz and her family! And I shall consider anyone who shows Almaz's family the slightest bit of sympathy an enemy of Ethiopia, deserving drastic punitive measures?' Would you in fact entertain such reasoning?"

Hailu sensed what Solomon was getting at. He had not given the *human* aspect of the Eritrea issue the consideration that it deserved. His position on the subject was that of a cold-blooded debater.

Solomon continued, "Do you now begin to see the dilemma in which many of the children of the younger sister in our parable on Eritrea find themselves? To expect that an Eritrean born and brought up in Ethiopia be grateful towards the country of his birth is perfectly in order. To expect that such an Eritrean play an active role in the healing of the deep wounds that are plaguing Ethiopia and Eritrea is also perfectly in order. But to expect that such children of the younger sister (i.e., the children of those Eritreans who had moved to and settled in Ethiopia) remain emotionally unmoved by what is happening in war-torn Eritrea is to expect the impossible."

The two were quiet for a couple, long minutes.

Chapter 2

"A crisis," continued Solomon, "is like smoke. As long as you are in it you tend to be smoke-influenced. Only if you can get above or under or outside of the smoke can you begin to reason sensibly. I think that this is true of the present crisis between Ethiopia and Eritrea."

Hailu looked at his friend, quietly. He sensed that Solomon had just gotten started with one of his meditative monologues. Hailu himself didn't always grasp what his friend was trying to get at. But he sort of enjoyed listening to him.

Solomon continued, "And you and I need to get out of the smoke, somehow. Outside of the heat and emotion and get some light instead. We have to help each other so that we can come to a readiness to listen to each other. You know how much talk there is about freedom on our continent. One of the profoundest aspects of freedom is freedom from fear—fear of one another. There is something tremendously liberating about being open, being willing to listen, without having to be defensive. You and I sit here and debate in the countryside in Sweden, the most comfortable society in the world, while the monster of war is reaping a terrible harvest among our brothers and sisters in Ethiopia and Eritrea. It does not take too much courage to debate an issue. I feel that you and I are cowards, deep down. That is why we are unable to contribute in a meaningful way to the solution of this problem. Deep down, we love ourselves, not our fellowmen."

Hailu noticed that Solomon's monologue was taking on a religious tone. This made him a little nervous. He was of course convinced that religion was "the opiate of the people." But as he sat and looked at his friend, he wished, for the first time in a long while, that there was a little more of what Christians called fear of God in this terrible conflict among Ethiopians and Eritreans. One thing was clear for Hailu. Fear of *men* had not helped to solve the problem.

Solomon continued, "There is a sense in which our identities as persons lie at a much deeper level than our tribal or ethnic affiliations. I don't mean to minimize the positive aspects of our tribal identities. But there is a deeper level at which a person's identity is determined. A person's true identity lies at the level where the person discovers his or her calling in life. And no calling, no mission in life, is worth the name unless it is governed by love. And by love I mean love for all—as far as this is humanly possible. When love for a certain tribe or ethnic group becomes hatred for another, then something has gone wrong. Such love is an idol. It is a selfish hobby. And pretty soon this idol will poison your relationship to your own people."

Hailu often felt that there was something unrealistic about his friend Solomon. For Hailu, Solomon was someone who had not tasted bitterness.

An idealist! But Hailu also felt that there was something engaging about Solomon's train of thoughts.

"Let us agree not to widen the gap on the Eritrea issue," Solomon added. "Let us rather build bridges among our peoples. Building bridges requires courage. What we need in this entire business are not more advocates but more bridge builders, if you get what I mean. And let us learn to think at the level of the stomach, at the level of the intestines as our parents used to say. Let us put a little more feeling into the whole thing. More humaneness! We seem to have developed into debating robots!"

It was getting late. They both got up to leave the café. Solomon saw an elderly Swedish couple across the room from where the two friends stood. "You know what?" he said, as he lifted his right hand to summon the waitress for their bill. "I wish these people would do something about this conflict between Ethiopia and Eritrea. I sometimes feel that they have forgotten that their own country once gave birth to such great bridge builders as Folke Bernadotte and Dag Hammarskjöld."

Hailu was quiet. He had received much food for thought.

Ezra Gebremedhin
November 6, 1975 (Stockholm)

Year 1975
Chapter 3

A Letter to King Carl XVI Gustaf of Sweden on the Ethio-Eritrean Conflict

Background

In their days of greatness, Swedish royalty had their contacts, directly or indirectly, with Ethiopia and what is today Eritrea, particularly in the decades after 1866, when the first Swedish missionaries arrived in Massawa.

Sweden's present monarch, Carl XVI Gustaf, was born on April 30, 1946. The forefather of the present dynasty, Carl XIV Johan, was Marshal Jean Baptiste Bernadotte, Prince of Ponte Corvo, and a former general of Napoleon Bonaparte. In 1810, he was elected to ascend the Swedish throne, which he finally ascended in 1818. Sweden's present monarch, Carl XVI Gustav, who ascended the Swedish throne on September 19, 1973, is the seventh regent of the House of Bernadotte. He is the youngest child of Prince Gustaf Adolf, who died in an airplane crash in Denmark in 1947 when the child was only nine months old. The son became second in line to the throne, when his grandfather, the then Crown Prince Gustaf Adolf, who had visited Ethiopia in 1935, ascended to the Swedish throne as King Gustaf V, in 1950. King Gustav V Adolf, the present king's great grandfather, had received Ethiopia's Regent Ras Tafari Makonnen in Stockholm in connection with the regent's visit to a number of European countries in 1924.

When I handed over a petition on the conflict between Ethiopia and Eritrea to the present king at *Östanbäcks kloster* (Östanbäck's Monastery) near Sala, on October 9, 1975, the king must have been 29 years old. He was held in respect in a highly progressive, just, and rich country, but he was no longer the bearer of decisive roles in the government of the country.

I was at said monastery to work on my doctoral thesis in a milieu that provided both quiet and opportunities for regular times of prayer and meditation. The Swedish monk in the picture attached to this background description, is Brother Johannes Lindell, then abbot of the monastery and a person who maintained close contact with the young king. On the day of his visit to the monastery, the monarch ate some *ärtsoppa och pannkakor* (Pea soup and Pancakes), the usual lunch menu in Sweden on Thursdays! Here follows my letter to the Swedish king.

The picture, attached to the following letter, shows me presenting a written petition to a Swedish monarch. The subject of the petition was a bitter and destructive conflict between Ethiopia and Eritrea.

The Letter

1975-10-23
Ezra Gebremedhin
Östanbäcks Kloster, Sala

His Majesty, The King of Sweden
Royal Palace
Stockholm, Sweden

Your Majesty,

I am deeply grateful for the opportunity that was given me to meet Your Majesty personally during Your Majesty's visit to the monastery at Östanbäck some weeks ago. At that time, I handed over to Your Majesty a brochure describing the needs of refugees in Eritrea. I also promised that I would write to Your Majesty concerning the war in Eritrea and its effects on the civil population of Eritrea. I am now writing on that subject.

This is a personal plea, a cry for help on behalf of Eritrea's civil population, which is suffering from a bitter war between Ethiopian soldiers and Eritrean guerilla. It is true that both parties are suffering loss in life and property in this war. It has been reported that the war in Eritrea costs Ethiopia one million crowns per day. I am deeply distressed by these losses that my homeland Ethiopia is suffering.

At the same time, I must confess that what weighs heaviest on my heart now is the suffering of the civilian population in Eritrea. It is there that conflict is in progress. In spite of the fact that no journalists are now allowed into Eritrea, I have learnt, from sources that I consider to be reliable, that there are 110,000 Eritrean refugees in the Sudan alone. The number of refugees in Eritrea itself is estimated at 300,000. The villages where these people once lived have been bombed out. Cattle have been killed and fields of grain and grass burnt. There have even been reports of the poisoning of wells and rivers. Farmers have, in many areas, not been able to sow and those who have sown haven't been able to harvest. In spite of the fact that Eritrea was declared a famine-area already in 1974, The Red Cross and other relief agencies have not been granted permission to come into Eritrea with relief.

The Ethiopian Government's basic argument has been that relief that is given to the civilian population in Eritrea can be used by their guerilla. One cannot deny that there is an element of truth in this argument. From a purely strategic point of view one can understand how the Ethiopian Government is trying to crush the guerrilla movement by maintaining a famine situation among the civilian population. Since I do not have first-hand information on these matters I shall not be quick to pass a sweeping judgment. Nevertheless, it is not difficult for Your Majesty to see the possible long-range consequences of a policy of intentional deprivation of relief on the civilian population in Eritrea.

I myself am an Ethiopian citizen of Eritrean parentage. In this sense I suffer with both conflicting parties. As a pastor of the Evangelical Church Mekane Yesus in Ethiopia—a church on which Swedish missionaries have left deep marks during a period of service extending over 110 years—I would like to see something done to heal this open wound in the lives of the people of Ethiopia and Eritrea. I plead with Your Majesty to make those responsible for such issues in The Swedish Government aware of the plight of the people of Eritrea.

Respectfully,

Ezra Gebremedhin

[I did receive a written reply from the king, a short letter of some five or six lines. He had forwarded my request to an appropriate instance within the Swedish government. Unfortunately, I have not been able to trace this letter yet in my files.]

Year 1974 (1994)
Chapter 4

Rain-Drops:
Extracts from My Diary

Strength lies in the ordinary, in that which has the commonness, firmness, permanence of mountains, fields, and trees. Yes, strength lies in those things in nature that are simply there—quiet, firm and regular. Dreams, fluctuating thoughts, ups and downs in convictions, a tempestuous mental and emotional life whipped into frenzy or shattered by ideology or philosophy or crusades, these are the enemies to watch out for. Letting others set our standards for us, having our expectations conditioned by the standards that are loudly proclaimed and advertised by others—these are the dangers we and our children face. These are the demons to be rescued from.

The courage that is required of us is not primarily the courage of martyrs. It is the courage of those who plod regularly—those who take the common, the daily, the routine seriously. What is required of us is the courage to live in rhythm with other rhythms—yes to live in rhythm with nature's rhythm and the rhythms of a given place.

23.1.74, Carolina Rediviva—the main library of the University of Uppsala
What we have given away is what will remain with us. What we have not laboured to consolidate will remain stable. It is the marginal things, those simple graces and virtues of life, that have durability. Only those aspects of our personal relationships that have the constancy and availability of sunshine, water, and air can last. Love to the poor, help to those who can't

repay us, a word of comfort that expects nothing in return—these are the treasures to pursue.

> And finally, before leaving the topic of mitigating aggressions, a word should be said for the saving grace of wit and humour, which are so bountiful a release for hostile impulses in some people. That they are sometimes employed cruelly does not lessen their great utility for those fortunate enough to have found this way out. (Karl Menninger, *Man Against Himself*, 1938, 376)

27.1.73, Roskilde, Denmark

Reports on violence and oppression are not the sort of emotional and mental diet that one can live on for a long time. Such reports can upset our emotions to such an extent that we cease to plan and work soberly. And power lies, primarily, not in stormy emotions, but in small things done regularly, in rhythm with other rhythms of life. It is the steady drops of water that eventually crack rocks.

17.2.74, Uppsala

Think of men and women of research! They are people who have limited themselves to a certain routine. They are people who win quietly and over a long, long period of time.

18.2.74, Geneva, Home of Dr. Herbert Schaefer, a former missionary to Ethiopia

I have noticed that I have a constant temptation to reduce problems from the concrete to the abstract, from particularities to generalities, from details to principles, from realism to idealism. I have a way of preaching about every concrete situation—about seeing the so-called depth of a specific problem. I am afraid that that sort of thing can make me lonely. It can lead to sermons that don't solve problems—unless of course I can push the process through to the stage at which principles become actions.

14.6.74, Hälsingborg, Sweden (City Motel)

The annual Conference of the Evangeliska Fosterlands Stiftelsen (EFS), also known as The Swedish Evangelical Mission.

Don't try to crowd the wisdom of a lifetime into a one-hour address held at an assembly. Give people as much as they can chew at the given time. Feel their pulses. An assembly is a living organism. Learn to detect its temperature, its appetite, and then plant that small particle of truth that should be planted there—that little impulse that is ripe for transfer. You can't do serious business where there are 1,000 people gathered. Policy statements should be worked out and made in smaller groups. A gathering of many people should be a festival, not a regimented parade.

22.6.74, Midsummer Day, Rättvik, Sweden
Every community that you come into has struck its own balance. It has come to terms with its tensions and arrived at some kind of *modus vivendi* (mode of living or being). Don't entertain the illusion that you can, by a wave of your magic wand, open the eyes of the community in which you happen to be, to a mystery that only you know. Don't ever be deluded into believing that you, the newcomer, have the psychological and physical strength to shake this group and reorganize it overnight. The best that you can do is to listen to its deep chords, to be attuned to it.

3.11.74, Löten Church, Uppsala
There is something suspect about the desire to be correct. We had a Family Service this morning. Children and all. And of course there was disorder. Why do we adults insist on order? Are we afraid of something? Is it possible that we are afraid that the child within us can escape and come out into the open—the child whom Jesus invites and embraces?

17.12.74, Uppsala
A crisis has a way of making us rush to a specific scene or centre of attention. In this sense a crisis is the creator of distraction. It draws our attention away from that which is of a work-a-day character. And yet we are slow to realize that it is precisely the neglect of the work-a-day world that precipitates a crisis.

21.2.75, Uppsala
A sense of reality. That is our rescue. To know one's limits and respect them is sanity. To wait if one has to, to tone down one's ideals to the rhythm of reality—that is wisdom.

18.7.75, The Diocesan Centre at Rättvik
Russian and American Astronauts have docked their spaceships. This is the result of a long process of regular, hard, steady work. America has gone through its Watergate and through its Indo-China agonies. And Russia has surely had its hidden struggles. But the goal of docking American and Russian spaceships seems to have occupied scientists from both countries in a quiet, unbroken effort. Now we see the fruit of this faithfulness to routine.

Lord, I would be faithful in my small daily tasks in spite of the commotion that events in Ethiopia are causing inside me.

5.10.75, Östanbäck Monastery
We live in a world, a milieu that is greater than everything we can do. I feel that there is a meaningful, sustaining reality waiting to envelope us. Just as the water in which fish swim is greater and more potent than the fish themselves, so is the quiet, undetected reality that surrounds us greater and more capable of sustaining us than are our frantic efforts at doing things.

2.2.76, An evening meal at the Östanbäck Monastery, Sala, Sweden
There were the tulips in the clean crystal vase on the table at which the abbot, Father Johannes, sat. And the quiet faces of people eating. The faces of monks, guests (both men and women) with candle light playing on them. And of course the sound of cutlery rubbing against the porridge bowls of glass and metal. Simplicity. Simple food. Simple light. Simple clothing. Simple music. And quiet faces.

13.4.76, Östanbäck
No one can accomplish great things if he has not learnt to carry small things through to completion.

8.11.75, Uppsala, Koinonia—a student-hostel for students of Theology
Here is a prayer that I uttered one week before a crucial meeting with Dr. L. Thunberg, my advisor, concerning my doctoral thesis.

> Lord! I would be like Elijah who gathered his stones, wood, meat and water for the sacrifice—and then waited for Thee (2 Kings 18: 30–34). Help me too to gather and pile up my academic stones, wood, meat and water properly—and to wait quietly.

Sometime during 1975, Uppsala
"The giving of a place to those who have none seems to me to be one way of defining our vocation as healers of persons. As we have seen, one becomes a person only if one really has a place." (Paul Tournier, *A Place for You*, 1968, 79)

11.11.78, Norrköping
Alongside our religious pronouncements runs the world of laws and natural necessities. The laws of cause and effect, the rhythm of night and day. Life

and death, heredity, pollution, or renewal. This is a strong world, a quiet, invincible world. As far as we know quite a predictable world.

But there is the world of our religious pronouncements, our confessions, our prayers, our admonitions. A world that is not guided by the same obvious laws that guide the world of nature and history. This spiritual world often gives the impression of a construction, a framework from which one glides away time and time again, because it does not have the same obvious down-to-earth, day-to-day character of our hunger and thirst, our fatigue, and our need of rest. Thus, to operate in this religious sphere can become a strenuous effort.

Now, Lord, I don't know if I have made a fool of myself again. But Thou who art Lord of nature—of what I call the obvious—and of all that is beyond, under and above the obvious—let these words rest in Thy presence.

1978, Uppsala
The problem with discarding all symbols in speaking about God is that we can very well lose our handles on Him.

17.7.82, On the train to Gothenburg
It is often either fools or saints who take drastic steps. When saints do so, they do it in all simplicity. I should think almost with ease. They do not act like those who must muster every ounce of energy to lift a heavy weight. They have been trained in making many small decisions in simplicity, humility, and obedience. And when the time for the big decisions comes, saints may go through anguish, but the decisions themselves are taken in utter simplicity—I presume, without calculations, subterfuges, or camouflages.

1982, Uppsala
No help is worth the name if it cannot be reduced into the kind of supportive routine that remains when you and your lofty words are gone. In this sense organization and law are paramount.

Thomas Merton writes in his *The Sign of Jonas* (2000): "The simplest and most effective way to sanctify is to disappear into the background of everyday routine." How true, and yet how difficult to accept!

1.11.82, Östanbäck
After reading C. S. Lewis's *A Grief Observed* (1961) I had to pray: "Lord! I too feel that I am rich in froth. Please get me down to solid ground."

Work, involvement in routine is an antidote to the sort of introversion and swaying back and forth in mystic heights that eats one's insides like acid. I guess that is why God gave Adam and Eve work to do (Genesis 2:15).

16.4.83, Lund
I presume that the words, "Well done, my good and trusty servant! ... You have proved trustworthy in a small way; I will now put you in charge of something big." (Matt. 25:21) apply also to our prayer life. Only when we gratefully receive our little gifts and use them faithfully can we pray for the greater things and greater openings.

10.11.83, Uppsala.
In his book *Surprised by Joy,* C.S. Lewis writes the following about one of his teachers: "Sirrah, as we called him, had been an admirable influence. He was what I would now describe as a wise madcap: a boisterous, boyish, hearty man, well able to keep his authority while yet mixing with us almost as one of ourselves, an untidy, rollicking man without a particle of affectation. He communicated (what I very much needed) a sense of the gusto with which life ought, wherever possible, to be taken. I fancy it was on a run with him in the sleet that I first discovered how bad weather is to be treated—as a rough joke, a romp." (1981, 58).

1983, Uppsala
"Perhaps if Man is finally to know the bodiless, timeless, transcendent Ground of the whole universe not as a mere philosophical abstraction but as the Lord who, despite this transcendence, is 'not far from any of us', as an utterly concrete Being (far more concrete than we) whom man can fear, love, address and 'taste', he must begin far more humbly and far nearer home, with the local altar, the traditional feast, and the treasured memories of God's judgements, promises and mercies. Since in the end we are to come to Baptism and the Eucharist, to the stable at Bethlehem, the hill of Calvary, and the emptied rock-tomb, perhaps it is better to begin with circumcision, the Passover, the Ark, and the Temple. For 'the highest does not stand without the lowest'. ... For the entrance is low: we must stoop till we are no taller than children in order to get in." (C. S. Lewis, *Reflections on the Psalms,* 1981, 75). How beautiful!

1985, Uppsala
John Newton, author of the hymn *Amazing Grace,* writes the following on dreams: "The most notable impulse which I have ever experienced

happened during a dream. Those who know the Holy Scriptures will verify that there have always been warning and miraculous dreams, which either prophesy or direct the future, apparently as communications from heaven. And those people who have wandered into the history of God's people know well that God has not restricted this communication with Him to any particular time period." (Quoted by M Kelsey in his *Dreams. A Way to Listen to God* (1978, 11).

January, 1988, Uppsala
"The year of the Nudges. Nudges from God, that is, or twitches upon the tether. Nine or ten of them, all having the effect of making me think about my distant God." (Sheldon Vanauken, *Under the Mercy*, 1985, 94)

August 1992, Collegeville, Minnesota
"Any mind that is capable of a real sorrow is capable of good." (Harriet Beecher Stowe, *Uncle Tom's Cabin*, 1965, 309)

May 1993, Uppsala
"But we must recognize that it is particularly religious people who, far from being joyously liberated by the good news of grace, are so obsessed by the fear of committing sin that all their spontaneity, their growth and their development is stifled." (Paul Tournier, *The Violence Inside*, 1978, 48)

September 7, 1993, Mekane Yesus Seminary, Addis Ababa
I have just returned from the customs section of the Addis Ababa International Airport. With the help of Ato Negussie of the Mekane Yesus Seminary, I managed to get out my unaccompanied luggage. A murderously time-consuming process. I was there alone in the afternoon. While there, I wrote the following words at the back of my almanac: "Slow, sleepy movements by workers. Fast, staccato exchange of words among those who were joking, teasing each other, without any offence being taken. There seems to be little respect for queues. The porters are those who work hardest and seem to be the most human of the lot—bound by a simple down-to-earth comradeship. Is it because they share the struggle and fatigue of everyday life?"

Can one possibly quote the words of Matthew 5:5 here: "How blest are those of a gentle spirit, for they shall have the earth for their possession" (Matthew 5:5)?

September, 8,1993, Mekane Yesus Seminary, Addis Ababa
I am sitting at the breakfast table at the home of the Nordlanders, a Swedish missionary couple. A teacup with its contents half-consumed stands to my

right. To my left lies the window with sunshine streaming in. Through the window, at a distance of a couple hundred metres, I see houses and huts clustered at the top of the farther side of the Mekanissa River—an elevated part of the river bank. The edges of the roof appear to jostle into each other. The rays of the sun are divided into different shafts of light that rest on corrugated iron roofs, bushes, eucalyptus trees, and whatever little piece of ground that happens to be exposed. Things are wet. The morning dew is strong out here, on both sides of the river. A very thin and soft blanket of dewy vapour fills the spaces between trees and roofs, softly. The refrigerator near me appears to maintain a steady hum. Outside I hear the gentle twitter of birds. The village looks quiet, even though it is already almost eight o'clock in the morning. I see a solitary man walking by, slowly, like many an Ethiopian on an early morning—a reminder of bodies and limbs that sleep has not yet left completely. Yes, nature, the ordinary, speaks to us in its own way. A book written in letters of many kinds. A scene so ordinary, and yet so strong. The ordinary, that which is of a workaday character, is also God's language.

September 8, 1993, Mekane Yesus Seminary, Addis Ababa
In one of his letters to an American lady, C. S. Lewis writes, "I love the empty, silent, dewy, cobwebby hours." (Lewis, *Letters to An American Lady,* 1971, 78). As I walked to my job early this morning, I noticed some hedges with, precisely, cobwebs! There is something strong about beginning the day early, even though I am no hero in this respect. The early morning is a reminder of the Biblical promise that God's mercies are new every morning. (Lamentations 3: 22–23).

September 25, 1993, Addis Ababa
A clear, almost totally blue sky. The high clear air of Autumn in Addis Ababa. I am sitting at a table at the Post Rendez-Vous, a café/snack bar combination. To my left, at a distance of almost a hundred metres, stands a massive monument with a red star perched on top. The giant stone-creation is "Tiglatchin" (*Our Struggle*), a reminder of the days of Mengistu Haile-Mariam, who was Ethiopia's Head of State during the dark Marxist interim of seventeen years. I also see a hammer and sickle some six meters below the star. About a quarter of an hour ago I had a closer look at the monument. I could read the words, "Down with Imperialism!" "Land to the tiller!" "Let him who does not work not eat!" The inscription at the foot of the centre-piece of the monument had been erased (or the letters plucked off). All over the spacious park around the· monument lay people on the grass,

many of them in rags. Some boys were playing football on the cement-court at the base of the monument.

I can understand the pathos behind the slogans. However, looking back on what did happen in Ethiopia, one is inclined to say: There is a pathetic kind of futility in all things that are loud and ostentatious. And this monument is a proof of that fact. If we only could understand that what a country needs, is not noise or bustle or flare, but loyal, dedicated people who work away quietly at little things!

November 20, 1993, Mekane Yesus Seminary
It is early morning again at the seminary. From the veranda of our house, I hear the engine of what appears to be a small aeroplane warming up. A thin mist lies between the eucalyptus trees and the buildings. Birds are chirping away and the shrill crowing of a cock pierces the morning air. I hear the engines of cars and trucks. A growing chorus of noises announces the beginning of a new day. The sun shines gently on and in between some eucalyptus trees, casting soft shafts of light diagonally on the sides of trees and buildings. Another day has started. An indirect reminder of the Psalmist, who writes of nocturnal animals who begin to seek their dens and man who goes off to his tasks at the beginning of the day. (Psalm 104:22–23.)

Sunday November 20, 1993, Mekane Yesus Seminary, Addis Ababa
Consider the following words from Jerome K. Jerome's book *Three Men in a Boat* (2013): "Sunlight is the life-blood of Nature. Mother Earth looks at us with such dull, soulless eyes, when the sunlight has died away from out of her. It makes us sad to be with her then; She does not seem to know us or to care for us. She is a widow who has lost the husband she loved, and her children touch her hand, and look into her eyes, but gain no smile from her."

Thank God that there is plenty of sunshine here in Addis! There is something wonderful about the high, clear Autumn-air at this altitude. Addis is, furthermore, a city of cool breezes, even when the sun is at its hottest. There is a dry and breezy cleanliness about the atmosphere—as long as one does not come too close to the ground! When I think of the fact that our children and grand-children have to cope with winter in Sweden, a surge of gratitude goes through my heart—and a longing that they too would get a share of this great gift of God.

March 19, 1994, home, Mekane Yesus Seminary
Hot sun. This recurrent feeling that there is something overwhelming and, in the long range, damaging about the stark heat of the sun here. Strange, in

Sweden we used to long for sunshine and warmth. And here we sometimes feel oppressed by the same sun whose warmth we have been longing for.

February 2, 1994, On the way home to Mettu from Dupa, Ethiopia
We have just passed the very small, primitive village of Suppe—the birthplace, according to my informants, of Be'alu Girma, a famous journalist and author. Among his most famous writings is *Oromai*—the story, in the form of a novel, of the Red Star Campaign of the 1980's, the unsuccessful all-out military and socio-political effort to crush the Eritrean struggle for independence. Be'alu disappeared shortly after the publication of the book during the years of the Derg. His car was found abandoned. His mother, I understand, lives in Suppe. Once again, Suppe is a proof of the fact that humble beginnings are no hindrance to greatness.

March 1, 1994, On our way to Addis from Nakamte
I see women dressed in second-hand Western dresses, carrying water gourds on their backs! One of the new examples of incongruence here in Ethiopia.

July 8, 1994, Nairobi
" '*Take Thou Lesson from the Tree,*' is worth laying to one's heart. The tree bears the heat of the sun and yet provides cool shade to us. What do we do?" (Gandhi).

> "Those who have the greatest measure of self-control or are most absorbed in work, speak the least. Speech and action go ill together. Look at Nature. She is continuously in action, never rests for a single moment, yet is mute." (Gandhi)

July, 1994, Uppsala
Rowan Williams writes the following on Luther's understanding of life in the workaday world: "His personal and theological affirmation of the Christian possibilities of life outside the cloister, in family and society, was for him an unavoidable consequence of the whole style of theological interpretation he had evolved. For countless others it was a message of liberation-perhaps cheaply and glibly apprehended by some, but none the less genuine and effective. Those who see Luther as the first exponent of 'secularizing' theology forget the profound and costly understanding of faith which underlies his 'conversion to the world'." (Rowan Williams, *The Wound of Knowledge. Christian Spirituality from the New Testament to St. John of The Cross, Cowley Publications,* 1981, p. 152).

August 5, 1994, Uppsala

The following are the words of Colin Wilson on the Russian monk, Rasputin: "As to mysticism and the Christian ethic of self-sacrifice and self-torment he was completely out of sympathy. His religion was sincere, but vital and primitive, closer to the ecstatic Dionysiansm described by Nietzsche in The Birth of Tragedy. It was an instinctive worship of the power of the universe, and it was logical that sex should play a part in it." (Cohn Wilson, *Rasputin and the Fall of the Romanovs*, 1966 , Granada Publishing Ltd. St. Albans. Hertfordshire. p. 133).

This is what happens when Nature is allowed to reign supreme and when Church, sacrament, discipline, penance have no normative value. Nature is powerful and she has throbbing allies within us. No wonder Rasputin has been described as "Saint, satyr, drunkard, miracle-worker, political schemer of Machiavellian proportions ...."

October 22, 1994, St. David's Retreat Centre, Rättvik

I am sitting in the living room, sipping at my cup of tea and listening to Mozart. In the centre of the room is the fireplace with its flames dancing. I thought of fire and water—these mighty and frightening elements. Fire that warms but also consumes. Water that quenches thirst but also drowns. I thought of the raging waves that recently swallowed *Estonia* with its hundreds of passengers on the Baltic Sea. I thought to myself: Fire, which warms us on this cold, northern Autumn evening, and whose dancing flames are a joy to the eye, is good and strong, as long as it remains what it is and, above all, as long as it *stays* where it should. Water too is good and strong, as long as it remains what it is and stays where it should! You and I too are good and strong, as long as we remain what we are and, above all, *stay* where we should.

Year 1997 (2020)
Chapter 5

Generators of Contact and Conflict among Swedes and Ethiopian and Eritrean Refugees (I)

This is the first of three articles based on a paper prepared for the 22nd ATEE (Association for Teacher Education in Europe) Annual Conference, held from the 26th to the 30th of August, 1997, in Macerata (Italy) under the Title Religious and Cultural Elements as Generators of Contact and Conflict among Swedes and Ethiopian and Eritrean Refugees. The theme for the 1997 conference was "The Implication of Migration Flows for Educational Practices and the Preparation of Education."[1]

A Small Digression!

We are in March 2020. Permit me to begin with a little story from the city of Macerata, where our conference was held in the last week of August in 1997. Some of those of us who had come from Sweden were out at an outdoor café somewhere in the city. I presume that we had taken a break and were eager to enjoy the sunshine of a historic place. Just a turn of my head brought my eyes within view of a stone pillar that carried some lines which even I, with my poor Italian, could understand. I was looking at a memorial stone for young Italian soldiers from Macerata who had died in an "unequal battle," fought on January 26, 1887 between Italy and Ethiopia, at Dogali, near Massawa, in present-day Eritrea! Almost 500 Italian soldiers were ambushed and killed by the troops of Ras Alula, a native Ethiopian commander of Tigreyan stock. Professor Bahru Zewde writes:

News of the Battle of Dogali provoked a frenzied reaction in Italy. The call for revenge was heard in the streets as well as in the government chambers. Parliament voted for an appropriation of 20 million lire for the defense of Massawa and its environs. A special force of 5000 men was organized to reinforce the existing troops. Roads and bridges were built and repaired in an effort to strengthen the infrastructure for future military action.[2]

I was deeply saddened by the ambush of Italian youth at Dogali but was relieved, as I sipped away at my cup of coffee, that at least the Italians in Macerata were no longer after Ethiopians and Eritreans who had killed their sons 110 years earlier! I could finish my cup of coffee in peace!

Here then is the article from 1997.[3]

Let me begin with some words on my background. The fact that I have lived in Sweden for the past 27 years, doing research in the field of Theology, teaching and working as a pastor at different intervals, has given me opportunities to associate with Ethiopian and Eritrean refugees.[4]

Previous Studies

A number of studies have been carried out in Sweden on the different ethnic categories of refugees or immigrants, on the process of their (successful or unsuccessful) adaptation to Swedish society and on the interactions between them and the Swedish people. In 1966, David Schwarz, one of the pioneers in the systematic study of immigrants and their integration into Swedish society with respect to their identity, edited a book entitled *Svenska minoriteter* (*Swedish Minorities*).[5] There is hardly anything about African groups in it. Of course, one could argue that there were hardly any African refugees in Sweden at that time. However, multiethnic or ethnological research projects at the main Swedish universities (whose work in this particular area is characterized by great vitality and variety) have not done much in the decades that followed Schwarz's work, as far as African groups are concerned.[6] A type-written study about Tanzanian students in Sweden by William E Hughes, *Relations between Swedes and Black Ethnic Groups,* is an exception to this statement, particularly in view of its approach.[7]

The work *Det mångkulturella Sverige: en handbok om etniska grupper och minoriteter i Sverige* (*Multi-Cultural Sweden: A Handbook on Ethnic Groups and Minorities in Sweden*), edited by Ingvar Svanberg and Harald Runblom, an otherwise excellent source book, hardly redresses this apparent lack of attention to African refugees, even though its short and instructive thematic presentations on immigrant issues cover, indirectly, also Ethiopian and Eritrean refugees. Eritrea is represented by one short article.[8]

A number of shorter studies or parts of studies on Ethiopia and Eritrea are available, however. These are of great interest, in spite of their brevity. The work entitled *Afrikaner i Sverige* (*Africans in Sweden*) includes an instructive article by Gaim Kibreab and Woldu Kidane, entitled "Eritreanska flyktingar i Sverige" ("Eritrean Refugees in Sweden").[9] The collection itself consists of shorter and longer articles published under the auspices of The National Aid to Religious Bodies (SST). I think it is an excellent presentation of the individual impressions and experiences of Africans who have lived in Sweden. It includes articles by both men and women and attempts not only to give information but also to analyze issues. Inger Björkegren's *Eritreaner i Sverige. En rapport om erfarenheterna av arbetet bland de eritreanska flyktingarna i Sverige* (*Eritreans in Sweden. A Report on the Experiences from Work Among Eritrean Refugees in Sweden*; 1985), Kerstin Björns's *Från Asmara till Heidenstamstorg* (*From Asmara to Heidenstams Square*; 1990), and Andrea Faber's *Från tanke till vardagen. Integrationsprocess bland eritreanska flyktingar* (*From Thought to Everyday Life. The Process of Integration among Eritrean Refugees*; 1991, are all well-written and informative essays.[10] Charles Westin, who takes up an "African" issue in a work that came out in 1990, chooses, interestingly enough, Ugandan *Asians* in Sweden as his subject.[11] Gambians in Sweden are the subject of a study in Ulla Wagner's and Bawa Yamba's article, "Going North and Getting Attached."[12] Africans have also been included in various studies on discrimination. Somalis in Sweden are, according to reports, becoming an increasingly interesting subject of research.

The works of the Chilean scholar Orlando Mella[13] are exclusively on immigrants or refugees from Chile. However, a quick glance at the table of contents of his two works, *Religion in the Lives of Refugees and Immigrants*[14] and *Searching for the Sacred: A Comparative Study of Popular Religiosity among Refugees in Sweden,*[15] suggests that his studies are partly applicable to refugees from Ethiopia and Eritrea. The subtitles "Involvement in the Sacred" and "Religious Rituals" are of particular interest in this regard. Lena Södergran's recent work from Umeå University, *Invandrar- och flyktingpolitik i praktiken: exemplet Umeå kommun,*[16] does not, unfortunately, give the national or ethnic categories of the refugees that are the subject of her studies.

All told, Africans (and, by implication, Ethiopians and Eritreans) are under-represented in the field of multi-ethnic research in Sweden. Is this a reflection of the great cultural distance between many African refugee groups and Swedes? Or is it a symptom of the feeling that the study of African refugees in Sweden is a subject for which there is very little demand or market? Or is the relatively small size of African refugees a possible explanation?

It has been pointed out to me by Ingvar Svanberg that most of the multiethnic research carried out in Sweden so far deals with immigrants who arrived in Sweden in the 1960s and that these studies cover mainly immigrants whose families have been in Sweden for more than one generation. This explains why research so far has concentrated on Fins, Greeks, Turks, and Yugoslavs.

Scope and Method

This paper will deal with Christian Ethiopians and Eritreans among the refugees in Sweden for the period extending roughly from 1974 to 1997. This limitation must be made for the simple reason that my contacts and my work as pastor and "elder" have been mainly among these groups. My contacts with Ethiopian and Eritrean Muslims in Sweden are very limited indeed. They should make an interesting subject of study.

My intention is to present some aspects of the meeting of the cultures and Christian faith of two East African groups with Swedish culture, religious views, and general attitudes. I do not intend to spell out, in any detail, the pedagogical implications of these encounters. To quote from Svanberg and Szabó's *Etniskt liv och kulturellt mångfald* (*Ethnic Life and Cultural Pluralism*), "To portray the everyday life of immigrants means focusing on their understanding of reality, cognitive reality, that which is sometimes called 'the mental map'."[17] This mental map is partly what I shall try to understand. However, I am confident that some of the questions I am going to raise will lend themselves to use for pedagogical purposes.

My method is very simple. I shall reason and write on the basis of almost twenty-five years of personal experience as pastor, teacher, and mediator among Ethiopians and Eritreans in Sweden. I have not used questionnaires, tabulations, or interpretations of any sort. Those who want to enter more deeply into the question of methods in immigrant or refugee research here in Sweden and other Nordic countries could consult the method sections in Lange and Westin's *Ungdomen om Invandringen*,[18] Runblom's *Synpunkter på norsk invandrarforskning*,[19] Svanberg and Szabó's *Etniskt liv och kulturellt mångfald. En handbok i invandrardokumentation*[20], and Kjell Magnusson and Orlando Mella's, *Invandrarungdomars verklighet:en metodstudie* (*The "World of Reality" of Immigrant Youth: A Methodological Study*).[21]

Chapter 5 41

A word on Literature: This work is being presented in English. However, much of the literature cited in it will have to be in Swedish, for the simple reason that the context for the encounter of Swedes, Ethiopians and Eritreans *is* Sweden. The readership I am thinking of is primarily Swedish and most of the literature on refugees and immigrants in Sweden happens to be in Swedish.

Statistics

It is not easy to get detailed statistics on Ethiopians and Eritreans in Sweden. According to the Statens Invandrarverk[22] (The National Department for Immigrant Questions), as of December 31, 1996, there were 4,371 Ethiopian citizens in Sweden. The number of Eritrean citizens was 698. The number of Ethiopians who had received Swedish passports up to December 1996 was 7,686. No information was available on Eritreans who had received Swedish citizenship. We can thus count on a total of 12,755 residents from the two countries as of December 1966. The Statens Invandrarverk had no information on the religious affiliations of these persons.[23]

The Ortodoxa- och österländska kyrkors ekumeniska råd (OÖKER= The Ecumenical Council for Orthodox and Oriental Churches), with its base in Stockholm, has only an Ethiopian Orthodox Church listed among the churches that receive financial assistance through it from The Cooperative Council for State Grants to Religious Denominations. There are 2,000 Ethiopians registered as belonging to this congregation, served by two priests and one bishop in exile. SST officials maintain nevertheless that such statistics are very preliminary.

The Eritrean Orthodox attend either The Swedish Orthodox Church, served by a priest of Italian origin, or the larger Eritreanska Ortodoxa Församlingen (The Eritrean Orthodox Parish) served by an Eritrean priest. On the basis of his report, there are about 3,000 Eritrean Orthodox attached in some way to his priestly functions. He maintains that the total number of Eritrean Orthodox throughout Sweden is higher. A total of 5,000 has been mentioned. Neither of these two congregations receives help from the SST through OÖKER. The SST could therefore not provide figures on their memberships.

Neither Ethiopian and Eritrean Muslims nor Catholics of either nation are registered by nationalities. Hence, it has not been possible to secure statistics on their sizes.

This applies also to the various Protestant groups. There are however several hundred Ethiopian and Eritrean Lutherans in Sweden. Those who are active churchgoers have found their spiritual homes in congregations like Lötenkyrkan in Uppsala, Betlehemskyrkan in Stockholm and Lutherska Missionskyrkan in Gothenburg. Others attend local churches of the Church of Sweden in their own parishes. There are also several hundred Ethiopians and Eritreans who belong to different Pentecostal groups.

The Eritrean Catholics have their own priest here in Sweden. He has a very wide parish, since Eritrean Catholics too are widely scattered in Sweden.

It should be stated from the outset that, according to the National Department for Immigrant Questions (*Statens Invandraverk* or SIV), among the 7,686 "Ethiopians" who have received Swedish citizenship, the majority are very likely to be Eritreans. In any case, Eritreans have always been in the majority here in Sweden but they have been registered as Ethiopian citizens, since Eritrea was a part of Ethiopia until 1991. I have received information to the effect that in many cases the computers still operate on the basis of older information on this subject and that, in spite of Eritrea's independence, a great number of Eritreans still find themselves registered as Ethiopians.

According to information from the Eritrean Embassy in Stockholm, a total of 5,931 had been registered as Eritreans up to July of 1997. This number comprises those who voted on the referendum for Eritrea's independence, Eritreans who turned eighteen after the referendum, and those who had not been registered as Eritreans before but have done so since. The number does not include Eritreans who have not turned eighteen. Of the total of 5,931, some 2,957 are male and 2,974 are female.

With this introduction as a basis, I shall now proceed to treat my overall topic of "Generators of Contact and Conflict among Swedes and Ethiopian and Eritrean Refugees" in parts II and III of this essay.

Notes

1 To the best of my recollection, I never got the opportunity to present this paper in full. (For more details on literary sources in some footnotes please see the partial bibliography that I have included at the end of this (whole) document!)

2 Bahru Zewde, *A History of Modern Ethiopia 1855–1991* (London: James Curry / Athens, Ohio: Ohio University Press / Addis Ababa: Addis Ababa University Press, 1991), p. 57.

3 When I first wrote this article, about 27 years ago, I felt that I was taking up a dreary but necessary subject, with a superabundance of dry facts. I was therefore encouraged when my friend Herui Tedla Bairu wrote the following comment in a private letter after reading the entire essay in the month of October, 2019: "Pastor Ezra's articles (*Religious and Cultural Elements as Generators*

Chapter 5

of Contact and Conflict among Swedes and Ethiopian and Eritrean Refugees) ... are a must to the researcher in this field."

4   Here in Sweden, I belong to The Church of Sweden and am on its roster of priests. Before Ethiopian and Eritrean refugees who belong to the Ethiopian Orthodox Church and (to a limited extent) the Catholic Church here in Sweden got their own priests, I was requested, on many occasions, to baptize children and perform weddings and funerals among them. My main duties were however among the members of the Ethiopian Evangelical Church Mekane Yesus and The Evangelical Church of Eritrea. Both are of Evangelical Lutheran persuasion and their churches trace their origins to the missionary efforts of the Evangeliska Fosterlands-Stiftelsen (The Swedish Evangelical Mission). The thoughts expressed in this paper are derived from my experiences as pastor among all the groups mentioned.

5   D. Schwarz (ed.), *Svenska minoriteter* (*Swedish Minorities*) (Stockholm: Aldus/Bonnier, 1966). See also his *Invandrar- och minoritetsforskning m.m.* (*Research on Migration, Minority Issues, etc.*), published in 1973 by Sociologiska Institutionen. Stockholms Universitet. Stockholm (The Sociological Institution of the University of Stockholm).

6   I. Svanberg, K. Magnusson, C. Westin, and H. Runblom are all men of research and prolific writers in the area of multiethnic relations, particularly in a Swedish context. Svanberg combines the study of themes or topics with the study of specific ethnic groups. Magnusson's strength lies in his study of peoples, particularly the ethnic elements in what was once Yugoslavia. Westin takes up a very broad spectrum of subjects. Perhaps he is the most phenomenological among the lot, even though much of his research is empirical. Runblom's specialty is Swedish emigration to the Americas. However, his research also takes up Baltic issues. See I. Svanberg (with H. Runblom), *Det mångkulturella Sverige: en handbok om etniska minoriteter i Sverige* (*Multi-Cultural Sweden: A Handbook on Ethnic Groups and Minorities in Sweden*), 2nd ed. Stockholm Gidlund. Uppsala Centrum för multietnisk forskning (Uppsala Centre for Multiethnic Research), Uppsala, 1990. See also I. Svanberg & K. Borevi (eds.), *Ethnic Life and Minority Cultures* (Uppsala Centre for Multiethnic Research, Uppsala, 1992) and I. Svanberg, *thnicity, Minorities and Cultural Encounters* (Uppsala Centre for Multiethnic Research, Uppsala, 1993).

7   Hughes, 1971.

8   Svanberg & Runblom 1990.

9   G. Kibreab, G. and W. Kidane, "Eritreanska flyktingar i Sverige" ("Eritrean Refugees in Sweden") in *Afrikaner i Sverige* (*Africans in Sweden*), SIV Pocket (Statens Invandrarverk, Stockholm, 1983).

10 See Björkegren, 1985, Björn 1990 and Faber1991.

11 Westin 1990.

12 U. Wagner & B. Yamba, "Going North and Getting Attached," *Ethnos*, 1986 (51:3-4) 199-222.

13 See his *Religion in the Life of Refugees and Immigrants* (1994) and *Searching*

for the Sacred. A Comparative Study of Popular Religiosity among Refugees in Sweden (1996).

14 Mella 1994.

15 Mella 1996.

16 L. Södergran, *Invandrar- och flyktingpolitik i praktiken: exemplet Umeå kommun* (*Immigration and Refugee Politics in Practice: The Example of Umea County*), published in 1997 by The Sociological Institution of Umeå University.

17 I. Svanberg and M. Szabó, *Etniskt liv och kulturellt mångfald. En handbok i invandrardokumentation* (*Ethnic Life and Cultural Pluralism—A Handbook on Immigrant Documentation*), published in 1993 by Nordiska museet, Stockholm, 1993), p. 183.

18 A. Lange & C. Westin, *Ungdomen om invandringen* (*Youth on Immigration*); a series in three volumes, covering 1991, 1992, and 1993, published by The Centre for Immigrant Research of Stockholm University.

19 H. Runblom, *Synpunkter på norsk invandrarforskning* (*Points of View on Norwegian Immigrant Research*), published in 1992 by NORAS (Norges råd for anvendt samfunnsforskning), Norway's Council for Applied Social Research, Oslo.

20 Svanberg & Szabó 1993. See also D. Schwarz, *Invandrar- och minoritetsforskning m.m.* (*Research on Migration, Minority Issues, etc.*), published in 1973 by Sociologiska Institutionen. Stockholms Universitet. Stockholm (The Sociological Institution of the University of Stockholm).

21 Magnusson & Mella 1982.

22 This is based on a letter written to the writer by Hans Nidsjö of the Economic Section, on June 25, 1997.

23 For statistical information on Ethiopians an Eritreans in Sweden after 2015, see Chapter 41 (below), "Integration (I): Sweden's Growing Challenge (2019)."

Year 1997
Chapter 6

Generators of Contact and Conflict among Swedes and Ethiopian and Eritrean Refugees (II):

Points of Contact

A Reservoir of Missionary Experiences

Sweden is a country with a long history of contacts both with what is now Eritrea and with Ethiopia. Swedish Lutheran missionaries came to the hot and humid coast of Eritrea in 1866.[1] Several of the missionaries were to proceed inland to Kunama only to fall victim to sickness and, in some cases, violence.[2] The graves of these missionaries still dot parts of the Eritrean countryside. The Evangelical Church of Eritrea is a fruit of the work of these missionaries. Swedes have played an important part in the introduction of basic education and health care into the country, in spite of severe limitations placed upon them by Italian colonial authorities.[3] At the same time, it may be of interest for the country that is hosting this congress to know that the Swedish missionaries in Eritrea had some highly appreciated Italian Protestant (Waldensian) co-workers, with their centre at Torre Pelice in Italy.[4] It has been maintained that the promotion of Tigrinya as a written language by some Swedish missionaries already in the 1890s and Swedish Church aid to Eritrean war-refugees both at home and abroad beginning in the early 1980s, may have contributed to the strengthening of an already mounting sense of Eritrean identity.[5] A considerable number of Eritrean refugees to Sweden (but especially the older ones among them) have some knowledge about Sweden's contributions to Eritrea. Not a few of them have parents, relatives, and friends among Eritrean Lutherans, commonly known as *Kenisha.*

An Eritrean Orthodox priest of Evangelical persuasion and some of his co-workers had arrived in Wolläga, Ethiopia, already in 1898.[6] The first Swedish Lutheran missionary entered Ethiopia proper in 1904.[7] It should be mentioned that Ethiopia, and particularly what is now Oromo territory, was the primary target of Evangeliska-Fosterlands Stiftelsen (the Swedish Evangelical Mission). In their plan for missionary work in Ethiopia, the mission stay in Eritrea was only a prelude made necessary by the turbulence that prevailed in Ethiopia proper when the first Swedish missionaries arrived at Massawa.[8]

Since the advent of the first Swedish missionary, an almost uninterrupted stream of other missionaries has found its way into Ethiopia—at first, into its capital city and later on into the western and southern parts of the country. When Italy invaded Ethiopia in 1935, Sweden was one of the first countries to send a Red Cross team to the country's southern front. International opinion was shocked and outraged when the team, its tents, patients, and Swedish and Ethiopian personnel were bombed ruthlessly by Mussolini's aircraft, in spite of the fact that the Red Cross tents were plainly marked.[9] For thousands of Ethiopians, the members of the Swedish Red Cross Ambulance became heroes.

A Reservoir of Development-Aid Experiences

After the Second World War, the Ethiopian government recruited several hundred Swedish teachers, medical personnel, officers, and civil servants to help Ethiopia build up its educational, medical, military, and administrative networks. Soon, Swedish government development aid found its way into the country and is still an important part of Ethiopia's aid reservoir. Books as well as reports by NIB (Namnden för Internationellt Bistånd or Commission for International Assistance)[10] and its successor SIDA (Swedish International Development Co-operation Agency) were sources of valuable information. Since the Ethio-Swedish Building Unit (= ESBU), also backed by SIDA, was actively engaged in the building of schools in Eritrea for a number of years, its reports contain significant information on Eritrea. SIDA's old organ, *Rapport*, has now been replaced by *Omvärlden*.[11]

Measure of General Preparedness to Receive Ethiopian and Eritrean Refugees

What we stated above meant that Sweden and the Swedish people had been exposed to news and information on Eritrea and Ethiopia for decades.

Chapter 6

Swedes of an older generation had managed to accumulate a reservoir of knowledge about and love for these countries. Three periodicals can be said to have played an important role (together for over a century) in providing popular, grass-roots information to Swedes about Eritrea and Ethiopia. *Budbäraren* (*The Messenger*), which previously had gone by the name *Missions-Tidning* (*Mission News*), began appearing under its present name in 1927. However, its predecessor had been started already in 1838. The other periodical (which was in fact a yearly publication in book-form), known as *Varde Ljus!* (*Let There be Light!*), began coming out in 1893 and ceased in 1959.[12]

As a result of a theological debate that had gone on within the Evangeliska Fosterlands-Stiftelsen (EFS) in Sweden, a new, break-away Lutheran mission organization by the name of Bibeltrogna-Vänner (BV, Bible-True Friends) was constituted in June of 1911. Its organ, *Bibeltrogna Vänners Missionstidning,* as well as books and pamphlets by its missionaries, were to become channels of rich information on both Eritrea and Ethiopia.[13] BV's organ has a new name as of January 1997. It is now called *Till Liv* (*To Life*).[14]

An organization that has contributed to the maintenance of a steady stream of general information on and contact with Swedes who have worked in Ethiopia is Svensk-Etiopiska Föreningen (The Swedish-Ethiopian Society). Its organ, *Tenaestelin* (ጤና ፡ ይስጥልኝ, the Amharic greeting that means, literally, "May He (God) give you health!", is, at the time of the writing of this paper, 49 years old.[15]

A Swedish-Eritrean Association has recently been established. It came into being in 1997. It envisages co-operation in the areas of economics, culture, and politics.

Part of Sweden's former store of knowledge and love for Ethiopia and Eritrea dates back to the earlier refugees who arrived in the country in the late seventies. Both the churches and the communal authorities had, in other words, a measure of preparedness to receive and accommodate these refugees and their children. There were Swedes who knew Amharic, Tigrinya, and Oromiffa. Many had worked as teachers, doctors, and nurses. They had knowledge of the histories, social structures, and educational and medical needs of these peoples.

However, the older generation of Swedes acquainted with Eritrea and Ethiopia was fast dying out. The reservoir of knowledge and the feeling of closeness for these refugee groups were diminishing with the shift of generations. A matter that complicated the scene where the Ethiopian and Eritrean refugees arrived was the conflict that now prevailed between Ethiopians and Eritreans, a result of Eritrea's struggle for independence. Whether they liked it or not, many retired and active missionaries or aid-workers to the two countries quietly took sides on the Eritrea-Ethiopia issue.[16]

At the same time, a new corps of mostly young Swedish relief workers under the leadership of older missionaries or aid workers was entering the area of refugee aid, particularly in Sudan and Kenya. These relief workers met Ethiopians and Eritreans outside of their homelands and saw their daily struggles to survive with self-respect under the often degrading circumstances which refugee life involved. These relief workers too were able to channel to the Swedish public fresh and valuable knowledge about the people among whom they were working.[17]

Studying Swedish as a Positive Point of Contact

The study of the Swedish language by refugees and the laughter and joking connected with the awkward attempts of the new beginners to express themselves in Swedish is a positive point of contact between Swedes and these refugees. Language study is also an occasion for the meeting of cultures and races. It brings together former enemies in a context in which the Swedish teacher and the content of the course (which usually covers a wide range of subjects!) play something of a mediatory role. The classroom becomes an occasion for refugees to experience solidarity as they try to explain how *their* ways differ from the *Swedish* ways represented by the teacher. On not a few occasions, Swedish teachers and their refugee students meet around food and entertainment representing refugee cultures.[18]

A Meeting of Christian Traditions

Among the facts that provided positive points of contact between these refugee communities and Sweden was, in the first place, Sweden's Christian tradition. Sweden's church buildings have, in the vast majority of cases, maintained and preserved the paintings, statues, and sculptures that are part of the country's pre-Reformation, Catholic heritage. Its liturgical practices (the use of liturgical vessels and vestments, handbooks, processions, the sign of the cross, and the like) speak to the Orthodox mentality of Ethiopian and Eritrean Christians.[19] Even though the Orthodox Churches in Ethiopia and Eritrea follow the Julian and not the Gregorian calendar, the churches in these two East African countries share the main Christian festivals with the Church of Sweden, which is an Evangelical Lutheran Church. Christmas, Epiphany, Lent, Easter, the Feast of the Ascension, Whitsun, and the Feast of the Transfiguration are all celebrated both by these Orthodox churches and by the Church of Sweden.

Here it should be added that those Ethiopians and Eritreans who had mission contacts with Swedes in their homelands had something of a head start in being able to adjust to Swedish conditions. However, an empirical study should be carried out to establish the validity of this statement.

Swedes in general are not very eager churchgoers.[20] However, they do observe some of the bigger church festivals. Baptisms, confirmation, church weddings, and church funerals are still very common among them. Swedish churches and cemeteries are very well taken care of. The fact that the Ethiopian and Eritrean Orthodox Churches practice infant baptism is one more point of contact with the Church of Sweden, which also baptizes infants. Swedish priests and church workers as well the families of Swedish children who have "refugee" friends enjoy being invited to baptismal feasts.

The coming of refugees who are adherents of an Orthodox Christian tradition to a country with (at least officially) an Evangelical Lutheran confession contributed to the clarification of a whole series of vaguely held views about these Orthodox Christians. The presence of Orthodox congregations, particularly in Stockholm, and the regular observance of the liturgy aroused the curiosity and inquisitiveness of Swedish priests, professional theologians, and interested laymen. Swedish Christendom now had a chance to ask specific questions and get specific answers from competent sources. To take only one example, Swedes were able to meet people who fasted not to reduce weight but for religious reasons. In short, the presence of these refugee churches contributed both to the volume and the quality of knowledge that Swedes had and may have had about the Ethiopian—and now also the Eritrean—Orthodox churches.

Some Attractive Features of Refugee Culture

Weddings are excellent occasions for meaningful contact between Swedes and Ethiopian and Eritrean refugees. Swedes have expressed great joy at the warmth, the festive spirit, the music and dancing, the unrestrained , and the abundance of food that accompany these feasts.[21] Many a Swede who had been critical about the extravagance of these wedding feasts has been deeply impressed upon discovering that the expenses for these undertakings are shared generously by relatives and friends—an example of the social dimension of the lives of these refugees. This is not to say that the *knytkalas* (pot-luck) tradition is uncommon among Swedes! It has been brought to my attention that guests and friends can in fact chip in and help even with expensive dinners to celebrate doctoral disputations. However, the pot-luck tradition is, I believe, far more common among the refugee groups named above.

The strong feeling of solidarity expressed in these refugee circles when someone becomes sick and the mutual concern that characterizes their mourning customs are also meaningful meeting points between Swedes and these refugees. These features of refugee culture have moved many Swedes and led them to wonder about the very restrained manner in which they themselves express their own feelings, not least in times of crisis.

A Common Respect for Antiquity and History

Sweden is a country of old traditions, buildings, and customs with a history of powerful kings. Gustav Vasa (1496–1560) and Carl (Charles) XII (1682–1718) can very well find their parallels in some of Ethiopia's emperors.[22] Sweden's museums and warships speak of a past era of military prowess and hero worship. Not a few Ethiopians and Eritreans find echoes of their own histories in the history of Sweden. With its rune-stones, castles, statues, churches, and well-preserved manuscripts, books, textiles, and artifacts, Sweden has succeeding in awakening memories of old, historic traditions among not a few Ethiopians and Eritreans.

Refugee Children and Youth as Bridge Builders

It is common knowledge that, in all cultures, children and youth are less inhibited and more direct in their ways of communicating with others than are adults. Furthermore, what unites children and youth also tends to unite parents and adults in general. Common undertakings *on behalf* of children provide bridges among adults from different ethnic groups.

In Sweden, this bridge-building mission of children begins already at the stage of pregnancy. Expectant mothers from different ethnic groups meet around common information sessions arranged by the maternal units at clinics and hospitals.

The so-called *dagmammor* (literally "the day mothers"), the *fritidsgårdar* (out-of-school-hours homes), Sunday schools, *kyrkans barntimmar* (the church's [weekday] childrens' hours), scout-groups, the so-called *juniorer* and *miniorer* (i.e., different categories of youth groups in congregations), the church choirs for different ages, the camps and outings, confirmation classes, parents meetings from kindergarten up to the secondary-school level, school feasts that require the help of parents—all these activities bring Swedish and refugee parents together at some time or another.

Ethiopian and Eritrean refugee families too share in these encounters, to varying degrees.

Refugee Associations as Bridge Builders

There are a number of associations for both Ethiopians and Eritreans in Sweden. In Uppsala itself (where I live and work) there is Föreningen för Etiopier i Uppsala (AEU; The Association for Ethiopians in Uppsala). On a national level there is Etiopiska riksföreningen i Sverige (The Nationwide Ethiopian Association in Sweden).[23] There are other Ethiopian associations in Sweden. However, I haven't had the opportunity or time to identify them.

There are at least three Eritrean associations that are registered under the SIV-Samarbetsorganization för Invandrarföreningar i Uppsala (The State Immigrant Authority's Co-operative Organ for Immigrant Organizations in Uppsala). These three are: Eritreanska Kulturföreningen (EKF; The Eritrean Cultural Association), Eritreanska Kvinnoföreningen i Uppsala (EKU; The Eritrean Women's Association in Uppsala), and Eritreanska Föreningen i Gottsunda (EAG; The Eritrean Association in Gottsunda). There are also nationwide Ethiopian and Eritrean associations, such as Riksförbundet för etiopier i Sverige (RES; The Nationwide Association for Ethiopians in Sweden) and Eritreanska Riksförbundet i Sverige (ERS; The Nationwide Eritrean Association in Sweden).[24]

Even though the stated goals of these organizations strongly tend to underline the preservation of the identity of the national groups that they represent, they also state their desire to directly or indirectly facilitate the integration of their members into Swedish society.

Some of the sub-goals of the Amharic version of the constitutions of the AEU are:

- To encourage and promote a good relationship among Ethiopians, Swedes and others.
- To encourage and promote ways that would enable Ethiopians to get to know and understand the Swedish way of life and Swedish social norms.
- To help Ethiopians who come to Uppsala in their contacts with Swedish authorities and in the process of their acclimatization to life in this country.

The EK includes the following among its statement of principles:

EKF is an organization that has a relation of solidarity with peoples' movements that fight for freedom, peace, justice, human rights and democracy.

Among the stated goals of EKU is the statement:

> The association was established so that women may be more easily enabled to adjust to Swedish society as far as language, equality and education are concerned.

Among the goals of ERS are the following:

> To work for cooperation between the association and Swedish society ... To be on the alert on and participate in the cultural, social and political developments in Sweden ...To work so that dual citizenship may be made possible.

To what extent these stated goals with particular emphasis on contacts with Swedish society have been implemented is another matter!

Cultural Exhibitions and Other Cultural Events as Positive Points of Contact

From 1989 to 1991 a mobile exhibition on Ethiopia entitled *Afrikas Tak* (Africa's Roof) toured almost the entire length and breadth of Sweden. Schools, churches, clubs, and study groups were able to take advantage of its instructive and colourful content. It was sponsored by The Church of Sweden Mission.

In the spring of 1992, The Museum of Uppland put on an exhibition on Eritreans residing in the county of Uppsala. The exhibition then moved on to The Nordic Museum in Stockholm where it appeared as part of the museum's exhibition, *50 Years in Sweden*.[25]

A cultural evening held every year in Uppsala on the first Saturday in September gives immigrant groups a chance to introduce themselves and their cultures. Ethiopians and Eritreans have started taking advantage of this opportunity.

The Association for Adopted Ethiopians—A Positive Point of Contact

The June 1997 issue of *Tenaestelin* (The organ of The Ethio-Swedish Association) carried a short report on the formation of an association for adopted Ethiopians in Sweden. Ethiopians in this category cannot be regarded as refugees but are nevertheless part of the picture of the meeting of cultures. It is interesting to read what one of the adopted Ethiopians, Sara Nordin, writes:

> The Association for Adopted Ethiopians is meant for you, who are adopted from Ethiopia, and feel that it would be fun not only to have to narrate and explain but also meet those who, like you, know what it feels like to have been adopted. There are a number of us, adopted children, who are now adults. We have many differences but also many similarities which should be interesting to share and discuss. We may also feel that it is important to get a picture of Ethiopia with more nuances. Ethiopia as it is today and (as it was) historically ... What we do at our monthly meetings is to talk about things which interest us, for example, adoption, Ethiopia, Sweden, racism and life on the whole.[26]

Here we have an example of an initiative that has its roots both in Sweden and in the homeland of the persons concerned—a truly positive point of contact.

A Growing Number of Ethiopian and Eritrean Academicians in Sweden—A Positive Point of Contact

There are an increasing number of Ethiopian and Eritrean academicians in Sweden. Among these are a number of medical doctors. The number of those who are getting doctors degrees in other fields seems to grow by the year, even though only a limited number of these have permanent employment. My brother, Dr. Mehari Gebre-Medhin, Eritrean-born but brought up in Ethiopia, is now (at the time of this writing) Professor of International Child Medicine at The Academic Hospital of Uppsala University.[27] He has a number of important consultative positions at a high level of Swedish society. The growing corps of Ethiopian and Eritrean academicians constitutes even morer points of positive contact with Swedish society.

Having pointed out the possible generators of contact and rapprochement between Swedes and Ethiopian/Eritrean immigrants, it is now time for us to move on to the third article in this series, namely, that regarding possible sources of misunderstanding and conflict.

Notes

1 Arén 1978, 130ff.
2 Arén 1978 144ff. Hellström 1996.
3 Iwarsson & Tron 1918. Arén 1978 288-292, 337 ff. Negash 1987, 72, 79, 82,

84, 90, 91. See also chapter 4, entitled "Newcomers and Pioneers in the Ethiopian Heartland 1920 – 1934)"; in Gustav Arén's book *Envoys of The Gospel in Ethiopia,* 1999.

4   Italian Waldensians like Alessandro Tron and Emilio Ganz are mentioned with reverence and love by old Eritrean Lutherans. Bruno Tron, a son of Alessandro Tron, is a retired pastor in Italy.

5   Most of the first Swedish missionaries to Eritrea used Amarinja, Ethiopia's main language, as a medium of communication and as a literary language. That the use of Tigrinja as a written language in Eritrea was also given impetus by Swedish missionary elements is witnessed to by the fact that it was Missionary Karl Winqvist who led the 'campaign', at times against strong opposition, from his colleagues, for the adoption of Tigrinja for purposes of literacy and evangelism. Arén 1978, 331 ff.

6   Read Arén's account of Gebre-Ewostateos' life and enterprise in Wollega. Arén 1978, 374 ff.

7   Arén 1978, 418ff.

8   Arén 1978. 211ff. and Zewde 1991, 27ff.

9   For an account (in Swedish) on this subject by the leader of the Red Cross team, Dr. Fride Hylander, see Hylander 1980, 143ff. Gustav Arén takes up the Swedish Red Cross and its history in Chapter 9 of his book *Envoys of The Gospel in Ethiopia, 1999.*

10   SIDA succeeded NIB around 965.

11   Halldin-Norberg 1977. SIDA's periodical *Omvärlden* is available from SIDA, Sveavägen 20, 105 25 Stockholm. SIDA has a special section for its work in East and West Africa. Furthermore it has a research office with archives open to the public on stated days and hours.

12   Both of these periodicals were published by The Swedish Evangelical Mission.

13   Anna-Lena Röstin's books in Swedish are an excellent source of information about country, people, and mission-work in Ethiopia. One need only read her book *Arvet i främlingars hand. Det fria Etiopien in memoriam* (*The Heritage in the Hands of Foreigners. In Memory of Free Ethiopia*), published in 1936 by Bibeltrogna-Vänners Förlag. Stockholm, to see the beauty of her style and the love with which she writes about Ethiopia. See also her *Svarta och Vita: abessinienskildring* (*Blacks and Whites. A Description of Abyssinia*), published in 1937 by SKD, Stockholm.

14   It is owned and issued by an association that is called *Till Liv.*

15   The Swedish Ethiopian Society cannot be said to have reached out widely among Ethiopian refugees to Sweden. There are several local and national organizations involving Ethiopians and Eritreans respectively. These are either of an expressly cultural or political nature.

16   The ethnic and language factor in Ethiopia's present organizational structure (the country's division into ethnic regions) raises the question of newly-awakened and intensified loyalties among missionaries to geographical

Chapter 6

or language-areas where these missionaries and aid-workers have worked previously. The entrenchment of such loyalties tends to create tension between Swedes and Ethiopians of different ethnic categories. This is however a matter that I can't go into at present.

17   Reports on work among Ethiopian and Eritrean and Ethiopian refugees in Sudan and Kenya are available with Lutherhjälpen (Luther-Help = Church of Sweden Help), the Swedish Evangelical Mission (EFS), and SIDA, which, by virtue of generous grants to refugee aid, required reports on the use of money granted for refugee purposes. Both Lutherhjälpen and EFS are now housed in Kyrkans Hus (= Church House) in Uppsala.

18   The files of such organizations as Arbetarrörelsens Bildningsförbund (ABF= The Educational Association för the Movement of Workers), Tjänstemännens Bildningsverksamhet (TBV= The Civil Servants' Educational Unit) and Kursverksamheten (KV= Course Activities) certainly contain interesting reports on the interactions between Swedish teachers and their refugee students!

19   For surveys of the history and religious life of the Ethiopian Orthodox Church, see Tadesse Tamrat, *Church and State in Ethiopia, 1270-1527* (Oxford: Clarendon, 1972); Ernst Hammerschmidt, 1967; Richard Pankhurst et al. (in Swedish), 1974; Aymro Wondmagegnehu and Joachim Motovu (eds.), *The Ethiopian Orthodox Church* (Addis Ababa: Ethiopian Orthodox Church Mission, 1970); Edward Ullendorff, *The Ethiopians* (3rd ed.), London, 1973; and the work entitled *The Ethiopian Orthodox Tewahido Church Faith, Order of Worship and Ecumenical Relations* which was produced in January 1995 under the auspices of the Patriarchate of The Ethiopian Orthodox Church. Gösta Hallonsten's short book in Swedish, *Östkyrkor i Sverige- en översikt*, contains a chapter entitled "Orientaliska kyrkor i Sverige", which also deals, albeit very briefly, with the Orthodox Churches in Ethiopia and Eritrea. Hallonsten 1992, 33–34.

20   It is interesting to note that one of the sub-titles in Kerstin Björn's essay *Från Asmara till Heidenstamstorg* ("From Asmara to Heidenstams Square" (the location of a specific church in Uppsala to which Eritrean refugees often come), reads "Till missionärernas land med de tomma kyrkorna" (= To the Land of the Missionaries with the Empty Churches). Of course the author is citing pious Eritreans who had hoped that the Swedes would display greater piety. Björn, 1990.

21   One Swedish tradition that attracts refugee-families in strength is Mid-Summer. This is one of the rare occasions on which refugees see Swedes of all ages singing and dancing with abandon.

22   Figures like Emperor Kaleb (Ellesbas) who dispatched a great expedition to Himyar in 525 AD, to champion the cause of persecuted Christians, Emperor Zer'a Ya 'eqob (who reigned from 1434–1468) and was a hard-handed, self-appointed church-reformer, as well as Emperor Tewodros (ca. 1818-1868) can, at the risk of some forced reasoning, perhaps be mentioned as reminders of these and some other Swedish kings. (See Jones & Monroe

1970 [1935], pp 30, 32, 34, 42, 44; Jones & Monroe 1970 [1935] 55-8 and Rubenson 1966).

23 The address of this association is Etiopiska riksföreningen i Sverige, S: t Eriksgatan 33B, 112 39 Stockholm.
24 The address of this latter association is Eritreanska Riksförbundet, Prästgårdsgatan 38, nb 172 32 Sundbyberg, Sweden.
25 See the work entitled *Uppsala som invandrarstad.* (Uppsala as a city of Immigrants). Boveri & Svanberg 1993. The pictures for the exhibition were in fact contributed by the Swedish Evangelical Mission.
26 *Tenaestilin* 1997 28. It would be interesting to study to what extent intermarriage between Swedes and Ethiopian and Eritrean refugees or immigrants constitute points of contact and conflict. In general, it can be stated that where the level of education and the religious convictions shared by the couples are comparable, the chances of a stable marriage are good.
27 At the time when this article was written!

Year 1997
Chapter 7

Generators of Contact and Conflict among Swedes and Ethiopian and Eritrean Refugees (III):

Possible Generators of Conflict

Flight from Scenes of Turbulence and Conflict

The launching of a Marxist revolution in 1974 in Ethiopia and the intensification of the armed conflict in Eritrea caused many Ethiopians and Eritreans of different ages to leave Addis Ababa and Asmara by plane for other countries or to flee, in far greater numbers, across the borders of Ethiopia into Sudan, Kenya, or Djibouti. Some of these refugees came to Sweden from their first countries of refuge. Others had stayed in some third country before arriving in Sweden.[1]

A Meeting Place for People of Contrasting Geographical and Cultural Backgrounds

By coming to Sweden, Ethiopian and Eritrean refugees moved to a geographic, climatic, and cultural context that was in stark contrast to the geographic, climatic, and cultural contexts that they had left behind. Fleeing to Djibouti, Kenya, or Sudan was enough of a culture-shock for many of them. However, in these initial, neighboring countries of their exile, they had at least the advantage of climatic and, in some respects, cultural conditions that were similar to those of their homelands.

Handicaps Resulting from Drastic Transitions

Many of the refugees who arrived in Sweden had come out of very traumatic experiences. A number of these traumas had been caused partly by the terrors of Ethiopia's Marxist regime and partly by the prolonged and often cruel war between Ethiopian troops and Eritreans fighting for independence.[2] A great majority of the refugees from Eritrea had fled through Sudan and many had incurred deep psychological wounds on their flight. All had left near and dear ones behind.

These two groups met in Sweden. Eritreans regarded Ethiopia (and often, by implication, Ethiopians) as oppressors and perpetrators of great crimes in Eritrea. Ethiopians regarded the Eritreans as rebels and traitors who were bent on destroying the territorial integrity of an old and respected country.

Memories of Past Conflicts

Many of the refugees who fled from their homelands had left behind them scenes of conflict related to politics, economics, and tribal loyalties. These conflicts were sometimes imported into Sweden and flared up, sooner or later, to the great surprise of Swedish communal authorities and social workers, who found it difficult to understand why refugees should be outraged about seemingly unimportant matters. A highly homogeneous society like Sweden, with basically one religion and Church, one basic language, one system of democracy and social welfare, and one national identity, could not easily understand why these refugees could not get along.

Memories of a Lost Status

Many of the men and not a few of the women among these refugee groups had left well-paying and prestigious jobs behind them. In Sweden they were reduced to what was, in effect, a type of functional illiteracy by the fact that, upon their arrival, they could neither read nor write Swedish. Consequently, they were denied an intelligent reception of the information provided by the media. Unemployment and the offer of jobs far below the level of the jobs these refugees were accustomed to in their homelands created a drastically impoverished self-image, with (not infrequent) depression as a consequence.

Summer and Winter—Light and Darkness

Sweden is a country with long, light-filled springs and summers and long, dark winters. The combination of darkness and cold is a formidable enemy to both the body and psyche of dark-skinned people. Warm, sunny weather is the African's shelter, clothing, and nutrition. In Sweden, the possibility of staying outdoors in sunny, warm weather with little clothing was denied for the entire duration of the winter months. Children and the young can readily develop the skills of ice-skating, tobogganing, and skiing. These sports are effective ways of defeating the physical isolation imposed by winter. The African might wish to see fire in an open oven or in a fireplace right at his feet, to warm, if not his body, at least his eyes and his spirit. In Sweden's well-built, well-furnished, and well-heated flats, he or she has to be satisfied with the heat from an invisible radiator or with the light of a Swedish candle, surely a rich symbol for the native Swede but hardly so for the Ethiopian or Eritrean who is used to resorting to candle light only after dark or if electricity fails.

The refugee from Ethiopia or Eritrea had to make the best of the short but (often) warm and beautiful summers, literally soaking in the sunshine and the sight of a country suddenly turned green. Soon the autumn would be here again, with its lengthening shadows, its rich but sometimes sad tapestry of colours, and its falling leaves, the heralds of winter's slow but relentless advance.

Isolated Refugee Wives

Refugee wives, who are often the last to get the opportunity to study Swedish on a regular basis, usually give birth to children in quick succession in Sweden's cold and dark climate. The possibilities to study and use Swedish are even more limited for them than for men. This tends to further isolate refugee women, in spite of the fact that communal authorities do their best to facilitate child care and social contacts outside of the home.

In the homelands of these refugees, breast-feeding mothers are respected and shown much love and care. Here in Sweden, their chances of any special treatment are limited, although working mothers do have about a year of maternal leave. Refugee mothers now have one more mouth to feed and one more person to take care of. Isolation and fatigue often results in sick wives and mothers. Sick wives are a great handicap in refugee homes where the ever-alert care of a woman is decisive in the proper functioning of a home.

No Longer Members of Religious Majorities

From having been citizens of countries with two big religious traditions, Orthodox Christianity and Islam (with large pockets of Roman Catholic and Protestant faithful), refugees from Ethiopia (in particular) and Eritrea are now witnessing the development of a galloping and confusing religious pluralism. There is still a strong, unofficial tendency among the majority of Ethiopians and Eritreans to believe that Orthodox Christianity and Islam are the two native and thus legitimate religions in their countries, and to resent smaller religious groups as intruders. In Ethiopia, one of the derogatory designations for these other religions, particularly in their Protestant variants, is metté (መጤ, literally a "Comer" or "Intruder").

Before coming to Sweden as refugees, Orthodox Christians and Muslims from Ethiopia and Eritrea were used to thinking that they belonged to respectable and unchallenged "majority" groups.

Here in Sweden however, adherents of both groups find themselves reduced to minorities. They are now simply two of the many smaller religious groups milling around the giant, The Church of Sweden.[3] Not all are particularly happy about being numbered among minority groups and resent the unrestrained missionary efforts of some of the smaller religious groups among the Ethiopians and Eritreans here in Sweden to win converts from among the Orthodox and the Muslims.

Identities Jealously Guarded

Under normal circumstances it would have been relatively easy for the Swedish communal authorities to accommodate people from the (Christian) highland regions of Ethiopia and Eritrea. These refugees share a common culture and religion. Their main languages, Amharic and Tigrinya, are of Semitic origin and share many common features. Highland Christian Ethiopians and Eritreans also have common habits related to food and dress.

The Ethiopians and Eritreans look very much alike. Furthermore, all Eritrean refugees were initially registered as Ethiopians, since no internationally recognized, independent country by the name of Eritrea existed at the time of their arrival. Swedes initially tended to address all or almost all of these refugees as Ethiopians, to which many Eritreans took offence.

Thus, the first years after the arrival of these two groups of refugees created dilemmas for Swedes and Swedish immigration and communal authorities. They often ran the risk of causing offence to one or the other of these groups by lumping them together under one national designation. The overall climate in this regard has, in my opinion, now improved. In general, Ethiopians and Eritreans in Sweden now treat each other with respect.

The Demands of Swedish-Built Homes and Buildings

At home, back in Eritrea and/or Ethiopia, many of these refugees were used to spending much time under the open sky. They worked, reasoned, and socialized in the open. Nature took care of much of the waste products that resulted from such a lifestyle. At the risk of some exaggeration, one can say that the traditional, rural African went indoors basically only if he or she needed to.

The saying "My home is my castle" is applicable to all cultures. Nevertheless, certain climatic circumstances place a particular set of demands on the construction and maintenance of homes. In Sweden, the home, the flat, the villa are not only residences but also shelters and domestic "fortresses," guarding their residents from the onslaughts of winter and, occasionally, the excessive heat of summer. Homes must be kept in a good state of repair if they are to protect their residents and provide them comfort during the long, cold winter months. The need for proper and regular maintenance as well as for cleanliness both inside and outside the home is an attitude that the Swede takes in with his or her mother's milk.

This does not mean that all refugees are disorderly or lacking in cleanliness, even by Swedish standards. Many of them make it a matter of honour to excel in this respect. However, it does mean that lack of regularity and thoroughness in meeting these high requirements in home care sometimes becomes a cause of conflict between Swedish landlords/landladies and refugees. This is especially the case with public facilities and meeting places, which must be restored to their original state of cleanliness and order after feasts sponsored by refugee communities. These are demands that can be difficult to fulfill for refugees with big families. As a rule, however, the longer these refugees have been in Sweden the more effective they have become in meeting Swedish standards of cleanliness and order.

Noisy Conversations and Food with Strong Odours

Like many other so-called Third-World people, the Ethiopians and Eritreans are gregarious. Socializing, eating with others, inviting friends and being invited, greeting each other at length and with a profusion of words—these are common features of the behaviours of people from both countries.

Sweden, on the other hand, is basically a society of few words and low voices. This is particularly the case during the winter. Initially, Swedes and these refugees are likely to become irritated with each other's ways of socializing. The refugees complain about the apparent lack of sociability and the exaggerated reserve of the Swedes.[4] Swedes, for their part, complain about the garrulousness and the level of noise among their refugee neighbours.

Moreover, the rather strong smell of the spiced foods prepared by these refugee groups is both a source of attraction and a deterrent. The Swedes may very well like the food but not the strong odour, which lingers long after the end of a feast and fills stairways and corridors.[5]

Different Concepts of Time

Cultures can be characterized, partly, by their understanding of time and space or distance. Many a traveler in Ethiopia and Eritrea has been taken by surprise in undertaking hikes or other forms of travel on foot on the basis of replies to questions like "How far is such and such a place?" or "How much time would it take to come to such and such a place?" Rural dwellers in both countries almost invariably give estimates of distance that are far lower than the actual distance to the envisaged destination. Statements like "Oh, it is quite near!" or "It is a quarter of a day's journey!" cannot be interpreted with any sense of exactitude by the clock. Much depends on *who* is giving the answer.

In these societies, and especially in the rural areas, time and space or distance are elastic concepts. Furthermore, they are associated with other considerations and not only with measurement as such. The whole concept of *time* and punctuality, both in arriving and leaving, often becomes a source of conflict between Swedes and Ethiopian and Eritrean refugees. Middle-aged and older people within these refugee communities sometimes behave as if time is a commodity that is as plentiful as air and sunshine—something that is measured not by clocks and watches but by sun-rays and the varying lengths of shadows or by signs of interest or boredom.

Weddings and other common gatherings can be notorious for being scenes of annoying delays, especially for Swedish guests. There seems to be an unwritten law [in Ethiopian/Eritrean culture] that a wedded couple have the right to come late to wedding ceremonies and feasts. Thus, sometimes Ethiopian and Eritrean hosts who invite Swedish friends to wedding feasts give their "white" guests a time of arrival that is different from the time of arrival known to the rest of the guests. The Swedes are simply advised to come later than the time indicated on their invitation cards!

What the Swede and many an Ethiopian and Eritrean are likely to forget is the fact that in the indigenous culture common to these peoples, coming early to a feast or a meal to which one is invited can be interpreted as a sign of greed, a sign of lack of self-respect! Though such an interpretation is not obvious among Ethiopians and Eritreans in Sweden, the *habit* of coming late is still deeply engrained in them. However, there is an apparent exception to this rule: coming "on time" to funerals, to money-paying jobs, and to appointments with the doctor, where absence without prior notice is penalized.

A more-or-less punctual arrival at funeral services can be explained by the seriousness with which one takes death and funerals. These are cultures in which enemies to a deceased person often relent momentarily from their grudges and spite to be present at funerals.

Can we then say, unequivocally, that where delay or absence *can cost money*, the same people tend to come in time? A friend who read this section took exception to this view. The punctuality in this regard is, according to this view, not that there is money in the picture but that the demand for arrival at a specific time has been clearly stated, *both orally and in writing*, as being very *specific* indeed. This may be a partially valid explanation. I would like to add that the weight of the *authority* behind the sources of this demand—e.g., Swedish communal and medical officials with the right to resort to *sanctions*—provides an additional impetus for punctuality in the cases mentioned above.

Should the Husband Put on an Apron?

Refugee husbands and fathers within the Ethiopian and Eritrean communities often regard Swedish society as a challenge to their status as men. One aspect of this question is the role of women in Sweden and the privileges that women have before the law in Sweden. Coming as they do from societies in which the roles of men and women are clearly defined, these husbands feel challenged and threatened in a country where one cannot employ cooks and washerwomen, and where Swedish men normally put on aprons to change diapers or help in the kitchen. Often the refugee husbands and fathers feel that their rightful authority is being taken away from them. In short, they can begin to develop a certain kind of resentment to Swedish society and its way of underlying the rights of women.[6]

Quick 'Justice' in Marital Conflicts

Ethiopian and Eritrean society provides social cushions, a protective network of relatives and other social role bearers, who can be of great help in times of conflict within the immediate family. In these societies, it is not unusual for a wife who feels wronged by her husband to move in with and lodge her complaints with the nearest relatives of her husband! In other words, the extended family plays a very important role in maintaining peace within the family and in providing a cooling-off period in times of conflict. The extended family and the institution of elders, so important in Ethiopia and Eritrea, are practically non-existent in Sweden. Often, wives and husbands do not get the cooling-off period they need to solve their problems. The wronged party or the party that *feels* wronged (often the woman) hastens to the Swedish communal authorities or to advocates with their complaints. These have the tendency to think in terms of rights and privileges and not primarily in terms of mediation. This means that conflicts are hastily raised to the level of legal or communal action. The conflicts are not given the cooling-off periods and mechanisms that life in Ethiopia and Eritrea would have provided. Such a state of affairs is resented by the men and, often, by the relatives of the couple involved.[7]

Tendency to Fall for Exhibitionism and Vanity

The average Swede is tempted to regard the use of clothes, cars, and furniture as well as the celebration of showy feasts among Ethiopian and Eritrean refugees as signs of extravagance. In general, we may be justified in stating that an educated Swede or someone in a position of leadership in Swedish society does not have to dress to show his status. Externals do not usually play a decisive role in his life, contacts, and thinking. Extravagance in such externals tends to irritate many a Swede and make him or her wonder not only as to where these refugees get their money but also as to the kind of judgment that these refugees have on financial issues.

The refugees in our two categories come from societies where occasional flares of festivity and exuberance are welcome interruptions to life's toil and monotony. At the same time, it must be said that these refugee groups are also very hard-working and frugal in their own ways. They are very frequent customers at shops that sell used clothes and articles. There are areas of austerity in their lives. Food is one of these. Ethiopian and Eritrean refugees also save and send generous amounts of money to relatives in their homelands.

Matters of Discipline

The desires of refugee children to enjoy the freedoms available to their Swedish peers create tension between the parents themselves and between parents and children. The general view among refugee parents that Swedish child upbringing is unusually liberal has led to one of two misunderstandings. Refugee families either resort to great strictness to save their children from what they regard to be the severe lack of discipline among Swedish parents and children, or they fall into the pitfall of an exaggerated permissiveness in their efforts to conform to what they regard to be the liberalism of Swedish child upbringing. These extremes have caused problems both within and outside the family. There have been cases where refugee parents have been accused by Swedish authorities either of repressiveness or irresponsibility towards their children.

Racism as a Source of Conflict

I am not sufficiently informed to speak with any measure of exactitude on this issue. However, racism is, by the admission of Swedish authorities, a rising problem. Groups like Vit ariskt motstånd (VAM; White Aryan Resistance), Bevara Sverige Svenskt (BSS; Keep Sweden Swedish), and elements within the "skinhead" culture are regarded as breeding grounds for racism. These movements have contacts with similar movements on the continent and in the United States of America. They are becoming increasingly organized and they spread their message through literature and music.

It is very difficult to say to what extent Ethiopian and Eritrean refugees are affected by the presence and actions of these groups. It is clear that individuals within these refugee groups cannot be immune from the ravages of racist groups in Sweden. Racism is indeed a point of conflict and an aggravator of the hindrances involved in the process of integration of refugees into Swedish society.[8]

Refugee Contributions to the Swedish Educational Agenda[9]

Flight is dislodgement, an uprooting. Those who flee from their homelands to save their lives can only save a part of it. A plant may be pulled by its roots and replanted in another soil. Nevertheless, it is replanted as a wounded, traumatized plant.[10]

The Ethiopian and Eritrean refugees who found their way to Sweden did indeed save their lives. However, they have also lost something of the joy, security, and supportive context that had been built up around them by generations of their forebears. To come as a refugee is therefore to arrive impoverished in body and spirit. The Swedish immigration, communal, and law-enforcement authorities are certainly the only ones who can understand the full implications of such a statement.[11] It has been pointed out to me that the very high percentage of unemployment among Ethiopian and Eritrean refugees (over 70% by one estimate) is an obstacle to positive contacts with Swedes.

Nevertheless, this is only part of the story. To receive refugees can also mean to receive riches and resources. My thoughts go back to the story of the great Hebrew "refugee" Joseph, who was carried into Egypt as a slave (Genesis 37). His contributions saved a whole nation from the ravages of a long famine. And yet he was a refugee.

It may not be presumptuous to say that the refugees who have come from Ethiopia and Eritrea to Sweden have started providing impulses and challenges to Sweden's educational agenda. They have brought new cultures, languages, foods, music, and patterns of relationships. Into Sweden's basically monolithic society they have injected further variety and a new world of concepts and presuppositions.

Pedagogically, the *positive points of contact* we have mentioned in this essay should be fully exploited and made to give the highest possible returns, for the mutual benefit of Swedes and refugee groups from Ethiopia and Eritrea alike. The flow of information from the various sides should be encouraged, structured, and specified. Furthermore, these attempts at sharing across cultural boundaries, orally and in writing, should be *rewarded* in some way within the school system. This would encourage both Swedes and refugees to become serious stewards and communicators of their cultures and religious views.[12]

The *points of conflict* we have mentioned should also be taken seriously and analyzed, particularly in view of the removal of clichés and oversimplified explanations of the problems at hand. Specific projects could be developed within the school system to encourage the analysis and possible solutions of the problems. These attempts should be *recognized and rewarded.*

The *how* of the implementation of this proposal is probably a methodological problem, on which I am not qualified to comment.

Swedish society is going to be, in the long run, the winner in the game of interactions and mutual adaptations. The impact that smaller ethnic groups can make is no match to the sheer size of Swedish society and its nationwide, monolithic presence. Time is also on the side of Swedish society.[13] Children are going to grow up basically as Swedes. Teenagers will take up, more and more, the ways of their Swedish friends. One should think of the pain that many parents and older relatives within these ethnic groups must suffer as they see a growing distance, a painful estrangement, between their children and themselves.[14] Adjustment to Swedish culture can, in other words, create isolation and tension within refugee families. This is particularly the case where refugee children abandon religious convictions and cultural norms dear to their parents and relatives. The older generation of refugees in these groups needs to be helped, also through a pedagogical awareness that attempts to build bridges between refugees and their children.[15] The provision of opportunities for instruction in the mother tongues of the children of refugees is an important step in this direction, as it facilitates communication between different generations among immigrant and refugee families.[16]

With the arrival of Ethiopian and Eritrean refugees, a part of the world has come not only to Sweden's shores but also to its bosom. The arrival of these refugee groups in Sweden has strengthened and broadened the basis of a growing pluralism within Swedish society. It has provided Sweden and Swedes a training ground, nearer home, on how to deal with other peoples further away from Sweden's shores.

Notes

1 On the background to the conflict in Eritrea see Gebre-Medhin 1989, Bondenstam 1989, Gayim 1993 and Negash 1997. See also Markakis 1988. For a description of the events which led to and followed the revolution see Spencer, *Ethiopia at Bay: A Personal Account of the Haile Selassie Years* (Algonac, Michigan: Reference Publications, 1984), pp. 327ff.

2 C. Westin's work *Tortyr och existens* (Torture and Existence) (Göteborg: Korpen, 1989) contains material that should be applicable to Ethiopian and Eritrean victims of torture. See also the short section entitled "Tortyr- och krigsskadade eritreaner" (Eritrean victims of torture and battle-wounds) in Inger Björkegren's essay, "En rapport om erfarenheterna av arbetet bland eritreanska flyktingarna i Sverige" ("A Report on Experiences from Work among Eritrean Refugees in Sweden"), 1985, 26.

3 On the special privileges of The Church of Sweden see the article in Swedish entitled "Svenska kyrkans särställning" ("The Privilege of the Church of Sweden") in Karlsson and Svanberg (ed.) 1997, 14 ff.
At the turn of the millennium The Church of Sweden will lose its privileged position as a State Church. However, as a bearer of the history and cultural life of the nation, it will be allowed to keep some of its former privileges. For a critical commentary in Swedish on the future privileges of The Church of Sweden see Beskow's articles in Swedish in Signum 1997 Nr. 1 Årg 23, pages 5-7 and Nr. 5 Årg. 23, pages 131-2) Beskow writes, presumably, from the point of view of a Catholic. See also Hallonsten's "Religionsfrihet, statskyrka och invandrarsamfund" (Freedom om Religion, State Church and Immigrant Demoninations) in *Östkyrkor i Sverige*. 1997, 54 ff.

4 An expression used for this alleged Swedish "characteristic" by one of

Björn's Eritrean interviewees is, "Svenskarna – det ljumma vattnet" (Swedes – the lukewarm water.) Björn, 1990, 26.

5 See the informative article "Invandrarmat" (The Food of Refugees) by Eva-Charlotte Ekström in. Svanberg & Runblom 1990 (1988), 164-174.

6 Some very interesting insights on the whole question of the relationships of the sexes in a Swedish refugee context are available in Kibreab & Kidane 1983, 68-69.

7 Kibreab & Kidane 1983, 81ff. Couples are, however, offered some kind of mediation and a cooling-off period.

8 See the article "Om termerna ras och rasism" (About the terms race and racism) in C Westin's *Skolan, hjärtat, världen*, (The shool, the heart and the world) and Lange & Westin's *Ungdomen om Invandringen*. 1991.

9 On the issue of the implications of multiculturalism in Sweden, see Svanberg (ed.) 1993 and Karlsson & Svanberg 1997.

10 Kibreab & Kidane 1983, 79.

11 In this connection it might be useful to look into J. Ahlberg's recent work on the statistical analysis of crime among refugees and their children. Ahlberg, 1996.

12 In this regard, works like C. Westin's *Ungdomen om Invandringen (Youth on Immigration)* and *Skolan, Hjärtat, Världen* (The School, the Heart and the World) may be sources of some useful ideas. (Westin's *Ungdomen om invandringen* (co-authored by Anders Lange) is a series in three volumes, covering 1991, 1992, and 1993, published by The Centre for Immigrant Research of Stockholm University.)

13 This in spite of the Swedish mass media's generous attempts to provide different ethnic groups with radio and television programmes in their own languages, and in spite of such shining examples as the TV programme known as *Mosaik*. Swedish communal authorities and so-called *studieförbund* (organizations that support study-circles) have been generous in supporting immigrant or refugee associations, be they political or cultural in character. There are a number of Ethiopian and Eritrean societies that belong to these categories.

14 Kibreab & Kidane 1983, 73–74.

15 In an article entitled "Identitet" (Identity) in *Det mångkulturella Sverige,* (The Multicultural Sweden), Anita Jacobson Widding maintains, "To co-operate in preserving immigrant-culture, at least temporarily, can therefore be an important measure towards the prevention of the problem of (loss of) identity, above all in the immigrant-circumstances of adults." Svanberg & Runblom 1990 (1988), 157.

16 See the article "Språk och Invandrare" (Language and Immigrants) by Erling Wande Sin *Det mångkulturella Sverige*. Svanberg & Runblom 1990 (1988), 402–408.

Year 2001
Chapter 8

The Undying Call to Dialogue— Some Parting Words

AHwat, aHat —Brothers, Sisters!

Greetings from an Uppsala that is now wrapped in the soft mantle of a late autumn—a season of changing colours, falling leaves, and lengthening shadows. Don't these things remind us of simple beauty available to all, of changing fortunes in the lives of human beings, and of the alternation of birth and death in the whole of creation? And of the hidden promise of Nature's coming to life again after a season of cold and darkness? Let this hidden language of sunshine and shadows, leaf-clad and naked trees, calm and storm spur us on to a life with a sober sense of reality, patience, and hope. We need the help of such symbols in pondering our personal lives and the life of our nation.

God willing, I shall be going into retirement on October 31, 2001. May I too speak of a late autumn in my life? In that case I do hope that I will be granted some more "late springs" and "late summers." My birthday falls in November, but regulations require that I retire in the month prior to the month of my birth. I want to thank the Network of Eritrean Professionals in Europe—Sweden (NEPE-S) for the privilege of access to a forum that has been stimulating and instructive. As a site for the exchange of ideas and as a platform for vigorous debate (at least when I first entered its company), NEPE-S has brought me close to the heartbeat of many an Eritrean—indeed, to the heartbeat of Eritrea itself![1]

The Price of Unity and Disruption

The tendency for divergent opinions and convictions among Eritreans to end up in confrontation is much more pronounced than the tendency to foster encounter and dialogue. Those of us who have followed what has appeared on the various Eritrean media and websites must recognise what I mean. This fact is so obvious that both Eritreans and non-Eritreans devoted to Eritrea's cause have pleaded eloquently for the reversal of this trend. Read the very moving and well-thought-out article, "Turn down the Volume," by former Peace Corps volunteer John Rude ("Memhir Yohannes") on *asmarino.com* (dated October 23, 1997, but posted on October 24, 1997). The risk is that an unchallenged and non-arrested tendency to confrontation will lead to galloping polarisation among Eritreans. On more than one occasion, this dangerous trend has made me think of the words in The Bible: "If a house is divided against itself, that house cannot stand" (Mark 3:25).

Building unity is a slow, demanding task. It can take generations. Disruption, on the other hand, accidental in its genesis or not, intended or not, is like a brush fire. All that such a brush fire needs is *ignition*. It then moves on by virtue of its own fiery momentum. What is taxing our people right now is not only a proliferation of physical needs (of which we have enough!) but also the risk of mounting polarisation and disruption, not least in the Diaspora. We need more encounters and less confrontation, more dialogue and less polemic. We need a deep, far-reaching, nation-wide *healing*.

We in NEPE-S should at least agree to resolve to avoid contributing to further polarization among our Eritrean fellowmen. One of the best ways to bring about a balance between confrontation and dialogue is to establish, promote, and maintain, wherever this is possible, permanent forums for the exchange of different views on a broad spectrum of subjects. The task is certainly not easy. Deciding what the place of a professional body like NEPE-S should be in the context of a highly charged political milieu is, in itself, an extremely demanding task. Nevertheless, is it too much to expect that NEPE-S could in fact be developed into a forum for continuing, progressive dialogue on a broad spectrum of topics among us here in Sweden? Doesn't the Swedish culture of dialogue by which we are surrounded constitute an encouragement and a challenge in this respect?

Some Words in Parting

Having said what I have said above in support of NEPE-S and the enhancement of its activities in the future, I must admit that what I am going to say below may betray a contradiction. What is the point of raising issues for discussion if one is not prepared to stay and take part in the discussion of these issues? I admit the validity of the question. However, I have no other choice. When I was penning these words, I was faced by the choice between a summary "Farewell!" without any message whatsoever, or a final appeal before the drawing of the curtains. I have chosen to include an appeal. Take what I have said above as counsel, as a humble bit of legacy from a retiring, elderly member of NEPE-S, not as a move from someone who wants to cast a burden upon you and then leave you to your worries.

I have finally reached the age of retirement. Life has taught me that the body is not made of metal. In spite of some useful things done here and there, I sometimes feel that I don't have very much to show for a great part of my sixty-odd years. It is as if many of these years have slipped through my fingers! Do you recognize the feeling? In any case, I need to take stock of things and see if I can use the time God pleases to grant me in the future more stringently. I must say with a sense of regret that I must withdraw from membership in NEPE-S, among other projects and activities.

I have requested that the termination of my membership in NEPE-S be effective as of the day of my retirement, i.e., October 31st. My loyalty to our Eritrean community in the Swedish Diaspora and to NEPE-S's stated goals remains intact. And I do hope that the contacts I have established and the friends I have made through NEPE-S will abide. I shall continue to use my present e-mail address. Those of you who want to contact me personally are welcome to use it. Stay well and God bless you.

Ezra Gebremedhin
Uppsala, October, 2001

Notes

1   NEPE-S is a non-political, non-religious organization of Eritrean professionals and academics living in Sweden. NEPE-S builds on the principle of voluntary and individual membership. It is an organisation under which Eritrean professionals and academics shall participate in the overall development of Eritrea by strengthening ties among Eritrean professionals in Sweden and between Eritrean and Swedish professionals in collaboration with the Eritrean people and its representatives. The Swedish branch of the organization, founded in 1997, is still on hold in 2020.

Year 2001
Chapter 9

Salt

I was shopping at The ICA Supermarket in Uppsala, Sweden. My shopping list contained the item "salt." Naturally I went to the spice stand and started looking for the usual, white plastic container with its content of salt and its labels in red. My eyes caught some plastic containers with the word "*Falsksalt*" (False Salt) written on them in dark blue. At least I *thought* that that was what I read.[1] My immediate conclusion was that what I saw was some kind of substitute salt, an equivalent to saccharin for those who don't use real sugar in their tea or sugar. But of course, I was looking for *real* salt, not for "Falsksalt." I knew that the shop used to offer its customers a good assortment of genuine salt. I was getting more and more irritated at not being able to find *real* salt. Where in the world had they placed their *real* salt?

At last I went to a female attendant and said to her, full of confidence on the rightness of my request: "I see that you have 'Falsksalt' (*false* salt), but I would like *real* salt!" The young woman smiled at me discretely and answered me: "But what you saw was not '*Falskt*salt' but '*Falk*salt'. 'Falk-salt', she repeated."

My embarrassment was immediate. I had seen a type of salt with the trademark "Falksalt," not "Falsksalt." *Falk* is a proper noun, whereas *falsk* is the Swedish word for "false." One single letter(s), accounted (I thought!) for the difference between these two words. As I have mentioned above, my embarrassment was immediate. My shame should have been even greater. In Swedish, "false salt" would have in fact been spelt "*falskt* salt," with a "*t*" at the end of the adjective "*falsk*."

So near the truth, and yet so far away! So sure of myself, and yet so far off the mark! And what misled me, I thought, was one single letter. I hadn't looked carefully enough. "After all," I thought, "I know what salt containers look like. There is nothing special about identifying them!" I had made up my mind. I had jumped to a conclusion in the absence of solid evidence. I had gone by appearances. True, the words "*Falk*" and "*Falsk*" look very much alike, but a whole world of meanings separates them.

How quick, how hasty, we can sometimes be in the conclusions to which we come! If we have some preconceived notions, some stored prejudices and already established clichés about our fellowmen, the platform is set for hasty judgments. At such times, appearances, similarities in wording and reasoning carry the day. Not meticulous attention to what is actually written, but a flippant glance at what *appears* to have been written becomes the decisive thing.

I had the good fortune to be corrected by someone who knew the shop and the spices offered in it. I succumbed to her verdict. Not all people, all issues, all topics are accommodated or serviced as effectively and conclusively as my mistake on the "salt" issue. Stubborn and prejudiced people fly off with their preconceived notions, with their own readings of things. Repeated pleas and requests don't seem to succeed in making them relent. Add a sense of false pride and a basic unwillingness to admit one's faults, and you have a recipe for continued confrontation.

Whatever our positions and standpoints may be, wherever our political camps may be located, it would indeed be a travesty of the rules of civilized dialogue if the views and arguments of our fellowmen were to be handled with the flippancy and haste with which I judged the salt-container.

Ezra Gebremedhin
Uppsala, October 16, 2001

Notes

1. In Swedish, the form of the adjective 'false' should in fact be '*falskt*', not '*falsk*', when it is used with the word 'salt'. But haste makes waste, even in trying to find faults.

Year 2002
Chapter 10

As We Move On (I):
Respect for Our Common Humanity

On May 24, 2002, we shall be celebrating Eritrea's 19th Independence Day. In a way, we are doing so with the sense that we are making a new beginning. Almost three years of turbulence, war, suffering, and displacement seem to be nearing their end. With the decisions of The Hague Tribunal on the border issue, hope is in the air. We can once more lift up our eyes and look with hope into the future. Are there some modest guidelines that we can follow? It is my conviction that there are.

I would like to take up two of them. The first one is what I would call *Respect for Our Common Humanity*. The second is *Respect for the Integrity of the Individual*. In this essay, I shall take up the first guideline.

On the evening of April 26, there was a programme on William Shakespeare's life and literary career on one of Sweden's national television channels. At one stage of the programme, a bleeding face appeared on the screen, a man with a battered face, emotionally broken, breathing with difficulty and gesticulating feebly as he began to speak in his own defence. He had apparently been mishandled. Soon, the man started declaiming some famous words from Shakespeare's *The Merchant of Venice*. I listened, enthralled, to the following words of Shylock:

> I am a Jew. Hath not a Jew eyes? Hath not a Jew hands, organs, dimensions, senses, affections, passions? Fed with the same food, hurt with the same offensive weapons, subject to the same diseases, healed by the same means? Warmed and cooled by the same winter and summer, as a Christian is? If you prick us, do we not bleed? If you tickle us, do we

not laugh? If you poison us, do we not die? And if you wrong us do we not revenge?

This programme happened to be about Shakespeare's *Merchant of Venice*, with a Jew, Shylock, as one of the main characters. His conversation happened to be with a Christian. My intention with this Independence Day greeting, however, breaks all such limitations and barriers. Many a human being in Shylock's situation (a Palestinian, a Colombian, an Afghan, a North Korean, a Muslim, a Christian, a Buddhist, an Animist) would be forced to utter similar words. The sentiments and appeals of Shylock touch upon our common humanity, our shared vulnerability as individuals in a cruel world. Let us think of our sicknesses and our pains! There is no *Jewish* fever or *Christian* cold or *Muslim* headache or *Animist* rheumatism. What we experience in our bodies and minds, we experience as members of one and the same species. At the root of our experiences of pain lies our common humanity that cries for understanding and help.

Consider further the specific contexts and traditions into which we human beings are born and through which we are molded. In time we become intensely loyal to these contexts. However, these loyalties can become not only bonds that unite and sustain but also chains that bind and limit. We were born into specific families, which (as far as specific countries are concerned) belong to certain clans, religious groups, and regions. We can neither despise nor wish these facts out of existence. In a way, our familial, tribal, and national attachments protect us from the invisible monsters of anonymity and alienation. They contribute to our identity and provide us with a measure of self-respect and security. However, in their specificity, they are not essential for our humanity. They are secondary, not primary values.

The famous Danish theologian and educator Nikolai Grundtvig (1783–1872) once said, "I am a human being first and then a Christian!" He was not downgrading his faith. He was not saying that the physical was more important than the spiritual. He knew that the attrition of spiritual values in a person could lead to the attrition of something in his innermost being.

No, in stating what he said, he was simply affirming that in the order of being, his humanity preceded his faith. His being human was more primordial than his being Christian. What united him with the *whole* of the human race was his humanity, not his faith.

I would agree with Grundtvig. I would be prepared to apply his philosophy to the question of an individual's attitude to such social and geographical phenomena as *Alyät* (ዓለየት – race, tribe), *quanqua* (ቋንቋ – language), *haymanot* (ሃይማኖት – religion); *Addi* (ዓዲ – home region); *awradja*

Chapter 10

(ኣውራጃ – district); and *hagär* (ሃገር – country). My motto too would be: "I am a human being first, and then …."

The surest way to be a good, loyal citizen of Eritrea is to strive to be a good, noble human being.

The sooner we begin cultivating such an attitude, the better. This is difficult homework and we have a long way to go. We are creatures prone to the herd mentality. The collective, the group has an enormous influence on us. For good and for bad!

People can feel, and rightly so, that they have been deprived of their due share of a country's or a region's resources and privileges. This can easily lead them to seek compensation in different social constellations and interest groups. Their moves are understandable. Nevertheless, if you and I entertain the idea that regionalism and religious elitism are the surest ways of securing lasting benefits for ourselves and our like, then it is time for us to wake up as we celebrate Eritrea's Independence Day. It is time for us to consider what countries like Rwanda, Liberia, Angola, Northern Ireland, and Yugoslavia (to name only a few) have gone through in our own lifetime because of exclusionist ideologies in matters of ethnic and religious affiliation. Respect for our common humanity is the bottom line, also for us as Eritreans. This bottom line is something sacred. It is our guarantee, our best insurance against fragmentation as a people.

Whenever respect for our common humanity is compromised in our relations to *guanot* (strangers or outsiders), it will, sooner or later, be compromised in our relations to our *ATSmä-siga* (kith and kin). I am reminded of the saying that a mother who is a thief does not trust her own child! If you are unjust to your immediate neighbour today, because he does not quite belong to your group, you will be unjust to your blood brother or blood sister tomorrow! If you are unjust to someone who does not belong to your religion today, you will be unjust to your coreligionist tomorrow. It is only a question of time before this reality comes to light. Especially in times of crisis, the sense of your own pressing needs (the instinct of survival) or the ingratitude of your blood brother/sister or co-religionist can push you into treating him/her like a *guana* (ጓና) – a stranger.

A person reaps what he or she sows. You cannot treat someone unjustly without becoming unjust. The moral law does not permit such impunity. Evil eventually cripples not only the victim but also the perpetrator. We cannot afford to allow *wägänawinät* (ወገናውነት – partisan thinking) to take root among us in any form. Today, on Eritrea's Independence Day, we have a wonderful opportunity to dedicate ourselves anew to the fight against *wägänawinät* in any form. Now is the time to discuss the problem calmly and intelligently and, where necessary, resist it calmly, in unity. Let us see to it that our secondary loyalties, which are good in themselves, don't become primary loyalties, tearing apart a small country like Eritrea, just trying to get on its feet again.

Engraved on the wall, high above the entrance to the main administrative building of Uppsala University, one can read the words "*Att tänka fritt är stort. Att tänka rätt är större.* (To think freely is great. To think aright is greater.)." Respect for our common humanity is an essential part of the right thinking that should accompany our celebration of Eritrea's Independence Day.

God's blessing on all of us, now and in the years ahead!

Ezra Gebremedhin
Uppsala, Sweden
May 20, 2002

Published on *asmarino.com*, on May 28, 2002.

Year 2002
Chapter 11

As We Move On (II):

Respect for the Integrity of the Individual

My first reflection on our Independence Day (2002) dealt with *Respect for our Common Humanity*. Here is my second reflection, which will deal with *Respect for the Integrity of the Individual*.

In his book *Tender is the Night*, the American novelist, F. Scott Fitzgerald writes:

> Either you think-or else others have to think for you and take powers from you, pervert you and discipline your natural tastes, civilize and sterilize you.[1]

These are hard words and cannot be flung around carelessly. We are all receivers, basically, and not innovators. Our parents, our teachers, our spiritual guides, our heroes and heroines, our customs and traditions, have all contributed to what we are. Culture—our *Higgi inddabba* (ሕጊ እንዳባ), our regional, customary laws—our religious and social rituals, have left deep marks in us. In short, our lives are not and cannot be solo performances.

However, I must underline my conviction that there is something very important in what Fitzgerald writes. There is something incomplete, yes something tragic about the individual who has not become himself or herself. And how many among us can say, with full confidence that we have become full-fledged personalities and not copies or imitators or "yea-sayers"?

To choose responsibly, in spite of all the risks involved in doing so, is one of mankind's labels of honour. Beasts live by their instincts. Man, at his best, dares to stand alone in obedience to the voice of enlightened conscience. The greatest kind of poverty is that which involves being robbed of one's freedom as an individual, of being tamed and being made into an instrument, a robot.

Not a few adults have been known to say to parents driven to despair by difficult and disobedient children:

> You must break his will, while he is still young. Otherwise you will nurture a criminal. The tender plant must be bent while it is still tender. Otherwise it will develop into a sturdy and unmanageable trunk.

The despair of parents and friends in the face of young lives tottering on the brink of ruin is understandable. The sort of advice given above can however lead to catastrophic results. The will is not there for us to break. To break someone's will is to do damage to national property. The will is there for us to mould, if necessary under very firm discipline. To break the will is to emasculate a personality and to impoverish a whole nation. This applies to all levels of life in society—social, political, cultural.

I have no first-hand knowledge of Eritrea's youths and their general attitudes to authority. I would nevertheless like to think of Eritrea as a family with members of different ages. Its leadership constitutes parents. It would be a pity if a conflict among the members of a family were to turn into a conflict among protagonists. The greatness of leadership does not reside primarily in its authority but in its magnanimity, a fatherly or motherly quality. The greatness of youth resides not in its courage, which can easily develop into recklessness, but in its humility and its willingness to learn.

Having said so, I would like to underline the virtue of genuine courage, wherever it appears in individuals in our society. The British man of letters and Christian apologist, C. S. Lewis, writes something to the effect: *Courage is the prince of all virtues.*

It would not be unreasonable to state that many youth who are rebellious can indeed develop into future leaders, if handled with care. Ponder this statement for a moment in connection with the different leaders of nations you can think of, not least in the countries of the so-called Third World. Many of them were once regarded as dangerous disturbers of the peace!

Youth can develop into serious liabilities if handled wrongly. They don't forget easily. Bitter memories can be the fuel that feeds the fire of the craving for vengeance. We have far too many examples of this phenomenon in history to dare to neglect it.

Stubborn and obstinate youth can also be the stuff out of which genuine personalities develop. Children who are "yea-sayers" may grow into quiet adults who create quiet around themselves. However, the real trailblazers, the pioneers and leaders are often those who were obstinate, rebellious, and stubborn. Many of us know the type from our own families!

The courage and/or recklessness of our individuals (young and old) are ours, to foster and cultivate or to demonise and squander.

Let us agree not to quench whatever virtue may have lifted its head among our individual citizens, young or old, learned or illiterate. Where virtue has made its presence felt, it is to be reckoned as our common wealth, to invest wisely. Where it has been tarnished by vice, it is ours to salvage. Are there signs of potential courage and independence of mind among individual Eritreans, young and old? Let us channel and foster them. Individuals with courage and an independent set of mind are plants to be pruned and trimmed, not weeds to be uprooted. To use another image, under the hard, stubborn externals in the behaviour of such people, there may be diamonds to be quarried. Such individuals are not "a dime a dozen." Where they do appear on Eritrea's social and political landscape, let us remember that they are our common heritage, a part of our national resources. Respect for the integrity of each individual is a wealth that we cannot afford to squander, as we move on.

Ezra Gebremedhin
Uppsala, Sweden
May 20, 2002

Published on *asmarino.com*, on May 28, 2002.

Notes

1. *Tender is the Night* (Middlesex, England: Penguin Modern Classics, 1972), p. 308.

Year 2002
Chapter 12

A Giver's Request:

Some Personal Words on *asmarino.com*

There are some things that I do daily, almost without fail. One of these is browsing through *asmarino.com*. I am one of the daily guests at its table. I have sampled its wide variety of dishes. Some of these have both substance and taste. Others are drastically lacking in both. Recently, *asmarino.com*'s sponsors have gone out with an appeal for support. For me they are in effect saying, "Help us to enrich our menu!" It is my personal opinion that *asmarino.com* is basically a *giver* and that its plea for support is the request of a giver that deserves to be listened to.

I know that there are those who regard *asmarino.com* as something far more dangerous and divisive than a harmless table with a menu of cyber dishes. Each and every one is entitled to their views in this regard. I don't intend to press my own on any one. And it cannot be denied that there is something ambivalent in the free word. It is powerful in the way that fire is powerful. Fire can both burn and give warmth. However, having used the services of *asmarino.com* for some time now, I would like to speak in favour of it by following one of the mild precepts of Eritrean tradition. The precept runs: "Has someone done good to you? Either do him good or tell others about his good deeds" (ገቲ ጽቡቕ ዝገበረልካ ወይ ግበረሉ ወይ ንገረሉ).

For at least two years now (2001–2002), *asmarino.com* has brought to my very study here in Sweden the voices of Eritreans on a wide range of subjects. Voices marked by joy or sorrow, anger or calm! Voices of Muslims and Christians! Voices of those who are masters of the written word, and those whose passions are stronger than their literary gifts![1] Voices of poets and voices of masters of prose! Voices of those versed in Eritrea's history and the lore of its bitter struggles, and voices grappling with its highly accelerated and puzzling developments in our days! Voices pleading for caution and patience, and voices crying out for words and deeds that have been long overdue! Voices castigating those of us in the Diaspora for not speaking out on behalf of those who can no longer make their voices heard and voices telling us, "Only wait until you hear of the sinister crimes committed by the so-called Reformers!"

Do you recognise what I am trying to say?

No Eritrean can escape the pain and anguish generated by some of these divergent voices. No conflict is as sad as that which obtains among siblings. The Bible uses the picture of the body and its different limbs in trying to underline how intimately related the pains and joys of the part are to the pains and joys of the whole. What affects Eritrea affects its sons and daughters everywhere. Its pains and joys are the pains and joys of its children. On the basis of this analogy of the relationship between the body and its limbs, it would make no sense to say or imply: "What is happening with the country as a whole is not your business! Just keep quiet and take care of your own daily callings!"

I think *asmarino.com* has contributed to making those of us who live in the Diaspora aware of the relationship between the body and its limbs, the part and the whole, as far as Eritrea is concerned. It has confronted us with the stark realities of a body wracked by pain. My impression is that it has not hidden things from us or tried to give us an unduly romanticized picture of our common reality.

My present concern however is *asmarino.com*'s role as a platform for ideas and information, particularly among Eritreans in the Diaspora. I personally feel that it has been and still is one of our most significant "classrooms." It has taught me more about Eritrea and Eritreans in the last two years than any other media had done in the preceding twenty. It has kept me awake. Sometimes it has set my heart pounding through the joy or outrage it has mediated.

Asmarino.com has been taken to task for lack of fair play. Let it answer to that charge. There were times when I was shocked by the highly personalized attacks that appeared on its pages. I think I have recently seen changes for the better, although the tone of many contributions even now is enough to dissuade less robust souls of my type from contributing, in writing, to the exchanges on its website. Having said that, I would like to put forth what I consider to be *asmarino.com*'s generosity as a website. I think it has made serious efforts to make available a platform for the free word.

It is true that no people can mature and grow into a cohesive unit without a wisely umpired use of this free word. Freedom without a sense of responsibility is bound to result in chaos. At times, what appears on *asmarino.com* has produced more heat than light. I therefore wish the sponsors of *asmarino.com* even greater mastery in their roles as umpires or referees, even though I am quite at a loss as to what to recommend in this regard! To open a platform for the free word and then set limits to this freedom must be an extremely difficult task. I don't envy the sponsors of *asmarino.com*.

One of our greatest needs is a culture of dialogue. And I am afraid that it is not just around the corner. Developing such a culture is going to require a great deal of wear and tear. However, it may comfort us to remember that no growth is possible without trial and error, pains and sighs. No child can learn to walk without a succession of tumbles. *Asmarino.com* has made a good beginning in providing us a training ground in communication. I personally would like to give it credit for that and provide it with the support that my circumstances permit.

Ezra Gebremedhin
Uppsala, Sweden
April 6, 2002

Published on *asmarino.com*, April 21, 2002.

Notes

1   A writer whom I found well-informed, serious, and instructive was Saleh Younis.

Year 2002
Chapter 13

The Years in Sweden—Have They Influenced My Theology?

This article is based on a Faculty Lecture held at Uppsala University on February 18, 2002. Let me begin with a story from the Bible. Jacob, the son of Isaac, is in flight from his brother Esau, whom he had deceived. He is on his way from Beersheba and makes his way in the direction of Haran. He comes to a place where he spends the night. God speaks to him in a dream:

> I am the Lord, the God of your father Abraham and the God of Isaac.
> I will give you and your descendants the land on which you are lying.
> (Gen. 28:13)

Jacob the deceiver receives a promise. He starts to tremble and says, "How awesome is this place! This is none other than the house of God!" (Gen 28:17).

What a person experiences at a specific place, at a definite locality, under particular circumstances can influence his or her understanding of God and the meaning of existence for the rest of their lives. And that was what seems to have happened with Jacob. In its turn this event has influenced the church's tradition of worship. To take only one example, the words "How awesome is this place!" have found their place in the Eucharistic liturgies of the Ethiopian Orthodox Church.

Factors That Have Influenced My Theology

Persons whom I met during my years in Sweden, events in which I was involved, books that I read, the research that I have conducted, worship services in which I took part, and discussions in which I have participated have all influenced my views on God and on myself. And they have done so in a Swedish context.

Think of Swedish hymns and poems. People in all nations sing and write about Nature and the seasons of the year in response to nature's wooings, whispers, smiles, and occasional roars. But the kind of theology that lies behind Edvard Evers' hymn, "*När vintermörkret kring oss står* (When Winter's Darkness Stands Around Us)" and Israel Kolmodin's (1643–1709) hymn "*Den blomstertid nu kommer* (Now Comes the Season of Flowers)" arises from Sweden's soul, as it were. The theology behind these hymns is both Swedish and Lutheran, in a specific way.

Last summer I read a collection of poems by the poet Dan Anderson (1888–1920). There is a lot of nature, a good deal of darkness, chill, smoke, wine, song, and moods in these poems. And a whole lot of implied theology!

In a way, it was here, at The University Library of Uppsala, Carolina Rediviva, that I met the Fathers of the Christian Church, far from their home villages, towns, or cities in Italy, present-day Turkey, Greece, the Middle East, and North Africa. Yes, far from the shores of Alexandria and from the shelves of the renowned libraries that carry their written works. Far indeed from the remote hermitages and monasteries of Egypt, Syria, Cappadocia, Latin Europe, and Germany! Sweden's libraries, and especially Carolina Rediviva, in Uppsala, have become meeting places for renowned theologians of antiquity.

I remember what Dag Hammarskjöld's close friend and co-worker, Sture Linér, said in a lecture delivered in Uppsala on the occasion on which he was honoured by a "Jubilee Doctorate." He said something to this effect:

> You people have said to me: You who have had the opportunity to travel widely and do research, to look with wonder at things ancient and rare, note down facts and write about them! You must be lucky indeed!

Sture Linér continued:

> I used to answer such admirers: You should know that it is you, who have access to extraordinarily well-equipped libraries and archives here in Sweden, who are lucky! Here you have more than enough material on which to do research!

He was right. In a sense, the whole world is available here in Sweden, in its libraries, museums, and centres of research on a great variety of subjects!

How has my theology been influenced during the years that I have stayed in Sweden? Let me set forth some examples!

- I think I have developed a more positive view of Creation and Mankind.
- I have arrived at a more considered view of the relationship between the communal role of the Christian Church as a steward of accumulated tradition and the role and right of the individual to have a say in this accumulated tradition.
- I, who was brought up in a low-church liturgical tradition, with an emphasis on the Word and the communion of the faithful, and on a simple style of worship, have come to appreciate the wealth stored up in older and more developed liturgies.
- My years in Sweden have groomed and pruned the polemical tendency in me.
- My years in Sweden have taught me the importance of seemingly small things—yes "crumbs"—in the realm of theology and worship.
- My years in Sweden have given me a deeper awareness of life's critical junctions, of the so-called border situations where light and darkness meet, where man is suddenly faced with the overwhelming and incomprehensible.

A Brighter View of Creation and Mankind

Let me begin with what I have called the brighter picture of Creation and Mankind. This awareness was strengthened in me by the theology of the Eastern Fathers. At the risk of some exaggeration, one can say that the West has tended to have a more or less dark view of mankind, not least in spiritual matters. I am not totally opposed to this "western" view. In spiritual matters, the human being is not only a resource but also a liability. Having said so, I would like to add that I am deeply grateful for the brighter view of Creation and Mankind that some Eastern theologians have mediated to us. One example is the well-known Church Father from the seventh century, Maximus the Confessor (580–662), whose theology has been very ably presented to a wide readership by my late mentor, Docent Lars Thunberg.[1]

According to Thunberg, the world for Maximus is *macranthropos* (mankind in big format) and mankind is *microcosm* (the world in miniature). Mankind was created as a mirror of the cosmos and has a mediatory function. Mankind was created to bind together opposite phenomena by linking or mediating between five different states of being:

- First mediation: between the sexes
- Second mediation: between Paradise and the inhabited world
- Third mediation: between heaven and earth
- Fourth mediation: between intelligible and sensible creation

- Fifth mediation: between God and His creation

Here we meet a deep and multifaceted anthropology that presupposes a unity between God and Man. Maximus sets forth the reciprocity that binds together not only God and Man but also God and Nature as a whole. The back-cover summary on the second edition of Thunberg's book *Microcosm and Mediator* (1991), reads (in part):

> Maximus understands man, as not only a being—a microcosm—who reflects the constitution of the created universe, but also as a being—a mediator—created in the image of God, whose task is, in Christ, to reconcile the spiritual and the sensible into one homogeneous unity.

This kind of Anthropology provides a meeting place for Theology and other disciplines that deal with Nature, disciplines that take up research related to the environment, the future of our world, and animal-related Ethics.

The Role of Tradition and the Individual in the Preservation of the Christian Faith

Let me use a quotation that I have already used in this book. F. Scott Fitzgerald, in his book *Tender is the Night*, writes the following:

> Either you think or else others have to think for you and take power from you, pervert you and discipline your natural tastes, civilize and sterilize.[2]

His point is clear. He is saying: "Don't let anyone steer or influence your thoughts. Seek on your own and arrive at your own conclusions." A weighty thought, but can it go unchallenged?

The Swiss theologian and disciple of Rudolf Bultmann, Edward Schweizer, writes:

> There is no doubt about the importance of clear formulations of confession, of doctrines and their focus on dogmas. I can never forget the enormous significance which the Barmen Declaration, with its crystal-clear statements and its clear differentiations, had with regard to what was right and wrong in the struggle against Hitler. The struggle of the Confessing Church in Germany would have never been possible without the confessional formulations of The Declaration.[3]

The *Barmen Declaration* was the answer of The Confessional Church in Germany to the so-called Arian Paragraphs, which forbade non-Arians, and especially Jews, to worship with the so-called Arian people. The point behind Schweizer's words is clear. There are times and circumstances when a Christian must make common cause with that which is said in common, in unison, for the benefit and survival of that which embraces all.

In the theological discipline known as *Patristics* (which deals with the Fathers of the Church and their theologies), we meet the terms *consensus partum* (the consensus of the Fathers) and *consensus ecclesiae* (the consensus of The Church) for the principle that lies behind the plea to maintain a united front in the church, not least in times of controversy around important points of doctrine.

The writings of the Church Father Irenaeus (c.130–c. 200) against the Gnostics and the work known as *Commonitorium* by Vincent of Lérins (d. before 450) underline the role of the Church and its unbroken tradition of teaching as the steward of Revealed Truth. Where then is the place and role of the individual Christian in this scheme of things? That no individual should be forced to believe or teach against the dictates of his conscience was taken for granted. However, primacy was clearly accorded to the united voice of The Church. This is a vital emphasis. And there is a dilemma involved in this position. Sometimes truth can have very lonely proclaimers!

On January 10, 2002, an author and member of The Swedish Academy, Kerstin Ekman, was interviewed by a journalist, Göran Rosengren, on Swedish Television. In the course of their conversation the two fell into a discussion of the "good narratives" in the heritage of nations. Ekman felt that it was a pity that people in present-day Sweden had forgotten the great (that is, biblical) narratives within the Christian Tradition.

A common church tradition, the fruit of centuries of hard work, should not be neglected. At the same time, such a tradition should be the subject of critical studies by individuals with a sense of responsibility. The Church's tradition cannot claim preferential treatment as far as academic scrutiny is concerned. Theology cannot claim its own preserve, protected from the questions and investigations of the mind. My years in Sweden and my work at the Theological Faculty at Uppsala University have helped me to realize this fact even more.

The Place of Liturgy in the Life of the Church

I have already stated that I come from a low-church background, in which the forms of worship were relatively simple. The making of the sign of the cross, bowings, burning incense, and similar actions were not in use in our Evangelical worship services in Ethiopia. I still appreciate the Evangelical Lutheran distinction between what is essential (mandatory) and what is optional in matters of worship and church practice. However, my studies in Patristics have taught me to appreciate the development and wealth of the liturgical traditions of the Church Universal. The Liturgy has been and is a treasure-house of the theology of the Church. Liturgy is teaching, concentrated! Many church traditions in the Middle East were able to survive because of their firmly established liturgies, preserved in the memories of priests and the faithful, in spite of periods of external pressure, persecution, and isolation.

I would like to suggest that teachings on the person and teachings of Jesus have been spelt in terms of two concepts, which can be designated as *Scheme* and *Drama*. The *Scheme* as far as the person of Jesus is concerned can be explained in the following terms:

> God is One, Eternal, Unlimited, and Indivisible Spirit. He dwells in Light that no one can approach. The Church has taught that in His divinity Jesus shares these attributes.

The *Drama* aspect of the person of Jesus can be explained in the following terms:

> God is Love, Creator, Risk-taker, and Rescuer, the One who seeks company eternally and comes out of Himself to have something to do with Mankind.

The Church teaches that the Incarnation (the taking of manhood) by The Son of God is the arena within which the drama of Salvation, the Rescue of Mankind, has taken palace. The divine drama in its different forms has become the source of the acts and rites of the Liturgy.

The Eucharist

Also known as The Lord's Supper or Holy Communion, mostly in Evangelical circles, the Eucharist has kept me occupied in theological and liturgical studies more than any other branch of Theology. My continuing interest in the subject is a result of my specific doctoral research from the time when I wrote my thesis, *Life-Giving Blessing: The Eucharistic Theology of Cyril of Alexandria* (1977). I am still working, though very intermittently, with the editing of some unpublished Eucharistic liturgies in Ge'ez, Ethiopia's ancient liturgical language. The years in Sweden have brought me closer to the Eucharist, both as a subject of research and as a life-giving gift.

Baptism

I have been a little worried about what seems to be the relatively secondary place given to Baptism in the field of theological research here in Sweden.

It is possible that such a statement reflects my lack of sufficient information on research on the topic here in Sweden. I am deeply impressed whenever I read about baptism on Easter Night, in such church orders as *The Apostolic Tradition* attributed to Hippolytus of Rome (d. 236).[4] The baptism of catechumens on Easer Night was a powerful rite of transition from the old to the new life in Christ, where the body and its exposure to the powerful words of confession in the Triune God, the use of water, oil, milk, etc., left a lasting impression on the baptized. For the world around the church, such a rite must have become a sign of the radical movement from heathendom to Christianity.

Some Concluding Words

Perhaps my most meaningful discovery in Sweden is what I experienced in a regular and deepened relationship with a spiritual guide. The place for the discovery and deepening of this experience is the Östanbäck Monastery, near Sala.

All discoveries in the spiritual realm, the excitement related to new experiences in private devotion and in worship, can grow cold or be reduced to lifeless routine. The Church has always taught that the uninterrupted, quickening function of The Holy Spirit, His awakening nudges, is essential for a meaningful spiritual life. The prayer hymn *Veni Sancte Spiritus* (*Come Holy Spirit*) is a treasure to cling to. My studies and experiences of worship here in Sweden have helped me to keep this truth in mind.[5]

Notes

1 See Thunberg's book: *Microcosm and Mediator. The Theological Anthropology of Maximus the Confessor* (C.W.K. Gleerup, Lund, 1965).

2 F. Scott Fitzgerald, *Tender Is the Night* (Middlesex, England: Penguin Modern Classics, 1972), p. 308.

3 Edward Schweizer, *Jesus Christ. The Man from Nazareth and the Exalted Lord* (1987). Published by Mercer University Press, Macon, GA. p. 71.

4 The document, believed to be from the early third century, was previously known as *The Egyptian Church Order.*

5 "Venite Sancte Spiritus" is the beginning of a prayer in the Roman Missal published in 1570. The prayer is used for the masses held around Pentecost.

Year 2002
Chapter 14

Recurring Festivals and Memorials:

To What End?

We are approaching June 20th, another landmark, a day to remember Eritrea's war dead. To speak or write about war and death is no virtue as such, no pleasant pastime. However, we have both the duty and privilege to remember those who gave their lives for causes that they considered dearer than life. June 20th is a reminder of the fact that Eritreans have paid a price. There is hardly any Eritrean family to which this statement doesn't apply, directly or indirectly. I have heard of families that lost all their children in the long war. I have been told of homes that were "closed."

I have no spectacular story to tell from my own family. I know of a cousin on my father's side who never came back. He was a very quiet young man, who disappeared into "the field" (ሜዳ) one day or night, without revealing his decision to any member of his family! One of his brothers used the expression "*Zigäbir nädi'ou näynägir!*" (ዝገብር ነዲኡ ነይነግር), a reference to the grim secrecy with which this cousin left home. The Tigrinya expression could be paraphrased in the words, "The one who has decided to act doesn't divulge his intention even to one who is as close to him as his mother."

When I think of my cousin, I feel a sad and quiet respect for him and his like. For me, he is a picture of the thousands of Eritreans, young and old, who quietly left home and hearth for "the field" (ሜዳ), never to see their near and dear ones again.

That Which Is Written

Here in Sweden I associate regularly with a grand old Eritrean, now almost ninety, who lost four of his sons, in Eritrea's struggle for independence. A fifth son survived but is physically handicapped. This father is a living example of what it means to have paid a high price for home and hearth. Whenever we take up the subject of Eritrea's losses in human life, he states:

> Father Priest: What is written must come to pass (ኣቦይ ቆሺ እቲ እተጻሕፈ ኣይተርፍን እዩ).

Not all may agree with my old friend about things being predestined. This is a theological issue, touching on the whole question of fate and the role of man's free will in the formation of his or her life. However, what my old friend says about "written things" being inevitable generates a train of thoughts within me.

Called to Be "Writers" and Recallers!

Those who died for Eritrea *had* already written something. Eritrea *is* the publication, the book resulting from their writing in their own lifeblood. And something *is* being written in the bosom of Eritrea every day, every week, every month—yes, every year. By what we say or do not say. By the things that we do or do not do! By careless moves and by considered actions! By the tendency to place ready-made labels on our neighbours or the willingness to give them the benefit of the doubt! By underlining the things that unite us or divide us! Yes, by promoting discord, knowingly or unknowingly, or by working tirelessly for dialogue!

These polarities in attitude and action are reason enough to make us ponder how we are writing Eritrea's future, in the wake of those who have written with their lifeblood.

In the first place, I feel that we must make a conscious effort to remember the war dead and what they have sacrificed concretely, and not only give them lip service. After all, those who died fighting for Eritrea's right to self-determination included young people who would have liked to study, qualify for different professions and trades, marry, have children, and enjoy a quiet old age.

They couldn't.

They included persons who already had professions or trades, families and children. They would have liked to continue to be husbands and fathers (or wives and mothers) and pursuers of different professions and trades, supporters of ageing parents, proud parents presiding over the weddings of their children and grandchildren.

They couldn't.

They included those who were only days away from the fall of Asmara. They had certainly started dreaming of a new life. Their dream was cruelly extinguished, within sight of their goal.

In short, the price that individual Eritreans have paid should be remembered in its naked reality, not reduced to soft tales of heroism. Those of us who have not looked death in the face are tempted to become lyrical about it. Taming death in that manner would involve "too little memory," as the French theologian and philosopher Paul Ricoeur has put it. It would involve a flight from reality.

Neither should death be remembered as a revelling in carnage and hate. An accentuation of death's monstrosities, however true they may be, would involve "too much memory," again to quote Paul Ricoeur.[1] Revelling in pain and bitterness can only bind our souls with invisible chains.

Where there is "too little memory" or "too much memory," we cannot move forward, healed from our inner wounds. We would be taking something unresolved with us into the future, the invisible chains of "flight from reality" and "unresolved anger" rattling at our feet.

Seeking Life-furthering Channels

We need, furthermore, to find ways of channeling our memory and grief into life-furthering activities. Once in a while I come across articles that deal with voluntary organizations. They range from associations for the prevention of suicide or of "drunken driving" to fund-raising for research into cancer or into heart diseases among children. There is one striking feature about these organizations. Among the founders and promoters of such groups, I often find individuals (parents, spouses, relatives, friends) whose children, spouses, or friends had despaired of life, succumbed to drugs or cancer or heart-problems at a tender age, or died through tragic car accidents in which drunken drivers were involved.

These are examples of situations in which death was used in the service of life. Here we see how grief and bitterness were converted into engagement for the living. These are possible examples of how we can continue to "author" or "write" Eritrea in the spirit of those who have already written with their lifeblood.

The Invisible *Baito* (Traditional Council)

I have been told that one uses the cry *"Ziban siwu'at!"* (ዝበን ስዉኣት; "Stop or desist, in the name of our Martyrs!"), although I don't know how widespread the practice is in Eritrea. In earlier days, one used to cry *"Ziban mängisti!"* (ዝበን መንግስቲ; "Stop in the name of the State or the Law!"). If it is indeed true that the cry *"Ziban siwu'at!"* is used in Eritrea, then it is perhaps a tacit recognition of an authority vested in Eritrea's martyrs. They now constitute a quiet, invisible tribunal. A council, a *baito* (ባይቶ), with both voice and vote!

Would it be wrong to permit ourselves some poetic license and imagine the company of the martyrs asking from its elevated tribunal, as follows?

> How are you all doing, down there, as you remember us on this moving day? Be assured that we too are thinking of you. We are at peace over the fact that the price we have paid has resulted in a home we can call our own. We are greatly relieved that Eritrea his regained its composure again after what amounted to a nightmarish repetition of the struggle we thought was finally over. That you are still one big family under one roof is our daily reward, and surely a cause for joy among you.

> But what are these echoes, reaching our ears from near and far? From young and old! Is there an unwelcome wind blowing among you? Don't tell us brothers and sisters are treating each other as enemies! Has camaraderie slipped into mutual suspicion and hatred? Where are some of our senior brothers and sisters of pioneer fame? What has become of those who once hungered and thirsted with us across Eritrea's wilderness, for love of freedom? Those who spent sleepless nights on sandy beds, got up with the sun, and stretched their weary limbs to wander over hot ground, into the scorching wind!

> Where are some of the more recent, warm-blooded youth who, according to winds reaching us, have, in their unsuspecting enthusiasm and through pointed words, provoked the displeasure of the more weather-beaten among you? Surely age must look with a mixture of severity and magnanimity on the young! Where are the youth that must be longing for the sight of open fields, the songs of birds, and the laughter of near and dear ones?

> Faint echoes have also reached us from people complaining about what they regard as the limitation of their rights to worship! Can this be true? The whole thing is somewhat puzzling, especially for us!

> We don't want to behave like those who know-it-all. We don't have all the facts. We are only asking questions, not giving verdicts. We hope that

you will understand our concern for our common home, acquired at such a price! Please, enlighten us and lighten our burdens!

Stay well!

As we remember the *siwu'at* (those who have sacrificed themselves), let us pray for harmony among all of Eritrea's children, and for the preservation and permanence of the good heritage left by her martyrs. Let us pray for lasting peace between Eritrea and her neighbours. May God bless and guide our future! May He make Eritrea an instrument of peace and reconciliation, near and far!

Ezra Gebremedhin
June 17, 2002

Notes

1. Paul Ricoeur (1913–2005) was an outstanding French philosopher. See his book *Memory, History, Forgetting* (Chicago: University of Chicago Press, 2006).

Year 2002
Chapter 15

On the Wings of New Year's Day (I):

Taught by Yesterday

We are still in a season between two traditions of celebrating Christmas. To those of us who have already celebrated Christmas I would like to say, true to Swedish tradition, *"God fortsättning!"* (A Happy continuation of the joys of Christmas!)" To those of us who are still looking forward to celebrating it, I say "A Blessed Christmas!" (ብሩኽ ልደት — *B'erouKH L'edät*).

The Gregorian calendar, according to which we shall be celebrating January 1, does not have any specific historical connection with Eritrea or Ethiopia. However, it does link us with a global network of personal, academic, political, and economic relationships. Those of us who live in the Diaspora function almost entirely within the borders of this calendar. We do well to allow this punctual guest from the realm of time to awaken both memories and hopes in us.

Time does fly. We can't slow it or stop it. We can however be lifted up on its wings and thus gain access to a panorama that extends backwards and forwards. With this picture in mind, I would like to share two reflections with my readers on the theme, "On the Wings of New Year's Day." The first is entitled "Taught by Yesterday" and the second "Poised for Tomorrow."

The If-only Syndrome

I remember a train journey from St. Paul, Minnesota, to some town in the American Midwest on a wintry evening at the very beginning of the 1960s. The time was a holiday season, although I don't quite remember whether we were celebrating Thanksgiving Day or Christmas or New Year. I started talking to a middle-aged white man who sat beside me. I found him to be friendly, mild, and dignified. After our conversation had started running smoothly and grown in familiarity, the man let me in on his earlier life. With a breath slightly scented by alcohol he told me about his family, his upbringing in a Christian home, and some of the highlights of his adult life.

On an evening, decades earlier, while he was still a young boy, he had gone out without his parents' permission. I don't remember whether he became involved in a fight or an accident. Be that as it may, that evening he lost the sight on one of his eyes. In a tone subdued, the man said to me, "If I had not gone out that evening, I wouldn't have lost my sight!"

I don't want to minimise the man's traumatic experience. What struck me, however, was what appeared to be smouldering regret, a painful backward glance, so many decades after that fateful evening. My fellow passenger was not demonstratively bitter. However, I got the impression that he had lost more than the sight from one eye. He seemed to have been deprived of the ability to come to terms with his past. At least in one respect! He appeared to have been caught in a nagging sense of regret over an irretrievable loss.

It is the "If-only syndrome," once more:

- "If only I hadn't been there at that time!"
- "If only I hadn't made that decision."
- "If only I hadn't married this man!"
- "If only I hadn't married this woman!"
- "If only I hadn't chosen my present profession!"

The list can be long. The backward glance to youth now lost. Beauty now faded. Health now eroded. And opportunities now squandered. Here we have the backward glance that is a liability, a defeat, a paralysis.

Salvaging the Painful in Our Memories!

It is 12:45 a.m., the morning after Christmas Day, and I have just finished reading the Swedish version of Imre Kertész's novel *Sorstalanság* (English title: *Fateless*; Swedish title: *Mannen utan öde* [The Man Without a Destiny]).[1] It is the story, with obvious autobiographical allusions, of a teenager who once looked devilry and death in the face. Writing later on as an adult (the book came out in Hungarian in 1975), Imre Kertész (b. 1929) describes the nightmare through which he went at the concentration camps of Auschwitz, Zeitz, and Buchenwald from 1944 to 1945. He writes with a detachment and objectivity that is ruthless and staggering. He writes as if he were "only brains," so meticulously rational is he. But he recounts details as if he were "only emotions and memory." Shouting, beatings, hunger, thirst, sleeplessness, fatigue, putrefying and smelly sores, boredom, and hopelessness—enough to drive anyone insane—are described clinically, almost without any self-pity or polemics, by the young Kertész, who almost died at Buchenwald.

Kertész, who has lived under the twin evils of Nazism and Stalinism, has succeeded in rendering his bitter memories fruitful. He was awarded the Nobel Prize in Literature on December 10, 2002. In an interview held on Swedish Television on December 6th of that year, Kertész spoke of memories of his childhood, youth, and adult life. I made notes on some of the things that he said. Below are some excerpts, rendered more or less word for word, into English:

> I have lived in periods in which the one dictatorship succeeded the other …. Totalitarian systems belittle and reduce a human being. They render man and his language infantile …. But there is always a way out …. We must face life's dark realities and snatch our own tale from the blows that history deals us …. Some of the greatest literature has emerged under systems that have opposed it …. To write is a joy, even if one writes about negative experiences …. Better to live one's life and try to relish it, instead of (wasting time) trying to pass a judgement on it …. There is something liberating in all my writings!

Two Men, Two Models

My stories above focus on two men who were severely tested in their youth. Let us go back to my fellow passenger on the train journey in the American Midwest decades ago. For him, an ordinary evening in his childhood ended in the devastating loss of the sight in one eye. We also have a fourteen-year-old Hungarian boy, whose life was suddenly plunged into a state of physical and emotional cataclysm.[2]

My fellow passenger on the train, whose name I don't remember, and Imre Kertész belong to two models for the tackling of the past and its painful memories. Permit me to call these two models "The Train Passenger Model" and "The Kertész Model."

A classic example of "The Train Passenger Model," taken to its extreme, is Judas, the disciple who betrayed Jesus. It is to be remembered that his backward glance, the memory of his guilt, pushed him to end his life in desperation (Matthew 27:3–5)—a case in which the backward glance and the guilt connected with it leads to self-destruction! I may be taking a case that is far too extreme, but we also have the example of Adolph Hitler and the consequences of the backward glances indicated in his book *Mein Kampf*. Hitler's life is an example of a phenomenon in which a backward glance of "The Train Passenger Model" leads to intense hatred and the destruction of others.

Luckily, we also have many examples of the positive, constructive "Kertész Model" of the backward glance. As a biblical counterpoint to Judas, we can refer to St. Peter (Luke 22:54–63; John 21:15–17). It is to be remembered that he had denied his Lord three times, in spite of his boasting that he would go to his death for the sake of his master. Peter was a person in whose life a backward glance of guilt, shame, and tears was converted into a forward look with a forgiven conscience, a restored self-image, and courage. In his life, failure was turned into faith and pain into power.

We have some other, extra-biblical examples. I remember the deep admiration for the dedicated and selfless individual that I felt, decades ago, after I had read Alan Paton's book, *Cry the Beloved Country*, a tale about common people in Apartheid's South Africa. Paton saw suffering, shared it, and decided to do something about it.[3] He turned a "prison" for delinquent young South Africans into a school. His suffering bore fruit. We have something of a twin spirit to Paton in Nelson Mandela. His autobiography, *Long Walk to Freedom*[4], is a moving witness to the fact that Mandela helped to turn a whole country, which had become a prison, into a school for life with dignity. Both Paton and Mandela conform to "The Kertész Model." Their lives demonstrate that suffering and painful memories can be used constructively. They can provide wings to the human spirit.

In accordance with the analogy of the two men whose stories I have narrated above, Eritrea too can be described as young and tested. It is a very young nation that has weathered some severe storms. For a small nation with a limited population and limited means, it has shown remarkable pluck, patience, and persistence. It surely has trophies to rejoice over and models to look up to. But it is also an aching body. It bears the marks of decades of bleeding and loss. Dislocation, disorientation, and disenchantment are still parts of the store of memories among thousands of its people, both at home and abroad.

Remembering is both unavoidable and necessary. And we can't deny that painful memories can either make or break a person. However, the memories of our yesterdays can also challenge and inspire us. They can give us wings. Out of the despair that they house, hope can emerge. Our memories are or can be our teachers. They can be raw material for many a beautiful edifice in our lives. It is remarkable how much music, how many works of art, how many sculptures, how many books, how many poems, how many plays, how many societies and fellowships have been born of painful experiences.

The end of each year reveals gains and losses, assets and liabilities in the lives of individuals and nations. This is surely the case with Eritrea and Eritreans at the threshold of a New Year. But I think it is always the losses and liabilities that we feel keenly. The decisive thing *now* is not what Eritrea and its people have suffered or lost but what they do with the pains connected with their memories. Which model are we going to follow in dealing with our past and charting our future? Will we follow "The Train Passenger Model" or "The Kertész Model"?

In his Nobel Speech on December 7, Kertész stated:

> Since we are talking about literature, after all, the kind of literature that, in the view of your Academy, is also a testimony, my work may yet serve a useful purpose in the future, and—this is my heart's desire—may even speak to the future. [...] Whenever I think of the traumatic impact of Auschwitz, I end up dwelling on the vitality and creativity of those living today. Thus, in thinking about Auschwitz, I reflect, paradoxically, not on the past but the future.[5]

What we say, propagate, and write about Eritrea and its memories, as groups and as individuals, is likely to influence the model that eventually prevails as one of the guides for its future. Are we prepared to make our past, with all its sufferings and losses, count for the future, in the spirit of Kertész? Or are we going to become people whose backward glances to old wounds foster continuing bitterness and polarisation?

The choice is ours, as individuals and as a nation.

A famous prayer runs: "Lord! Give me the power to change what I can change, the patience to accept what I can't change, and the wisdom to know the difference."

A good prayer indeed to remember at the threshold of a New Year!

Happy New Year and God bless you, one and all!

Ezra Gebremedhin
December 27, 2002
Uppsala, Sweden

Notes

1. Swedish version translated by Maria Ortman (Panpocket, Norstedts. Stockholm, 2002). The English version, *Fateless*, was translated by Tim Wilkinson and published by Vintage Classics in 2016.
2. Kertész' parents were divorced and he lived with his father and stepmother. On the day on which he was picked up, his father had already been at a "work camp" for some time. In short, the young man was virtually an "orphan," though his stepmother was evidently loving and considerate.
3. Alan Paton, *Cry the Beloved Country* (Simon and Schuster, 1995).
4. Nelson Mandela, *Long Walk to Freedom* (Little Brown, Boston and New York, 1994).
5. Nobel Speech entitled *Heureka,* delivered on December 7, 2002. See the website of The Swedish Academy (svenskaakademien.se).

Year 2002
Chapter 16

On the Wings of New Year's Day (II):
Poised for Tomorrow

In my first reflection I maintained that the threshold to a New Year was a station between our yesterdays and tomorrows, a vantage point from which we could look both backwards and forwards. In this reflection I would like to say a few words about some simple, home-grown guidelines for our journey into the next year. First some words on the need for humility at the threshold to a New Year.

Those of us who have attended Eritrean engagements, weddings, certain religious ceremonies, graduations, the laying of foundations and the like, surely remember the words:

መፈጻምትሉ የጸብቅ —*MäfäTSämti'ou YäTSäb'eqo*

Roughly translated:

> May God make the end or outcome auspicious!

There is no guarantee that a good beginning will always lead to a good end. Our forefathers arrived at this truth through painful experience. And they were not alone in this insight. Sayings like *Man proposes but God disposes, All is well that ends well,* and *He laughs best who laughs last* reflect something of the uncertainty that we all sense around beginnings. New Year's Day is a good beginning. But we cannot take its festive entry into our midst as a guarantee of sustained joy and success. Too many New

Year's Days have been celebrated among us, and too many periods of twelve months have passed, for us to be naive about the possible outcome of a New Year. In the years that have elapsed, some hopes have borne fruit in our lives as individuals and as a nation. And some have remained stunted or have shrivelled altogether. By now, we should realise that events with far-reaching consequences can run out of our control. Let us move into this New Year with hope and optimism, but also with quiet and prayerful humility.

Poised with Time as Our Ally

To think of a New Year is to think of Time, of events, and of the emotional contents of these events. Time may not heal all wounds, but it can in fact accomplish a whole lot of good. In the first place, it is a guarantor of change and ageing. In this regard, no one or nothing can stand in its way. All must eventually bend under its steady but powerful hands. The proud and the humble, the wise and the foolish, the powerful and the powerless, the rich and the poor, must stand, grey-haired and weather-beaten, before Time's tribunal. Even conflicts have their time limit. They too age, praise God! And eventually, all must make their final exit from life's stage to Time's quiet nod.

To make Time our ally is to let it do its work in people, circumstances, and places, without permitting ourselves to sink into passivity. You surely remember the saying:

ንነዊሕ መገዲ ኣይትጐየዩሉ ንክቢድ ነገር ኣይትተሃወኽሉ

Roughly translated:

> Is your way long? Don't start running! Is your case (errand) demanding? Avoid haste!

It has been said that haste makes waste. And this is in fact the point of the saying quoted above. But there are also occasions when delaying action makes waste—not striking while the iron is hot is, symbolically speaking; wasting golden opportunities. Having said that, I must add that I personally feel that the greater and more frequent risk is that I act hastily under critical circumstances! The saying of our parents quoted above is therefore appropriate. At the threshold to this New Year, let us lift the banners of wise caution and well-considered moves.

Chapter 16

Poised with Openness for Mutual Trust and Respect

በይኑ ዝምጉት ዝረትያ ነይብሉ ።

በይኑ ዝጎዪይ ዝቕድሞ ነይብሉ

Roughly translated:

> He who argues his case alone has no one to disprove him!

> He who runs alone has no competitor to defeat him!

I don't have the slightest doubt about the necessity of a critical attitude, a healthy dose of skepticism, in reading and responding to written discussions on Eritrea in these troubled times. However, without a basic element of openness and trust, no genuine communication is possible. Where there is no serious intent to listen to what others are saying, we are condemned to talking past each other.

Our different cyber media should be forums for us to sharpen our pencils and ideas, not our swords and spears. They should be meeting places, not battlefields. Those of us who live in the Diaspora and are surrounded by traditions of the free word and open forums, have a heavy responsibility in this regard.

We who write on the different Eritrean cyber media don't have umpires or referees with the unquestioned authority to put a quiet stop to our stubborn opinions. Neither is it desirable that we be dependent on such umpires in the pursuit of our political or social debates. We could, however, use some very stringent self-censorship in what we say and write. To write is to take a heavy responsibility upon oneself. Ten, twenty, thirty years from now, I hope Eritreans will read a number of the written contributions to the different cyber media with benefit and pride. However, I am afraid that many are going to ask some pointed questions on the way as to whether we have used our common mental resources and the forums available to us.

Poised with Openness for Objectivity

The Swedes have the very telling word *saklighet*, which builds on the word *sak* ("thing" or "object"). This word is a badge of honour in the Swedish news media and in the pursuit of all academic work. Taken literally, *saklighet* means "thinginess," something that has to do with the very being of an object or an issue! It is another word for objectivity. A culture of sober dialogue, sincerely sought and cultivated by all of us, could foster minds that are more open and accommodating towards others, as we move into the coming year.

This is one of the main points of Gherense Asfaha Neguse's impressive article in Tigrinya, ከስዒ ኣደ ጉራምራ (Roughly translated: "A mother's stomach [womb] is many coloured"). The article was originally posted on November 20, 2001, and posted again on *asmarino.com* on December 3, 2002. It takes up the task that is incumbent upon the present generation to contribute to an edifying culture of debate and dialogue.

Happy New Year and a fruitful exchange of thoughts!

God bless you, one and all!

Ezra Gebremedhin
December 27, 2002
Uppsala, Sweden

Year 2002
Chapter 17

Where Is My Mother? (I)

It was one of those light summer evenings here in Uppsala, Sweden, only some weeks ago. I thought that the main door to our flat was locked. Suddenly it was flung open and a little Kurdish boy stood before me, with an ice-cream cone in his left hand. To say that he was taken aback would have been an understatement. He was frozen in his tracks. Wondering if he had come to ask about a stray ball that perchance had landed in our fenced backyard, I inquired gently, in Swedish, "What do you want?" Trying to compose himself he asked, "*Var är min mamma?* (Where is my mother?)"

For a split second he must have experienced the horror of the possibility of having lost his mother, irretrievably. His hidden anguish and his moments of controlled panic stung my father's heart. I felt a tremendous sense of relief at the fact that things were not as bad as he might have suspected.

He had been out playing in the children's court and interrupted his pastime to run back to his mother in our apartment complex. This time he dashed into the wrong stairway entrance and headed, unknowingly, for our flat. His bewilderment at seeing me instead of his mother was luckily short-lived. I took him by the hand and led him out. A neighbour's son recognized him right away and promised to deliver him at the right address.

After the child had left, one association after the other rushed into my mind. I thought of the Tigrinya saying:

ንዘረባ ዘረባ የምጽኦ ንሓመድ ድጉሪ የውጽኦ

Roughly translated:

> Thought begets thought as the ploughshare digs up soil!

The child's question, "Where is my mother?" was simple and yet profound in its implications. In his disorientation there was a focus of certainty. In his momentarily stormy surroundings there was a firm anchor. The name of this quiet centre, this firm anchor, was *Mother*.

A Country as Mother

The term Mother stands for the rule of love written in the heart (ልቢ, *libbi*) and bowels (መዓንጣ, *Mä'AnTa*). By some wonderful arrangement beyond man's engineering, something of a mother's love is shared by a further category of people with a kindred spirit: a faithful baby-sitter, a doting grandmother, a devoted older sister, a loving aunt, or a just and generous stepmother. That is why they are all addressed as *Mother*. Sometimes even a man is called *Mother*, because he radiates the love and concern of a mother. Such is also the case with a school that has nurtured grateful students. Hence the term *Alma Mater* (a loving, nurturing mother) applies to the institution of learning to which an individual looks back with appreciation and gratitude!

One of the loftiest symbols of the mightiest nation on earth today, the United States, is that of a woman, a mother, represented by the Statue of Liberty.

It was Gustav Vasa (d. 1560), patriot and warrior, and his successors from the sixteenth to the earlier part of the eighteenth century, who shaped Sweden into an independent and powerful nation. And yet, it is not they who are the primary objects of the love and adulation of the Swedes in our days. In the popular mind it is Sweden itself as *Moder Svea* (Mother Sweden) that rules with primacy in the hearts of its subjects. Swedish TV reporters in a good mood accompany their reports on home news by cartoons of *Moder Svea*, crowned and seated on a low stool in her flowing dress of blue and yellow, Sweden's national colours.

We have Eritrea's national anthem, sung with rapt attention and quiet pride on official occasions. It is striking that this anthem repeats the name of the nation more often than many anthems of its kind, as it narrates the high exploits of a people personified as a woman.

In short, by some primeval instinct unquenched by the passage of millennia, countries have preserved the archetype of Mother, deep in their being. The question is how and to what extent this fact influences the policies of nations and the treatment of their citizens.

Chapter 17

Womanhood and Motherhood as Humanizers of Sentiments

War should never be a subject of rejoicing. It has its grim and frightful aspects. At the same time, it cannot be denied that Eritrea's decades of military struggle (launched according to a commonly accepted tradition, on ባሕቲ መስከረም (The First of Mäskäräm, i.e., September 1, 1961) have, after the analogy of the rose among thorns, molded many an Eritrean character.[1] The war years have destroyed many. But they have also purified and ennobled many an Eritrean soul. They have contributed to a growing sense of Eritrean identity, in which a *shared* goal and *shared* suffering are important factors.

However, we should not forget the fact that all prolonged armed conflicts constitute two-edged swords. They spell not only the trophy of independence but also a dark, subconscious heritage of violence, assimilated or suppressed. The post-Vietnam experience of the United States, unfolding in the turbulent lives of many of its war veterans, is one telling witness to this oft-forgotten truth. Pacifying and taming this dormant monster, this substratum of traumas, is one of the pressing needs of the future. Eritrea will need more than programmes and projects to be able to do so, good and necessary as these are. It will need more than its men and fathers, dedicated as these are. It will need the heart of a Mother. It will require the patience, dedication, and untiring love of a ወላዲት ("giver of birth").

In view of this fact, we must ask ourselves, "How seriously does Eritrea take the rich and mighty symbol of the woman, the mother, which is such an obvious part of its national anthem? How much of its national life and the treatment of its citizens is dictated by the sentiments of the heart (ልቢ , *libbi*) and the bowels (መዓንጣ , *Mä'AnTa*) of a *wäladit* (ወላዲት , literally "giver of birth," i.e., mother)?"

I realize that sound statecraft cannot mix the juridical and the maternal indiscriminately. However, all successful leadership is a sound combination of the resources of the *head* and the *heart*.

Just now, in the year 2002, upholding Eritrea's image as a Mother and fostering a "mother mentality" in high and low places is, in my opinion, a matter of urgency for the country. Not to take one's cues from a tradition of nurturing, nursing, and pleading Eritrean mothers may be missing a God-given opportunity. Metal and muscles are not always the best means of creating harmony and maintaining stability within a nation. At times, motherliness may do a far better job.

Healing comes from a motherly attitude, also on a national level. Stay well and God bless you, one and all!

Ezra Gebremedhin
August 28, 2002
Uppsala, Sweden

Notes

1. See article in *awate.com* under the title *In Memory of Awate, The History-Maker*, by Taher Journal, Washington D.C., September 1, 2001. On August 16 of this year, I was happily surprised to find an article entitled *A Bit of Eritrean History*, at Bridgeport U.K., with interesting glimpses into the earlier part of Awate's military activities. See *asmarino.com* for August 15, 2002. The article was posted by Alemseged Tesfai, who had it published first in *Eritrea Profile* on August 11, 2002.

Year 2002
Chapter 18

Where Is My Mother? (II):
The Necessity of Reciprocity

John F Kennedy once said, "Ask not what your country can do for you but what you can do for your country!" There is something equivocal about this famous statement. It can be used to confirm and reinforce an authoritarian system of government. But there is also a deeply positive aspect to it. Indeed, a country has the right to ask, "Where are my children?" and expect a loyal response. However, it is equally important that the citizens of a country too can ask, like the little boy in my first reflection, "Where is my Mother?" and do so with an unabated sense of security and confidence.

There must be some kind of meaningful give-and-take, some measure of reciprocity, for even the most altruistic of relationships to function and last. We human beings are creatures of flesh and blood, not angels or spirits. We have a proven tendency to lose interest in, tire of, and give up on enterprises and relations that are no longer "paying propositions." I am not trying to equate citizenship and business. Nevertheless, the fact remains that the most ardent love can cool; the embers of the most burning patriotism can slowly turn into ashes, *unless they are sustained by a meaningful give-and-take!*

Every human experience has its own pain barrier, a point beyond which endurance becomes extremely difficult or impossible. In recent weeks we have been hearing of draft dodging and of the flight of youth from Eritrea. I cannot vouch for the statistics behind such news. Neither am I prepared to sit as a judge at a tribunal set up to identify the guilty party in the set of interactions leading to draft dodging and flight!

That these phenomena exist cannot be denied. What do they show? Are they results of factors that are beyond the control of any person or institution or country? Are they indications of sheer cowardice or ingratitude on the part of young Eritreans? Or are they the unfortunate and completely unintended results of the moves of a government trying to carry out its rightful duties under the most unfavourable circumstances? Can draft dodging and flight be the results of pain barriers reached and crossed? By many they have been interpreted as the expressions of the deep grief of parents and the hopelessness of youth.

These questions must be asked fairly and objectively.

A state has both the duty and the right to see to it that reasonable measures are taken to maintain its rightful borders. The trumpet call has its time and its place in the life of a nation. But so has a people's longing for life under normal conditions, for answers to nagging questions, for the hum of festive gatherings and the sound of joyous music! A people must be challenged, when occasions demand that they be. But they also need to be encouraged. A nation's subjects can be taken to task, when occasions demand that they be. But they also need to be commended. A country is a fortress to be protected. But it is also a home in which one can recline. It is a field to be cultivated by the sweat of one's brow. But it is also a garden to be enjoyed at leisure.

To say these things is to repeat the obvious. But there are times when the obvious must be repeated.

Avoiding a Prolonged State of Conflict

Until about two weeks ago, I did not know that the book known as *The Art of War* even existed. This classical work on warfare was written over 2,500 years ago by the famous Chinese military strategist, Sun Zi. I shall not be presumptuous enough to enlighten men and women in uniform about any part of its contents. Permit me, however, to refer to it.

A relative of mine happened to mention the book to me while I was working on these reflections. Out of sheer curiosity, I secured and started browsing through the Swedish version of the book. Among its 383 maxims on the art of warfare, I found a couple simple and down to earth ones, which I felt could have a bearing on what I am trying to say.

In the chapter entitled "Conducting War," Sun Zi writes:

> There is not a single instance in which a country has been known to have derived advantages from a prolonged state of warfare.[1]

Furthermore, in the chapter entitled "On Manoeuvres," Sun Zu writes:

> A soldier's energy is at its highest in the morning; at midday it starts to diminish; and in the evening his senses are set solely on returning to camp.[2]

Bear with my folly, but here is my layman's interpretation of Sun Zi. Take it with a grain of salt, since even I know that I won't get a grading of "A" on it!

Instead of "soldier" in the quotation above, read "the people of Eritrea"! Instead of "energy," read "stamina" and ሓበን (*habbo*—guts, decisiveness, perseverance)! Instead of "morning," read ባሕቲ መስከረም (*BaHti Mäskäräm*, 1961)! Instead of "midday," read "the bitter mid-years of the 1970s"! Instead of "evening," read "2002"! Instead of "camp," read "normal, everyday life"!

It is true that Eritrea is not engaged in a shooting war just now. In fact, it is co-operating in the demarcation of its border. It has its hands more than full in setting a ravaged house in order. The fact remains, however, that war has also seriously depleted the emotional and psychic resources of large sections of the population. Eritrea stands not only before *buildings* but also *hearts* in ruin. For people who have experienced war and its effects, directly or indirectly, for over three decades, this state of things is hardly surprising. It is precisely these people and their children who are longing to return to camp, to normal, everyday life.

Avoiding the Last Straw

The author of the biblical book of Ecclesiastes writes:

> To everything there is a season, and a time to every purpose under the heaven [...] *A time to weep, and a time to laugh; a time to mourn and a time to dance.* (Eccl. 3:1, 4)

Blessed is the country that can do the right things at the right time. Enviable is the nation that can harmonise duties and privileges, fasts and feasts, sighs and smiles. Such a country is indeed a Mother.

I know that these things are more easily said than done. I am thinking aloud, not trying to hurl ready-made answers from a high horse. But I am convinced that the things I have said are better said than unsaid.

"It is the last straw that breaks the camel's back," as the saying goes. These words are applicable not only to the moods and sentiments of individuals but also to those of a nation as a whole. Stress over a very long period of time can be devastating. It is not hard work that wears us out. It is rather the haste, the anxiety, the uncertainty, the fear, the perennially tight circumstances connected with what we are and what we do. We can all witness to this fact.

Sweden is perhaps the world's most accommodating nation as far as the care of its citizens is concerned. And yet, the phenomenon known in Swedish as *utbrändhet,* a state of being psychically and mentally burnt out, has become a matter of national concern. That the problem appears to hit educated, gifted, ambitious, and hardworking citizens in the first place doesn't make things better. The problem is being discussed in the public media and ways are being sought by state, county, and private organisations to counteract it.

We cannot compare Sweden and Eritrea. Nevertheless, how much more should a country like Eritrea, poor and war-torn as it is, stay on the alert against the depletion of human energy? The country must face the emptying of psychic resources resulting from stress, sorrow, and disappointment over a long period of time and find remedies for them!

A Cause for Vigilance and Not Hopelessness

Does Eritrea need to be reminded of these things by its children in the Diaspora? A good friend of mine said to me after returning to Sweden from a recent trip to Eritrea:

> Our leaders and our people are slowly nursing a nation back to normalcy. They are trying to make ends meet, against enormous odds. Things are slowly moving in the right direction. As you very well know, the economy had ባይቱ ዝቢጡ (hit rock bottom). What point is there in showering criticism on an enterprise that is sincerely trying to get a nation on its feet again? Shouldn't people try to be part of the solution instead?

I respect my friend's views and the concern out of which he spoke. All voices should be heard in these matters. I am convinced that there are good things happening in Eritrea. And a criticism that is not constructive, in its basic intentions, is best not voiced.

This does not mean, however, that crucial questions should not be discussed. To take up such issues is to be a part of the solution. Whether we like the fact or not, whether we are prepared to admit it or not, there is severe turbulence in the heart and soul of many an Eritrean—at home and abroad—these days!

Let us take one example. Not so few are the Eritrean families that are experiencing the pain of separation anew. It is very sad indeed to read of Eritreans becoming refugees once again, when we thought that the phenomenon of flight had at last been reversed. It is to be remembered that thousands had already returned from Sudan in recent years.

Regardless of where the final blame for this reversal is to be put, the reversal itself is highly regrettable. It is not to be minimised. It is a serious setback.

A setback or a series of setbacks do not imply the end of the road or the end of the world. Someone has said that Eritrea's greatest natural resource is her people. And she still has this natural resource. Her people are a resource worth handling with extreme care and respect. One of the things I can say with certainty about my fellow countrymen is, "If you can help it, don't provoke an Eritrean!" Eritrea has survived poverty and hardship in the past because of the sustaining power of a common goal and the durability of the psyche of its people.

Edward Denison's testimony reflects something of what I am trying to say:

> If you begin to comprehend the immeasurable suffering that these people have had to endure and the degree of success with which they have been able to put this tragic history behind them, it makes it even more remarkable that their compassion towards visitors is so resolute.[3]

These are indeed words that should warm our hearts. The question is how much longer one can count on the binding factors and the psychic stamina of the past decades. Cries and pleas are emerging from the heart of the nation. And it takes the heart and wisdom of a Mother to realize that pleadings neglected tend to become plagues protracted. There is every reason to ponder this matter. After all, it is the last straw that breaks the camel's back.

An Appeal

I want to go back to the words of John F Kennedy, "Ask not what your country can do for you but what you can do for your country!" These words are valid and must remain valid in the heart of every Eritrean. But there is another question that must also remain valid. Today, in the year 2002, it is the right of every Eritrean to ask, in full confidence, "Where is my Mother?" And the task of contributing to a loud and clear answer is a challenge to all Eritreans, leadership and citizenry alike.

Stay well and God bless you, one and all!

Ezra Gebremedhin
August 28, 2002
Uppsala, Sweden

Notes

1 Sun Zi, *The Art of War* (Swedish Edition), Arctic Reprint (London: Acturus Publishing Limited, 2016), number 22, p. 6.
2 Ibid., number 28, p. 63.
3 Edward Denison is a very close friend and colleague of my brother Naigzy. Their years in the Cultural Assets Rehabilitation Project (CARP) in Eritrea and their work together in assessing the architectural heritage of Asmara can be said to have led to Asmara's recognition as a World Heritage site, a final achievement in which Edward was a *primus motor* (main actor).

Year 2003
Chapter 19

Encounter or Confrontation?

I shall not say why I didn't write earlier. What I can say right now is that I am writing these words out of a sense of futility—the feeling that nothing useful can come out of one's efforts. A sense of futility because I am going to say something that hundreds, indeed thousands of Eritreans and their friends have said before me, without seeing their wishes and pleas for serious dialogue fulfilled. A sense of futility because I am writing in the face of a *fait accompli* (something done and finished)! Members of the so-called G-15 have already been put under arrest and Eritrea's young, private newspapers have been placed under a ban.[1] There are either some extremely serious (but to us unknown) risks to the national security of Eritrea, which we of the grassroots should of course not minimize, or the parties to this conflict in high places (and I am now thinking particularly of our leaders) have their own rules of political action, apparently immune to the pleas and petitions of serious-minded Eritreans all over the world. In short, I am writing out of a sense of frustrating ignorance and uncertainty and a desperate desire to make a minute dent in what appears to be a citadel of animosity in high places.

I am also writing out of a sense of apprehension because I know, as a reader, what sort of verbal slaughter can result from exchanges on the Eritrean cyber-media. The ease and superficiality with which derogatory labels are being flung around in our cyber-media nowadays has become not only ridiculous but also lacking in decency. One is tempted to stay out of the whole fray. However, I have felt more and more that refraining from commenting on Eritrean affairs, even as an amateur in political matters, out of fear of such labels would be tantamount to succumbing to blackmail. It would be bowing to cheap intimidation. Hasn't someone said that politics is too serious a matter to be left to politicians? I remember a piece of advice that was given to me by a relative some years ago, on the risky business of getting involved in verbal duels on Eritrean politics: ኣብ ዉራይካ ኣይትጋየሽ። (*Ab werayka aytigayesh*—Don't behave like a guest at a feast of your own making).

The Need of a Clear Choice

The Jewish philosopher Martin Buber once made the classic statement: "All real living is meeting!" In other words, *All real living is genuine encounter.* The implications of these words should be obvious to all serious-minded people, societies, and countries. Time-honoured institutions of mediation, which saw to it that people in conflict were offered the help of a third party, are a confirmation of this insight. Mediation or arbitration, the creation of contexts for "meeting" or "encounter," is a feature of life on all levels of interaction—social, economic, religious, and political. Our ባይቶታት (*baitos*—traditional forums for discussions and decision-making) in Eritrea stand in the same tradition. Age and grey hair were once signs of authority and not of purported incompetence or senility. Individuals bowed their stubborn wills to the seasoned pleadings of the old.

Even those who felt that they had not been granted their full share of justice out of the *baito* proceedings were grateful receivers of the blessings uttered by the elders. It was part of the sound, primeval instinct of our ancestors that humility and respect for the *vox populi,* the voice of the people, expressed through sacred tradition, was part of the in-built guarantee for the communal and social health of our people. This insight was built on the understanding that the leadership of a country is the privilege of the collected wisdom of the community, not the power of individual actors. Where the channels for this collective wisdom are absent or fall into disuse or disrespect, the fist or sticks take over. Where imagination, fantasy, traditional stories, and myths in the rustic rhetoric of our elders are neglected, the language of polemics, hard logic, and the law book take over. These latter instruments are deaf to healing lore and merciful arbitration. Theirs is primarily the language of confrontation or capitulation.

My question is: "Has the order of the day for relationships in high places in our country become not *Encounter* but *Confrontation*?" Or have I completely misunderstood the present state of things in Eritrea?

For Eritrea, its people, its different factions and its leaders, there is no alternative to "meeting" or "encounter" in a cordial, open, generous spirit of dialogue. Are we Eritreans, on all sides of the current conflict or conflicts, so absolutely sure of ourselves that we would be caught dead rather than give the counsels of others a chance? If so, woe is Eritrea! If so, the relentless writing on the wall may read: "Communicate or perish!"

What shall we who are Eritreans in the Diaspora do? Shall we speak? Shall we keep quiet? If we decide to keep quiet, what would our motivation be? If we do speak, how do we know that what we are saying makes sense? We live at a great distance from Eritrea. We feed or have been fed on reports from official and private newspapers, from radio broadcasts, from Eritrean websites, etc. All reports are, willy-nilly, modifications, exaggerations in some direction or another. We who live abroad can therefore be victims of the embellishments or aggravations that accompany all retelling. To live far away from a country and its daily developments, especially in times of crisis, is to live, partly, in a dream world. It can lead to a state of being "cocooned" in an atmosphere of half-truths and myths. People who have recently returned from visits in Eritrea have cured many of us from a number of myths and exaggerations, in all directions. And of course, added some new myths and exaggerations, depending on those they have met and the places they have visited in Eritrea!

However, in spite of the misinformation and misinterpretation that distance can create, keeping quiet in the face of ominous developments can entail its own price. The virtues of wisdom and courage are rare. We have been told by the wise and courageous in the past that, under certain circumstances, the silence of the good can be as criminal as the outright transgressions of evil people. The question is: "What shall we do?" How can we be sure that our silence is not a concession to evil? What subjects shall we take up? Shall we take up the apparent lack of dialogue among the so-called G-15 and the Government? The Asmara University students at Wi'a? The whereabouts and state of Semere Kesete, the chairman of the student body of Asmara University? The arrest of members of the so-called G-15? The ban on private newspapers?

Where There Is Smoke, There Is Fire

Our questions are manifold. Weighing their pros and cons endlessly can paralyse us into total passivity. However, inaction cannot be a viable alternative at this time. We have the saying, "Where there is smoke, there is fire"! And surely a lot of smoke has been reaching us these days. Lately the smoke has become suffocatingly thick. The incidence of smoke in the present political and social atmosphere of our country witnesses to the presence of fire somewhere, in some form or another. And no one can neglect a fire. Not even those who want to avoid being called alarmists.

There is one more issue to consider, as I have already indicated. All kinds of alarm have in fact been sounded on the conflict within our leadership in Eritrea—alarms by politicians, military personnel, academicians, the elderly, religious leaders, grassroots people, etc. What then is the point of coming up with one more cry of alarm? Isn't it plain hypocrisy to try to be counted among those who have spoken by writing now? Wouldn't speaking and writing now be tantamount to the barking of the dog after the departure of the hyena?

Worried

I have my own reasons for having kept my peace so far. However, in light of recent events, I feel that no Eritrean can maintain total and unqualified silence at this time [see footnote 90, above]. As many of us as possible must continue to say that we are very, very worried. Expressing our worry can't mean incriminating our government *a priori* or supporting just any protagonist in the current conflict. To say that we are worried is to say that we share in the sighs and inner torments of our country's evolving history. We are worried for the simple reason that things are accelerating ominously and we don't know what the end of this whole development may be. We are worried because we know that an atmosphere shot through with suspicion and bitterness cannot, in the long run, augur well for a country like Eritrea, whose people have been and are going through the traumas of a recent conflict. The present development can literally poison the emotional life of the country.

We are worried because we know, from numerous examples in the histories of countries like ours, that a persistent lack of rapprochement and cordial dialogue in a situation of tension at high levels of society can easily lead to a deep-rooted national crisis, sooner or later. Those of us who are married can't be ignorant of the emotional state that a domestic stalemate (marked by silence, glum faces, mutual recriminations, needling comments and reactions) can lead to in the relationship between strong-willed couples! Raise this scenario to the millionth magnitude and you can get a very faint idea as to where festering conflicts on a national level can lead. A persistent lack of a structured, sober and progressive dialogue and the launching of punitive measures against those who have raised uncomfortable questions can sow the seeds of thirst for vengeance in the hearts of coming generations. The French Philosopher Paul Ricoeur said in a lecture some years ago that the bitter conflict in the Balkans was the result of *Memory*.

Chapter 19

Is Silence Always Golden?

As far as the present state of tension in high places in Eritrea is concerned, one can be silent because one is convinced, in spite of news of general unrest, that things are basically all right, that those at the helm of government are in full control, that they are sensible, farsighted people, possessed of good judgment, that the members of the so-called G-15 were actually motivated by ulterior and personal motives. One can keep silent because one does not know the whole truth or because not all details behind controversial issues have come out in the open. In short, one can keep quiet because one agrees with the position, tacit or overt, which can be interpreted as reflecting our government's attitude: "Take care of your own specific callings and wait. Surely, you should have enough confidence in your government to give it time to sort things out."

Theoretically, the presuppositions and arguments mentioned above could be valid. The plea that we encounter from time to time, "Don't rock the boat 'Eritrea' too much at this hour of crisis," may indeed have some validity. But only "may." Beyond entertaining such a benevolent attitude towards those who seem to be telling us not to be too worried, we cannot say anything with certainty. Even if we were to give our government the benefit of the doubt in the present conflict in which repeated calls for serious dialogue appear to have been turned down, the element of doubt is bound to remain high.

It must be said that expecting an unquestioning attitude on the current conflict from the Eritrean public at home or in the Diaspora is making a high demand. It is like saying: "You need not worry about the smoke which has already reached your eyes and started scorching them."

What was and still is at issue is the necessity of open, serious, cordial, extended dialogue, on high levels. The arrest of members of the G-15 and the closing down of private newspapers has been justified by a reference to concerns for national security. This is indeed a very weighty matter, even though we of the grassroots cannot be the final judges of the validity of its being raised right now. Be that as it may, not to aspire to dialogue in the sense mentioned above is to go the way of confrontation and not encounter. A blanket suggestion that an open, detailed, and cordial dialogue on high levels among former equals is "unrealistic" or "untimely" or "western" or "imported" or a camouflage for "sinister motives" and that the only way to solve the current conflict is the use of punitive measures strikes one as an oversimplification that thinking Eritreans would find very difficult to accept.

Silence Blindly Accepted?

Silence on our part at this time appears to require acquiescence to the sort of message that seems to imply: "Trust us when we say or imply that no serious, planned, all-embracing dialogue is warranted or needed at this time. Trust us when we say or imply that no serious mistakes have been committed. Trust us when we say or imply that all the alarms that have been sounded so far on the possible risks of lack of an open, detailed, structured dialogue are not to be taken seriously. Trust us when we say or imply that the best stance you as Eritreans can take, at home and abroad, is to keep calm and to minimize the alleged seriousness of any expressions of unrest inside and outside of Eritrea. Do your business and wait until Eritrea's political atmosphere clears up. Simply trust and wait."

I want to ask the question: "Do all the points I have raised above reflect, without exception, the presuppositions out of which our leadership is operating as far as the present conflict is concerned?" I hope not. If our leaders are expecting *unquestioning* acquiescence and silence, in good faith, from all of their mentally and emotionally preoccupied compatriots, at home and abroad, on the present political tension in our country, I am afraid they are expecting something out of the ordinary. Serious questions have been raised and serious answers have to be given. Isn't there a risk that taking punitive measures against those who have asked the questions becomes an avoidance of the crux of the problem? Or are people like me completely in the dark as to what has been transpiring in Eritrea during the recent years, in spite of my efforts to follow developments closely?

I have also a question for those who have challenged our leadership, particularly the members of the G-15. Are they expecting us to accept the charges they have brought up, lock, stock and barrel? I hope not. If so, they too are expecting something out of the ordinary. Only after an open, clear, and cordial dialogue, made known to the public, can we who belong to the grassroots of Eritrea speak of some possibility of judging the nature and implications of the various questions and accusations. It is to their credit that the G-15 have, from what I understand, repeatedly requested dialogue. Whether their basic motives are totally genuine or not, is another matter.

In academia we have the saying: "Publish or perish!" Who knows, the writing on the wall right now to us as a people may read: "Communicate or perish!" Surely, it would be a tragedy of tragedies if Eritrea, having thrown off previous shackles, should be enmeshed in the snares of fratricidal conflict and chaos as a result of lack of genuine encounter among her own children. We don't want to believe that of Eritrea or of her leaders, who have paid too high a price in their lives to have it squandered at the eleventh hour!

Hawkum (Your brother)!
Ezra
2003, Uppsala

Notes

1. My understanding is that the group known as the G-15 attempted to initiate dialogue with the President of Eritrea on national issues at a crucial period in the history of the country. They were members of the Central Council of the Ruling Party, People's Front for Democracy and Justice (PFDJ). Seven were former cabinet ministers. They were arrested in September of 2001 after publishing an open letter to the government and President Isaias. Their claim was that they had requested democratic dialogue. Their move was interpreted as an action directed against the security of the nation. At the time of publication, twenty years later, the fate of the G-15 remains a question mark.

Year 2003 (2020)
Chapter 20

Bus Eritrea

The date was November 21, 2002 and fresh snow covered the countryside. I was travelling on Bus Number 61, heading for the Monastery of Östanbäck, a ninety-minute journey by train and bus from Uppsala.[1] After watching buildings, cars, shrubbery, and people slip by in the wintry space outside for some time, I settled back in my seat. Soon, a sign on the windshield of the bus caught my attention, a round sticker that read "*Bromsar kontrollerade september 2002* (Brakes Checked September 2002)."

I had noticed similar, larger stickers on the bodies of inter-city buses in Stockholm and Uppsala before. The signs were placed on the body of the bus, often to the left of the main entrance where passengers could see them before climbing on to the bus. I intentionally took a closer look at the larger stickers after I had started working on this reflection. The authority that carries out the inspection of brakes on buses here in Sweden is *Bilprovningen* (Car Inspection), which also requires that, under normal conditions, the brakes of buses should be checked every six months. The stickers on the bus imply that a responsible, qualified, and neutral authority has approved their issuance and that these small certificates are trustworthy.

But why was the sticker on the bus placed where everyone could see it? Was it intended to assure passengers that the vehicle in which they were travelling was safe? Was it a reminder to the driver about the next date for the inspection of brakes? Why wasn't there a label declaring equally conspicuously when the *wheels* were checked last? Or the *gearbox*! Or the *steering wheel*! Or the *accelerator*! Why this particular attention to brakes?

[2]

Unassuming But Indispensable

In recent years, Sweden, a country that just now occupies the highest place in the world as far as traffic safety is concerned, has had some severe bus accidents with fatalities. Brakes played a decisive role in some of these.[3] The traffic authorities are on the alert against neglect in matters related to the care of vehicles, particularly as regards brakes. To take only one example, on February 22nd of this year, buses on the roads of the Swedish province of Värmland, where our son Emmanuel and his family happen to live, were stopped without warning. They were released after the brakes and the steering capacity of each bus had been checked thoroughly.

Brakes are not particularly conspicuous. Neither are they objects of special beauty, although I understand that nowadays they come in different grades of sophistication.[4] The brakes that I knew during my youth were associated with sharp noises and heating. Brakes are more exposed to wear and tear than any other part of a car, probably with the exception of tyres. Furthermore, they must function unseen and unsung. And it is precisely their lack of visibility and their unassuming character that tempts us to underestimate their significance. There is no glamour involved in taking time to have our cars (and their brakes, of course!) inspected. I can witness to that fact, having owned a car once. I would rather have spent the time in doing something more enjoyable, like attending a concert or a movie or having a meal with good friends!

And yet, brakes are indispensable for the proper functioning of traffic and for the preservation of life and limb. Many a life owes its survival to brakes that functioned well on critical occasions. Many a gravestone is a witness to brakes that failed. Many a mother has shed bitter tears and wished that brakes had functioned on that fateful day when a daughter's life was extinguished. Many an aspiring athlete, now confined to a wheelchair, has deeply regretted those seconds when the brakes of his vehicle were found wanting.

As with vehicles in traffic, so too with everyday life! The fact is that deviations in nature and vices in private and national life are natural tendencies and virtues gone wild, for lack of brakes.[5] Let me give some examples.

Large stretches of impoverished farmland in many parts of the world are a result of cultivation without brakes. The pollution of the environment is, in many cases, the result of the exploitation of nature without brakes. Cancer, often the result of the pollution of our environment, is the multiplication of cells without brakes. Drug addiction is the search for excitement or relief without brakes. Drunkenness is "thirst" without brakes. Gluttony is appetite without brakes. Prostitution (one of the main causes for the spread of HIV-AIDS) is passion without brakes. Tribalism and racism are pride in one's identity without brakes. Religious fanaticism is piety without brakes. Corruption is the urge to own without brakes. Misuse of authority in high and low places is the urge to control without brakes.

A Bus on the Road—A Picture of a Nation on the Move

All analogies limp. They either say too much or too little. In spite of this fact, I intend to use my bus journey as an analogy. A bus in traffic can be taken as a picture of a nation on the move. Twelve years have now elapsed since Eritrea gained her independence, *de facto* (in actual fact). The Referendum, it will be remembered, came two years later. It then became independent *de jure* (by virtue of law). Eritrea is now a "bus" in its own right. She has her own drivers and her passengers are on board. She has her own roads and highways to drive on. She also has her own roadmaps and traffic regulations. Bus Eritrea is involved not only in domestic but also in international traffic, as it were. She has taken her place among the 'drivers of an international car pool: "The United Buses." This is also true of her movements on a regional and inter-African level. Her registration plate is no longer a puzzling cipher. More and more buses and passengers are being acquainted with Bus Eritrea and its passengers. Bus Eritrea is slowly moving ahead and seems to be gathering speed.

Against All Odds

I remember some of the slogans on the licence plates of vehicles in the United States. The state of Minnesota, where I once spent five youthful years, had the words "Ten Thousand Lakes" on its licence plates. Such words capture something of the identifying characteristics of the state in question. Bus Eritrea is a young vehicle, with a moving story. This story is fitly summarised by the title of a book on Eritrea, a formulation that would eminently fit Bus Eritrea's licence plate. I am thinking of the phrase "Against All Odds."[6]

The slogan "Against All Odds" has characterised Bus Eritrea's history so far. It will have to guide its future journey. A bus can put up with occasional bumps and jolts, be they severe or mild, expected or unexpected. It will surely have to make allowances for changing an occasional flat tyre. A bus can sustain holes, gashes, and other types of disfigurement on its body, without losing its character as a bus. Paint that fades or crumbles can affect its public image but not the quality of its journey. Shortage of fuel may limit the movements of a bus and reduce the distances it can cover. A bus can survive, if necessary, with creaky doors and windows, with windshield and headlights marked by cracks, with seats and furnishings that betray the wear and tear of time. A bus can roll forward on recycled tyres. If the times and circumstances demand, it can even drive with patched tyres. There is, however, one thing that a bus simply cannot afford. It cannot afford to be on the road with brakes that are not checked regularly, at the right place and by the right persons.

This was the truth brought home to my mind by the small round sticker on the Swedish bus in which I was travelling. The sticker issued by Bilprovningen (Car Inspection) underlined two facts: regularity and stringency in the inspection of brakes.

The Place of Brakes in Statecraft

I recently asked someone who was well read in constitutional matters here in Sweden how he would relate the laws of a nation to my analogy of brakes. Without having read my reflection, he replied, "The most important brake or system of brakes is, of course, the Constitution itself." I was struck by the quick and short reply to my question. I was, furthermore, impressed by his explanations of the division of labour among the Legislative, Executive, and Judiciary branches of government. This discipline is of course not my area of competence. However, I have been told on more than one occasion that there is an effective system of brakes applicable to all and every one of these spheres of statecraft, in all soundly formulated and soundly operating constitutions.

Many of the passengers on Bus Eritrea are convinced that the use of the brakes so far is fully defensible. "A beleaguered country, a country whose security is at stake," they maintain, "has the right to suspend certain obvious rights. We must get our priorities straight."

Other passengers take strong exception to this view. "When used honestly," they maintain, "this argument can only warrant exceptional measures whose time limits must be strictly monitored. An exception cannot be made into a rule. The brakes of Bus Eritrea, i.e., the restrictive and punitive prerogatives of her authorities, have indeed been used far too arbitrarily so far."

There is a third category of passengers whose views lie somewhere in between these two widely divergent opinions. Many are the passengers of Bus Eritrea who are quietly waiting, brooding, praying, grieving about former fellow-passengers whose whereabouts are unknown. Fellow passengers, now "locked up" at the back of the bus.

Chapter 20

My heart goes out particularly to passengers of the third category. As a person who occupies many roles at the same time, (I am a husband, a father, a grandfather, a brother, an uncle, a pastor, an elder, etc.), I can easily put myself in the place of individual passengers of Bus Eritrea and identify myself with their pains. We know how lonely, how exposed and utterly defenceless the individual can feel before the roar of challenged power. For the individual, all states are power giants, be they benevolent or not. No individual can match the power of a whole state apparatus. A state, anywhere in the world, is never at a loss when it comes to speaking for itself, and has, moreover, hosts of people to speak for it.

This simple fact is not true of the individual. This is not to say that the individual is an angel. Neither is it to deny that subversion can in fact begin with individuals. It is not to maintain that a state cannot speak on behalf of its citizens. But it does mean that, in his state of total powerlessness, the individual needs someone to speak for him. He needs someone who can keep asking questions on his behalf. Worthy of respect is the country that has a political culture that does not leave the individual to his fate before an overwhelming challenger or accuser. In Sweden, every person accused of criminal action is offered legal counsel!

In tackling some of the thorny questions that I brought to him, my spiritual guide used to tell me, "Sobriety is of the essence. You should neither exaggerate nor minimise the issues at hand." One thing has however become more and more obvious to me as far as the journey of Bus Eritrea is concerned. The reactions of drivers and passengers alike are *primarily* reflections of different views of the ways that the *brakes* have been used. The use of brakes on Bus Eritrea has been one of the most crucial factors in the evaluation of the journey of the bus so far. This is true of both domestic and international views on the subject. Brakes are indeed a topic of heated and bitter discussions both among passengers on Bus Eritrea and among their kith and kin in the Diaspora. The spirit of the continuing journey of Bus Eritrea will surely depend on how its brakes are used and on how passengers feel about the use of these brakes. I can't see how a discussion of the issue of brakes can be postponed.

We human beings have at least three possible reasons for obeying restraints placed upon us. In the first place, we may obey because we believe that these restraints are just and warranted, either directly or by implication. This is the *principle-based approach* to restraints. Secondly, we may obey because we feel that we can derive some kind of benefit from bending our wills to these restraints, regardless of our reservations about certain aspects of the restraints. This is the *pragmatic approach* to restraints. Thirdly, we can obey because we are afraid of the consequences of disobeying these restraints. This would be *the survivalist approach* to the restraints. Psychiatrist Erich Fromm (1900–1980), a man of erudition, writes:

> Freedom does not imply lack of constraint, since any growth occurs only within a structure, and any structure requires constraint …. What matters is whether the constraint functions primarily for the sake of another person or institution or whether it is autonomous—i.e., that it results from the necessity of growth inherent in the structure of the person.[7]

Fromm is, I think, telling us that brakes are necessary for life and growth, on both the individual and national or societal levels. The crucial question is whether these restraints are in line with the natural and genuine needs of the individual or whether they are burdens imposed on him and his fellowmen solely in the interests of others.

Driving Steadily into the Light

At the beginning of this article, I wrote that I had been travelling on Bus Number 61, heading for the Monastery of Östanbäck, a ninety-minute journey by train and bus from Uppsala.

I wanted to meet my spiritual guide, who happens to be a monk. He deals, among other things, with the "brakes" in the life of the individual. These inner brakes bear the name "conscience." Only a conscience kept trimmed on the personal level can enable the individual to use those brakes wisely and justly on the social and national level.

God Speed to Bus Eritrea as it moves into the future.

Ezra Gebremedhin
May 23, 2003
Uppsala, Sweden

Bus Sweden—April 2020

Today is April 23, 2020. When I woke up this morning, I wished for some kind of parable, some narrative pattern, to further exemplify my reflections on "Bus Eritrea." And my heart (or was it my mind?) said: "Why not write about 'Bus Sweden'?"

We are in the midst of the modern-day pest known as CoronaVD-19. The past weeks have been times of widespread restrictions in the use of the "brakes" of Bus Sweden. Restrictions (application of brakes) have been introduced into practically all areas of life: domestic, communal, regional, national, and international.

But what has impressed me is the abundance of information, guidance, warning, and encouragement about the pandemic on all kinds of media here in Sweden. The restrictions are qualified by a basic respect for the right of the individual and for the protection of these rights by law, even in times of emergency! Citizens in this country know that they have a constitution that has been both ratified and put into practice. And that "brakes" made necessary by the present pandemic will be "lifted," without any unreasonable delay.

The constitution of Eritrea, which, I understand, was ratified in 1997, has been on hold since then. The way the constitution came about, a process that must have involved an enormous amount of work, has been a subject of severe criticism, especially on the part of "the Opposition." As far as the Eritrean Government is concerned, the main reason behind the postponement of the implementation of the constitution appears to be the risk of constitutional privileges playing into the hands of subversive foreign powers.

On the occasion of the celebration of Eritrea's 23rd Independence Day in 2014, President Isaias announced that the country would draft a new constitution. The new constitution would use important lessons acquired from hostile external schemes aimed at derailing the nation-building process and would chart out the political roadmap for the future. Six years later (in 2020), one is eager to know about measures taken towards the formulation of a new constitution.

I personally feel that our trying times, not least around "Bus Sweden," can give us much-needed lessons on life, both as individuals and as citizens of a country. As far as Eritrea is concerned, we need to take a good look at the following works by Professor Bereket Habte Selassie and Professor Tesfatsion Medhanie, to acquire some basic knowledge of the *history* of the formulation of constitutions. The works are:

The Making of The Eritrean Constitution. The Dialectic of Process and Substance. (Red Sea Press, 2003), the fruit of a richly documented and multifaceted dialogue under the chairmanship of Professor Bereket Habte Selassie. See also Bereket Habte Selassie, "An Exclusive Interview with Dr. Bereket Habte Selassie," awate.com. May 17, 2001.

Professor Tesfatsion Medhanie's paper, "Constitution-Making, Legitimacy and Regional Integration: An Approach to Eritrea's Predicament and Relations with Ethiopia. Development, Innovation and International Political Economy Research (DIIPER)," Aalborg University, Denmark, DIIPER Research Series, Working Paper No. 9, 2008, is an instructive and vigorously written work.

Notes

1. The majority of the Swedes are Lutherans, at least nominally, the country being an heir to the Reformation. Monasteries, banished from the country for almost four hundred years, have been on the return for over fifty years now. Most of them are of Catholic vintage, but there are some orders within The Church of Sweden. The one I was heading for belongs to the latter category.
2. I know that every vehicle inspection does in fact cover also these parts of a vehicle. I have purposely chosen brakes for special attention.
3. In the autumn of 1990 The Reverend Stig Jonsson, Dean of the Parish of Kista, a suburb of Stockholm, and Mrs. Annika Hagström, a journalist with the Swedish evening paper *Expressen*, published a book entitled *En bro över mörka vatten* (literally: *A Bridge Over Dark Waters*). The book is the story of a bus accident that took place in a tunnel at Måbödalen, near Bergen, in Norway on August 15, 1988. Twelve Swedish school children on holiday and four adults were killed in the accident. Nineteen persons suffered severe injuries. A potential adventure turned into a nightmare. The authors describe an unfolding drama of shock, denial, hope and resignation among the family members, relatives and friends of the deceased and the injured. There are almost always both human and technical factors involved in an accident. In this case there were clear indications that the brakes were in not in optimal form.
4. Examples are Drum Brakes, Disc Brakes, Hydraulic Brakes, Power Brakes, and Anti-Lock Brakes.
5. It is interesting to note that most of the Ten Commandments are formulated in "preventive" language. "Thou shalt not ..." There is something of the character of brakes in them.
6. The name is taken from Dan Connell's book: *Against All Odds. A Chronicle of the Eritrean Revolution* (Trenton, N.J.: The Red Sea Press, 1997).
7. Erich Fromm, *The Anatomy of Human Destructiveness* (Greenwich, Conn.: Faucet Crest, 1975), p. 225.

Year 2003
Chapter 21

Roots Unlimited

I could hardly believe what I read. The phrase hit me with the force of a contradiction. The man had died at 90 at his home in Soweto, South Africa, on May 7, 2003. I had taken it for granted that he fitted the common pattern, that he fell within "the standard distribution," to use a statistical term. Here, however, was this obituary, quietly smuggling in the sort of revelation that many would utter in whispers. That, in any case, was how I felt after I had read the phrase *"the son of a white foreman."*

Taken by itself, the phrase should hardly awaken special attention. It was a plain statement on parentage. It comprised 5 words in a BBC report consisting of 478 words. It occupied about one-third of one line in a text consisting of fifty-two lines. But it was a pregnant phrase. A little packet of verbal dynamite! Whether I was prepared to admit it or not my reaction must have implied the sort of thinking that runs: "So he was not a *real* South African! He was not a *wäddäbbat* (ወደባት), a Tigrinja word that, translated literally, means *"the son of a father* (i.e., a native-born)."

I don't think I am alone in this very subtle tendency to place people, almost automatically, in loaded, ethnic or racial categories.

I am thinking of Walter Sisulu. According to a BBC report, Mandela visited Sisulu's bereaved family at their home in Orlando, "looking old and frail."[1] If Mandela's body looked old and frail, his words, his sentiments, his camaraderie, as reflected in his own obituary, were certainly not. There was freshness and mellowness about these words from the lips of an old warrior. His tribute to his old friend and comrade is a legacy to all of us.

I remember reading about Walter Sisulu some years earlier. He was already an elderly man, who had suffered a stroke and become paralyzed on one side of the body. I don't recall whether he suffered his stroke before or after the final collapse of apartheid. But I do remember thinking, "What a pity that this misfortune should befall him when victory was at last within sight. He surely deserved a better reward!"

And now I was reading about his death in a short report from the BBC (05/06/2003), published on the website *asmarino.com*. I also happened to see the newscast about him on Swedish Television. The film reel used by Swedish Television must have been from an earlier period because the person in question looked healthy and well preserved. He was of middle height, or even short, with ample grey hair preserved on a head fitting both face and body. He had somewhat aquiline features and his skin colour was not of blackest hue. He was born in 1912, the year the African National Congress (ANC) was inaugurated.

Let Mandela speak about this old, seasoned combatant, a *tägadalai* (ተጋዳላይ), a "struggler," a "combatant") on this side of the grave. He was a comrade without a trace of bigotry. Let Mandela help us to remember our *siwu'at* (ስውኣት), one of "those who had sacrificed themselves," as he remembers his friend Walter Sisulu:

> Xhamela (Walter Sisulu) is no more. May he live forever! His absence has carved a void. A part of me is gone. Our paths first intersected in 1941. During the past 62 years our lives have been intertwined. We shared the joy of living, and the pain. Together we shared ideas, forged common commitments. We walked side by side through the valley of death, nursing each other's bruises, holding each other up when our steps faltered. Together we savored the taste of freedom. From the moment when we first met he has been my friend, my brother, my keeper, my comrade.[2]

The man had died at 90 years of age. The obituary stated that the deceased had risen to the position of Vice President of the African National Congress (ANC) and that it was he who had recruited Nelson Mandela early in 1940. Upon hearing of the death of his compatriot and fellow contender in the fight against apartheid, Mandela calls him "friend and mentor." The two had spent twenty-five years at the notorious prison at Robin Island, off the coast of South Africa, following their conviction for sabotage in 1964. They had been engaged in the same cause for over sixty years.

What captured my attention in the obituary was the statement that Sisulu was, "The son of a white foreman who came to his native village in the Transkei to supervise black road workers." Could this be true? Didn't Sisulu fight *against* the white man? Wasn't he an *enemy* of apartheid? And wasn't apartheid a creation of "the white race"—more specifically, of the Boers of South Africa, who were, for many, a pernicious branch of the tree known as White Supremacy? How could the son of a white foreman in

South Africa fight for the rights of the black man? Just look at his surname, *Sisulu*. There was nothing white about that name!

Our Brittle Myths

Discrete as the sentence in the obituary may have been, the thought it contained was true. Walter Sisulu was indeed the son of a white foreman. He was the son of a white father and a black mother. A case of white blood and black blood flowing together in the same arteries and veins! If there is indeed "white" and "black" blood to speak of! Here we have a tale, indeed a saga, of white blood fighting against white blood. White blood fighting against itself! Or, perhaps, fighting *for* itself, at the deepest possible level! White blood fighting for the kind of human dignity that does not know of blood boundaries!

I do not need to convince anyone of the fact that life-giving blood does not follow colour barriers. I am writing about our attitudes, yes, our prejudices, clichés, myths, and unexamined presuppositions. Mandela was the son of a South African tribal chief, a true, genuine, pure South African. From him we would surely expect solidarity with and dedication to the cause of blacks in South Africa. Mandela was "sure fire," the genuine stuff. A son of the soil, a true *wäddäbbat*, as we say in Tigrinja!

But Sisulu's father was white. His mother was black South African. Was he a true, genuine, South African? What does one need in order to be a true South African? What does one have to do to qualify as a genuine member of a national community, a people with a cohesive understanding of its identity? Can any good accrue to a community of oppressed black people in South Africa, from the life of a person whose father was a white foreman?

And yet, it is precisely such a person who spent a whole lifetime fighting for the dignity of black South Africans. It was precisely such a person that Nelson Mandela called "friend and mentor." Walter Sisulu was a "half-white man" who came to be regarded as a father of South Africa.

Sisulu, brought up by a single mother, apparently neglected by his white father, had evidently fought his own battle in his own person and therefore could fight for others. He was not blinded by hatred, but fired by a noble enthusiasm for the dignity of fellow Africans. Perhaps he had no *pater*, no "father" who admitted his paternity, but he had a *patria*, a fatherland to fight for.

Identity, Not Idols

As we think of those who died for Eritrea, we honour and revere the blood they shed. It is no wonder that blood is called "lifeblood." To shed one's blood is to pour out one's life. Tracing *types* of blood and bones is not, however, our most pressing problem in Eritrea right now. Besides, there is something futile in the whole enterprise. Something of a ridiculous merry-go-round! And I don't want to give the subject the attention that it does not deserve. We have other matters to attend to.

But the "new light" on Sisulu's parentage was too good an object lesson to miss. I didn't have the slightest idea that this great name in the fable of black South Africa's struggles had white parentage. And if the obituary hadn't named the fact, I would have remained in innocent bliss about the whole thing. But we cannot discount the fact that bitterness and dark ambitions are often great promoters of genes and genealogy. This is especially true among populations where there is a lack of a just sharing of power and resources.

Africa has had and still has some frightening examples of this phenomenon. Rwanda, Liberia, Sierra Leone, and Congo (to name a few countries) have become bywords in this respect. Secondary loyalties have their places in our lives. The families, the clans, the regions from which we come, our languages, are not to be neglected. In fact, reducing these items into a thought world of taboos, making the very mention of these things *anathema*,[3] may have completely undesired results. Sentiments and emotions suppressed are often sentiments and emotions abandoned to the forces of darkness. Once again, the families, the clans, the regions from which we come are not to be neglected. They are the contexts in which we first become aware of a much-needed personal identity. If maintained in a sound and healthy spirit, they can create a sense of self-respect in us and promote respect in our attitudes to others. It is a fact that the person who accepts and respects himself finds it much easier to accept and respect others.

However, whenever these secondary loyalties are lifted up to the level of primarily loyalties, then we are in trouble. When they are made into idols in our lives, then they become destructive. Making idols of our tribal and national identities takes us back to some dangerous instincts, to behaviour that reminds one of the aggressive behaviour of animals that are driven to protect their territories by the use of their teeth or horns. We are not called to build altars to our secondary loyalties. We have a common homeland to build. We have nobler and healthier truths to pass on to new generations of Eritreans. We have a common humanity to cultivate and nurture.

Of Leaders and Factions

"All are yours" (1 Corinthians 3:22), writes St. Paul in trying to counteract the building of personality cults in the Christian congregation in Corinth. It is as if he were saying to the faithful:

> All [things] are yours. If you had realized this truth, you wouldn't pride yourselves in your exclusive claims and vaunted banners. By saying, "I follow Paul; I follow Apollos; I follow Cephas," you are in fact impoverishing yourselves. They are all yours. The potentials, resources, gifts and experiences in each and every one of these leaders, are your common wealth. Why live with the blinders of factionalism when you can broaden your horizons? Why fix your gaze at your feet when you can lift your eyes to the stars? Why sit at a meager table when you can share a feast?

As we commemorate *BaHti Mäskäräm* (ባሕቲ መስከረም), the first day of Meskerem, let us remember that *all* Eritreans are ours, whether they be of the Sisulu Type or of the Mandela Type. Let us think not only of genes and genealogy but also, and primarily, of vows and virtues, of those qualities that are durable and capable of inspiring in a lasting way. Let The Apostle speak to us again:

> Whatever is true, whatever is honourable, whatever is just, whatever is pure, whatever is pleasing, whatever is commendable, if there is any excellence and if there is anything worthy of praise, think about these things. (Philippians 4:8; New International Version of the New Testament)

"Think about these things!" Yes, "pursue these things!" These are the norms to go by, these are the tests to demand in judging fellow Eritreans. Other standards are bound to be short-lived and undependable.

God bless Eritrea and all its roots!

Ezra Gebremedhin
Uppsala, Sweden

Notes

1. *BBC News*, World Edition, May 6, 2003.
2. Nelson Mandela's Tribute to Walter Sisulu, *BBC News*, World Edition, May 6, 2003.
3. A Greek word which means, among other things, "object of a curse".

Year 2003
Chapter 22

For Light and Life:
Portraits of Four Women

I remember a song from my days in Sunday School in Addis Ababa, Ethiopia. The first verse of the song runs:

> This little light of mine, I am going to let it shine.
> This little light of mine, I am going to let it shine.
> This little light of mine, I am going to let it shine.
> Let it shine, shine, shine, let it shine.[1]

I remember how we children sang this song with energetic gestures, our hands tracing movements in the air, a finger acting the part of a candle, the palm of a hand covering or uncovering the imagined light. A picture of a virtuous Christian life lived openly for others to see, and not covered because of shame! I even remember a point in our singing, when we blew vigorously on a finger, adding the words: "Don't let the evil one blow out your lamp!" (or something to that effect).

That was decades ago. Now I am writing these words from Sweden. My language and my perceptions have changed. One fact has, however, remained unchanged. I know that darkness is strong. But light is even stronger. The flame of a small candle may not be larger than the top half of a finger. However, such a flame can disperse thick darkness in a large room, to the extent that we can make out the outlines of all sizeable objects in the room. Darkness is strong. But light is stronger. As in the physical, so too in the world of human relations! To be a promoter of "Light" is to be an advocate of Life. This, in short, is the substance of my present reflection.

A Sicilian in the Wintry North

Why did I begin to think of Light at all? My answer would be: "The month of December." In December, Sweden is a dark place, more or less. Were it not for some hours of daylight, an abundance of electricity, and the bright celebration of an Italian martyr saint called *Sankta* Lucia, darkness would reign unchallenged.

["Sankta Lucia" is the Swedish variety of the name. The name Lucia comes from Latin *lux*, which means "light." According to tradition, Lucia suffered martyrdom in Syracuse, a seaport on the southwestern coast of Sicily, around 300 A.D., during the reign of Emperor Diocletian (A.D. 243–316). She was a virgin of noble birth. When her mother was miraculously healed from a severe illness, Lucia gave away her dowry to destitute Christians. Her outraged fiancé accused her of having become a Christian, a crime at the time. She was placed in a house of prostitutes, but no one dared to touch her. A fire was lighted around her, but her body remained untouched by the flames. Finally, she was put to the sword. A later legend narrates that Lucia once plucked out her eyes, with which a youth had fallen in love, and had the eyes sent to the enamoured youth, on a platter. He was so moved that he became a Christian. And Lucia got her eyes back. All that according to legend! Dante regards Lucia as a representative of the heavenly light, after The Virgin Mary. People with eye-maladies once implored Lucia. She is also regarded as a patroness of farmers.]

There are areas in Northern Sweden where the sun is hardly visible during some months of the year. Fortunately, however, the Nordic people have a wonderful candle culture, which reveals itself in all its imaginative variety especially in the month of December.

Early in the morning on December 13, white-clad, candle-bearing boys and girls, led by a light-crowned Lucia, glide gently into many a Swedish bedroom. The measured movements of their stockings on the floor and the soft shuffle of their gowns keep tact with the rhythm of the well-known verse:

> Night makes its heavy round
> Through sleepy farmstead
> As shadows, silence-bound
> Brood, unmolested
> Then, to our dark abode
> Enters, with light adorned
> Sancta Lucia, Sancta Lucia

> Then, to our dark abode
> Enters, with light adorned
> Sancta Lucia, Sancta Lucia[2]

The singing company serves *bullar* (sweet buns) and coffee or tea to pyjama-clad beneficiaries, struggling to keep their eyes open. Since this festival falls during the week in which the Nobel Prize is awarded, candidates to this prestigious prize are also treated to the early morning ritual in their hotel rooms, or in rooms where different families have received them as guests. In 2002, one of the candidates for the Nobel Prize in Physics was an Italian by the name of Ricardo Giacconi. My guess is that he too was entertained to this Swedish ritual that has its historical roots in his own homeland.

The feast of Sankta Lucia links past and present, light and darkness, night and day, cold and warmth. Lucia brings together The Mediterranean Sea and The Baltic Sea, Latin Italy and Nordic Sweden, senior Rome and junior Stockholm. Indeed, Lucia has the unusual distinction of uniting Nobel Laureates, the world's foremost men and women of science and letters, and even youth still in the early dawn of their search for knowledge.

"Lucia" is a promoter of Light and Life.

A German-Brazilian in Sweden

Lucia will surely greet the Swedish royal couple early on the morning on December 13th. Perhaps one of the two daughters in the family will act the role of the martyr saint. The queen, Sylvia Renate Sommerlath, is of mixed German-Brazilian parentage. In other words, she cannot be counted among the *däqqäbbat* (ደቀባት), the native-born, here in Sweden.[3] However, in her person, three strands of rich history and culture (those of Germany, Brazil, and Sweden) have been interwoven harmoniously. She has won the hearts of the Swedish people. Her special concern for the wellbeing of handicapped children and youth has already won her worldwide acclaim. A fund set up on the day of the wedding of the Swedish royal couple, June 19, 1976, has brought light into the lives of thousands of children in this age of child exploitation, neglect, and abuse.

Sylvia is a foreigner on Swedish soil. However, if there is any family that feels Sweden in its very hearts and veins and is prepared to give life and limb for the country, it is the Swedish Royal House that she represents. She is motivated by vows and virtues, not by genes and genealogy.

Sylvia is a promoter of Light and Life.

A Moabite in Judah

Here in Sweden, the feast of Sankta Lucia is regarded as an unofficial precursor of the celebration of Christmas, the birthday of the Light of the World (*Lux mundi*), according to the records of The Gospel of John.[4] One of the ancestors of Jesus was a woman by the name of Ruth. And she was a Moabite, not a Jewess.[5] We have her story in the Old Testament book that bears her name. Naomi, a married Jewish immigrant to the land of Moab, loses her husband and two sons, and is reduced to a sad, childless widowhood. Totally dejected, she decides to return home to Judah. She urges her two daughters in law, Orpah and Ruth, also widowed and childless, to remain in their homeland, Moab. Orpah heeds Naomi's advice and stays at home. Ruth refuses to be dissuaded. Who can remain untouched by the reply that Ruth gave to Naomi?

> Don't urge me to leave you or to turn back from you.
> Where you go, I will go, and where you stay I will stay.
> Your people will be my people and your God my God.
> Where you die I will die, and there I will be buried!
> May the Lord deal with me, be it ever so severely,
> If anything but death separates you and me."
> (Ruth 1:16–17; New International Bible)

In deciding to follow her mother-in-law, Ruth was not belittling her own roots. Her entire tradition, indeed the entire Semitic world, was and is highly conscious of genealogy and of the honour rightly due to *inddabba* (እንዳባ), the home of one's forefathers. At the same time, Ruth is the meek iconoclast, the breaker of racial, tribal, social, and cultural idols. Her spirit is so free, so generous, that she could feel at home literally anywhere. In her, we have the quiet neutralizer of noisy prejudice. Love is her compass, deep commitment her rule of life. She brought the light of hope and comfort into the life of her mother-in-law. She is a representative of our common race at one of its noblest moments. Her world is human, through and through.

Ruth is a promoter of Light and Life.

An Eritrean in the United States

The person I am thinking of is perhaps more than an Eritrean. Perhaps an Eritrean-American! I don't know. But there is one thing that I am sure of. Her poems are a welcoming call. They are the open doors of a hospitable home. Her language is clean, soft, simple, and economical. There is nothing of the impatient and pushy elbow in her short compositions. She writes like a mother, a daughter, a sister. After being quiet for some time (or is it I who have been delinquent in my reading?), her voice has emerged again. Strikingly enough, some of her latest pieces of writing take up the subject of light, both as a creator and an expression of a healthy relationship among peoples. And she lets children show the way.[6]

Feven Afewerki is a promoter of Light and Life.

What Am I Getting At?

I leave that to my readers to decide. I have sketched simple portraits of four female representatives of our race, promoters of Light and Life. May there be thousands more of their kind! Our times are in desperate need of Light in individual, communal, national, and international relations. In letting their lights shine, women the likes of Lucia, Sylvia, Ruth, and Feven may very well inspire the rest of us to light our small, individual candles and keep them shining. For, indeed, darkness is strong. But "Light" is even stronger.

Or am I dreaming?

God bless you, one and all!

Ezra Gebremedhin
December 11, 2003
Uppsala, Sweden

Notes

1. It is very possible that there are different melodies to this song. The repetition of words and phrases in this version depends on the melody that I remember.
2. This is my "free" translation of the first verse of the well-known Lucia song, *Natten går tunga fjät*.
3. The word *däqqäbbat* is a reference to those who can trace their paternal line to the country which they claim as their own. The "Forefather" of the present "Swedish" dynasty, Carl XIV Johan, was Marshal Jean Baptiste Bernadotte, Prince of Ponte Corvo, and a former general of Napoleon Bonaparte. In 1810 he was invited to "candidate" for the Swedish throne, to which he finally ascended in 1818. Sweden's present monarch, Carl XVI Gustav, who ascended to the Swedish throne on September 19, 1973, is the seventh regent of the House of Bernadotte. Indeed, the present Swedish Royal family can hardly be called *däqqäbbat*.
4. See The Gospel of John 9:5.
5. The Moabites and Ammonites lived east of The Dead Sea, south of the river Arnon, which flows into the Dead Sea. The date of the composition of the book is unknown. However, it appears to be from the period after 1050 BC. Her selfless love was in fact rewarded. She married Boaz, a man of good

standing in his community and a relative of Naomi. Obed, born to this marriage, was the father of Jesse who was the father of David. Thus the royal house of the Jews is connected with both Bethlehem and Moab. Incidentally, an excellent source of quick information on biblical characters is the book *Who's Who in The Bible*, by Peter Calvocoressi (London / New York: Penguin Books, 1990).

6   In her poem, *Eritrea and Ethiopia, may all your children bathe in light and be light*, Feven Afewerki calls down blessings on people in these two countries, summoning each colour of the spectrum to her aid. Her poem *Children of the infinite wisdom of Eritrea and Ethiopia* which appeared on November 30, 2003, also contains the theme of Light. Her other poems are available on *asmarino.com*, under "Poets", Eritrean Internet Mirror Site.

Year 1973–1996
Chapter 23

The Body and the Self:
More Rain-Drops

We who regard ourselves as Christians live out of our raw inclinations to a degree that we can hardly imagine. I suspect that many of our so-called spiritual views and pronouncements are a spiritualization of purely human emotions and problems. But, of course, I must also ask myself: What do I mean by "purely" human? Where does the boundary between the human and the spiritual run?

So much can be said with certainty: A Christianity that does not take our humanity seriously cannot be essential Christianity. And by our humanity I mean our body, our nerves, our entire subconscious being, and our personality (in contradistinction to the personage we put on). The body is an ally on our spiritual pilgrimage. And it simply refuses to be neglected, even in the name of spirituality.

2.1.73, Uppsala
The worst thing you can do is to give a touched-up picture of yourself, of your dreams, your weaknesses, and your strengths. True, you are under constant pressure to do so. You don't want to disappoint people. You want to maintain a constant image. But who has such an image? Aren't we made of an ever-changing series of images? Aren't we much more fragmented and unstable than people think we are? No, we should rejoice when it is time to rejoice, weep when it is the time to weep, doubt when it is the time to doubt, and believe when it is the time to believe. It is only when we dare to be ourselves that we can say that we are walking in the light.

26.3.74, At the Diocesan Retreat Centre in Rättvik, Sweden
Sacrifice everything—but not your life-rhythm or the life-rhythm of your neighbour. Don't pay more than your body and your psyche can afford to pay. If you spend too much in this regard, you can eventually become an angry person—angry with those whom you have tried to serve.

14.6.74, At the Retreat Centre of the Lutheran Church in Alsace, Lieb Frauenberg, France
I often feel terrified. I am afraid of making sacrifices, of giving up my life. But I also have one assurance. I am a gift. I am a bundle whose existence, whose placement in this life has a givenness about it. I did not place myself here. I am a tool with the possibility of being used by the Great Artisan. I am His raw material. God grant that this raw material, for whose origin I am not responsible, may be used to the fullest and best.

28.11.74, Svettis (The Student Sports' Hall), Uppsala
We don't help turbulent people by jumping into their turbulence. We help them by being centres of calm, of stillness, in the midst of their turbulence.

Don't believe that you are indispensable, even if people would tell you that the world would collapse without you. Sit lightly on your saddle, ready to be moved away. The only sense in which you might be considered indispensable is the obedience that would be expected of you at a specific point of time that is absolutely ripe for your action.

We are destroyed when our composure is destroyed. The world collapses when our world collapses. Man is a pivot—a vital, decisive point of departure. To know one's self and to control one's self, to become an organized, functioning, harmonious unit—that is our great challenge.

12.12.74, Uppsala
Notice how sure writers in *The Ethiopian Herald* (The main government-sponsored English paper in Addis Ababa) sound as they write about a people's revolution that has unanimous support. If each person is a bundle of contradictions (and each one of us knows that from personal experience), what bundles of contradictions there must be among a big group that tries to govern!

The things that are operative in today's "Revolutionary" Ethiopia are not only principles, plans, and ideology, but also fear, nervousness, egos with a history and egos in trouble. Perhaps egos put on the spot. To expect a thoroughgoing solution to a country's problems from a group of such a composition, as if the group were a calm, integrated, and homogeneous body, is an illusion.

1.2.75, Uppsala
To be involved in mass hysteria is to lose one's footing, to be taken out of oneself and to be enslaved by a master dangling in the air. Only when each person is rooted in himself or herself, established and convinced, in the deepest sense of the term, only then can he or she accomplish anything lasting.

10.3.76, at 4.45 a.m., The Monastery at Östanbäck, Sala, Sweden
"Lord, I would live in the sign of love—of a calling in which my body and psyche, with all their weaknesses, become a sacrifice of love. Save me from living in the sign of decadent cells and a melancholic psyche. Give me the grace of self-mortification, which is another name for love."

8.4.76, Uppsala
Our true self can't be bribed by anything. We may suppress its voice. We may impose silence upon it. But the true self cannot be bribed.

12.12.76, Uppsala
I long to hear news from Ethiopia, now in political and social agony! I wish I could get insights from that troubled place. I seem to forget that those who are in the midst of trouble are not necessarily those with the clearest insights. Perhaps it is those who are far away, those who have distance at their disposal, who can make a sound judgment about a given situation.

February 1981, Uppsala
Archbishop Fénelon (1651–1715) writes, "Denying the body is bitter for most weaklings and for worldly people. For these weak people nothing is more constitutive of the self than the body which they satisfy and adorn. Even when they have seen that the body has lost its beauty these people maintain such a love to the bodily life that it creates shameful cowardice in them and it is going to cause them to shake at the very mention of the word death."[1]

14.11.83, The Diocesan Retreat Centre Breidagård (near Uppsala), Sweden
Those things or people whom we regard as the sources of our problems, as the causes of our bitterness, are, often, only triggers. They are not the root causes of our problems because they cannot account for the whole of our identity, our wholeness, our context. Our problems lie within us. Things and people often simply help to precipitate them.

We don't become humble by suppressing our feelings and urges. We become humble by choosing humble outlets for them.

May 1989, Uppsala
"Here one can ask why it is desirable that a person individuates himself. It is not only desirable but even absolutely necessary, because through his identification with others he is put on the spot and commits acts which bring him into disunity (conflict) with himself." [2]

July 1991, Collegeville, Minnesota, USA
"But what if I should discover that the least of all brethren, the poorest of all beggars, the most insolent of all offenders, yes even the very enemy himself—that these live within me, that I myself stand in need of the alms of my own kindness, that I am to myself the enemy who is to be loved—what then?"[3]

May, 1993, Uppsala
"...suffice it to say here that self-effacement and 'goodness' invite being stepped on and being taken advantage of; further, that dependence upon others makes for exceptional vulnerability, which in turn leads to a feeling of being neglected, rejected, and humiliated whenever the excessive amount of affection or approval demanded is not forthcoming."[4]

August 2, 1994, Uppsala
"To respect the secrecy of whoever it may be, even your own child, is to respect his individuality. To intrude upon his private life, to violate his secrecy, is to violate his individuality."[5]

March 27, 1995, Wettershus Retreat Centre, near Jönköping, Sweden
It is late evening and I have just finished reading the Swedish version of the book *Kroppen minns det du vill glömma* (*The Body Remembers What You Want to Forget*) by the Norwegian journalist, Solveig Böhle.[6] If what she writes on the basis of interviews with patients and specialists in the medical world is true (and she sounds very convincing), we have one more confirmation of the fact that we simply can't neglect the body if our psychic and spiritual life is to be healthy and to flourish. According to this book, the body seems to be a storeroom for memories of poignant and sometimes frightening experiences. In many cases, these memories have to be activated and worked through if health is to be restored.

But I sometimes wonder if there are not cases when it is best *not* to open certain rooms in this storage of memories. Sometimes it may be merciful to leave some memories coded and disguised. I don't know.

December 16, 1996, Uppsala
Blessed, thou advancing age, who doest talk to us through aching limbs and steps that labour up a flight of stairs! Thou cooler of our ambitions, liberator from the slave driver whose name is "Achiever"!

Notes

1. From the Swedish, *Kristliga Råd och Betraktelser / Christian Counsel and Devotions*, a selection from the writings of Fénelon collected by Ernest Naville and translated into Swedish by Anna Bohlin, Stockholm, Diakonystyrelsen), 1930), p. 41.
2. C.J. Jung, *Jaget och det Omedvetna;* a translation into Swedish of Jung's *Die Beziehungen zwischen dem Ich und dem Unbewussten / The Relationship between the 'I' (Ego) and the Unconscious* (Stockholm. Wahlström and Widstrand, 1967), p. 131.
3. C. G. Jung, quoted in C. W. Baars, M.D. *Born Only Once. The Miracle of Affirmation.* Franciscan University Press. Steubenville. Ohio. 1989, p. 9.
4. Karen Horney, *Our Inner Conflicts.* Published by W. W. Norton and Com. London. 1992, p. 55-56.
5. P. Tournier, *Secrets.* 1976, 24. John Knox Press. Westminster.
6. Bokförlaget Forum, Stockholm. 1994.

Year 2003
Chapter 24

While We Wait

Wait, says a plaintive voice, patriotic to the core.
The times are hard,
We dare not low'r our guard.
Reveal our cracks before the evil eye?
Come now, refrain! Put words on hold.
Those distant guns are ominously warm.
Wait until peace its solid entrance makes
Full-feathered, tall, with triumph on its face.
Speak, says a strident voice, patriotic to the core.
Speak, time is ripe, high vigil still our lore
Speak, words are due,
Delay can only lead to hearts that go their separate ways,
And deeds which love subdue.
Speak for our cherished land,
Which though perturbed by wind and sun,
Knows what it is to struggle and to stand.

I am not a poet but the two stanzas recorded above are actually mine. And (excuse me!) I am a little surprised at my literary product! But attracting praise is not my aim. Please read the lines again and try to catch what I am trying to say.

Two lines of thought! Two arguments that run like red threads through much of the material that has appeared on asmarino.com's home page in recent months! Many have spoken for one of the two arguments. Not a few have done so eloquently. Not a few with quiet fervour. Others with cutting words and scorching rage.

One thing is clear. Whether we are among those who speak critically at this juncture of Eritrea's history or those who choose not to, we must all wait, willy-nilly. For the simple reason that time is the common medium through which we all must pass as we anticipate and argue for what we feel to be a matter of priority for Eritrea. The question is: What shall we do while we wait? How can we put our turbulent waiting period to proper use? Are love and hate, friend and foe, 'pros' and 'cons' the only alternatives left to us?

We can, among many other completely justifiable and urgent options, do one thing. We can develop the rare and noble discipline of listening. We can make a serious, objective, respectful effort to hear what the other party says, without hastening to label him or her. I say "listen to," not necessarily "approve of." It has been said that we can get the truth about ourselves from two categories of people: our best friends and our worst enemies. Of course, we must take such a statement with a grain of salt. But it contains much more truth than we are willing to accept.

"Let every man be swift to hear, slow to speak, slow to wrath," pleads the Epistle of James (James 1:19). This is a good, time-honoured piece of advice. Any elder from any of our traditions, lowland, highland, or coast-land, Muslim, Christian or Animist, would confirm that fact.

"Lend me your ears!" pleaded a well-known Roman statesman (in the words of Shakespeare) before his colleagues over two millennia ago. Yes, we can lend our ears, even if our hearts may be full of bitterness and our tongues aching to speak. Even if we feel that the one who is speaking is not worthy of our ears! It takes courage and nobility to listen to those persons whose views we don't like. If we cannot listen to our opponents now, on the cyber-media outside of Eritrea, we won't be able to listen to our friends later on in Eritrea, when we (by necessity) must some time end up in some unexpected conflict of interests. True to the wise among our fathers, let us practice the discipline of listening carefully and interpreting things in the best light before lashing out at any speaker or writer.

We can learn from all, even though what remains with us may sometimes amount only to seemingly marginal facts. Take, for example, my exciting little discovery (from my base in Sweden), thanks to asmarino.com, that there is a female Eritrean by the name of Almaz Hale, who has her own TV show in the USA! Or that the mother tongue of the Rashaida is Arabic. Or that we have an Eritrean poet by the name of Dr. Reesom Haile, who writes from Brussels, which he, to my repeated chuckles, calls the Hembirti of Europa. Or think of my discovery, from my Swedish corner of the world, that the abbreviation BTW does not stand for some compact chemical formula but, from what I understand, for the expression "by the way." Or that the Arabic *Allah yerHamu* has the same function as the Latin

R.I.P. (*Requiescat in pace* = May he rest in peace!). Thanks, Saleh Younis, for this last item of enlightenment, among many other, weightier things!

"Crumbs!" you may say about these small details of information that I have mentioned above. Aren't there more important things to say, especially at this time of Eritrea's trial when people are discussing extremely weighty matters? Why waste our time with such crumbs?

Surely! But let us not despise our crumbs. Mind you, crumbs, though small in size, have the character of the bigger "loaves" from which they fall. They are more potent than we think. Together they can be meals. Meals that slowly, imperceptibly nourish heart and mind! If we are prepared to feed on them! While we all wait.

With sincere greetings from Sweden!

Ezra Gebremedhin
Uppsala, 2003

Year 2019
Chapter 25

Pentecostalism:
Risk or Resource? (I) —

Introduction

On Wednesday, July 18, 2018, the first flight of Ethiopian Air Lines (EAL) from Addis Ababa to Asmara in over 20 years touched ground at the Asmara International Airport. From what I understand, the flight consisted of a fleet of two passenger planes. The leading plane carried Ethiopia's former Prime Minister, Haile Mariam Desalegn, his wife, and other dignitaries and retinue.

Joy was pervasive already on the planes in flight. Passengers left their seats and crowded the aisles of the planes. They took photos and so-called "selfies" to record this great event. Hostesses distributed flowers. People were offered champagne. Loud talk and singing filled the inner space of the flying birds. The planes landed after a flight of just over an hour.

What struck many news watchers and spectators on the ground was the demonstrative presence of a preacher who answered to the name of Prophet Suraphel Demissie. He was among those who stood at one end of the aisle, presumably in plane number 2. He uttered his religious slogans, with hands and voices raised. He had evidently started preaching on the plane.

Scenes at and following the debarkation from the planes were almost tumultuous with joy. Hugging relatives, caught in the thrill of a longed-for reunion, moistened each other's faces with tears. Flowers were exchanged, children and grand-children introduced, hugged and kissed. Long-separated relatives, prospective businessmen, cameramen, and journalists bustled on the tarmac nearest the planes.

But what struck many a news and video watcher, in Ethiopia, Eritrea, and abroad, was the behaviour of Prophet Suraphel Demissie. Let us borrow some words from an article that appeared (around July 28) in awate.com under the title "PM Abiy and the Rehabilitation of Dictators," written by the Awate Staff. According to the article, not only were Eritreans taken by utter surprise by some of the unexpected words of President Isaias Afewerqi during his visit to Ethiopia on July 14:

> ... but also stunned by another man who claims to be a prophet, a healer, and an exorcist ranting about how the Gospel will be victorious, in front of the Asmara Palace Hotel, upon his arrival to Asmara from Addis Ababa, aboard the first Ethiopian Airlines flight that landed there after a 20-year absence.

I have personally heard a video recording where Suraphel utters the slogans, ([Wängel yashän'efal] The Gospel shall be victorious!), ([Wängel yibar'ekal] The Gospel blesses!), ([Sälam yamätah antä näh] You [i.e., Jesus] are the one who brought peace!" during his outdoor, mini-rally. Already in the plane he had announced, with hands and voice raised, ([Houloun tadärg zänd Chai näh] You are capable of doing everything!). At one point he shouted, ([Asmära kä'eng' 'edih wädih bäwängel t'enawätaläch] From now on, Asmara will be shaken by The Gospel!)

These expressions belong to the kind of language commonly used among religious communities that go by the names Charismatic or Pentecostal. Such groups have indeed been under the severe scrutiny and censorship of the authorities in Eritrea. A number of their leaders have spent years in prison. One of the reasons for the government's measures against these Pentecostal Christians can be their alleged tendency to downgrade other religious bodies and to evangelize with vigour and success among them. The freedom with which such groups associate with Christians of all nationalities, with hardly any political caution, has resulted in some of them being accused of lack of patriotism, a charge which they reject vigorously.

About Suraphel Demissie, the Awate article maintains:

> A controversial preacher, who calls himself Prophet Suraphel Demisse, took to the street of Asmara in a rally, unhindered by the Eritrean security forces that do not even allow a private religious congregation of those who share Suraphel's faith, in a private home ... a flamboyant pastor, a charlatan who exploits gullible followers with his riveting, and often hyperbolic, fiery sermons appeared in Asmara.

Chapter 25

.... We are apprehensive of the guy who thinks other people of faith, particularly the Orthodox Christians, are not genuine and have to become Christians again. We know that the 'Ancient Orthodox Christianity' has not produced modern-day flashy entrepreneurs of televangelism with gaudy suits who mesmerize audiences and air their skits on television, but it's traditionally homegrown, a spiritual and a genuine faith, and it has more history and gospels than the rest of the world.

Our Awate article winds up its verbal attack with the following words:

Under the PFDJ rule, Asmara is not known to accommodate any religious expression outside of prayer houses, particularly the Pentecostals, whose Eritrean preachers are languishing in jail, and the sect is banned from any public expression of their faith. How would anyone who is supposed to know the state of affairs in Eritrea be bold enough to fly in aboard the first flight to be received by crowds who seemingly were notified of his arrival? That was not coincidental, and it is difficult to think the security forces did not know about it. Or, was it a deceptive show of tolerance to cheating the world that Eritrea respects religious freedoms? Perhaps, the relaxing of the security regiment was a gesture to appease the current Ethiopian prime minister who is an evangelist! In addition, Hailemariam Desalegn, the former Ethiopian Prime minister, who is also an evangelist, was in the same flight and warmly greeted Suraphel on the airport tarmac. ...

Suraphel had expressed his plan to continue preaching his inflammatory messages across Eritrea as he does in Ethiopia. He also indicated he had an appointment to meet with the Eritrean government officials and was planning to meet with other evangelist leaders in Asmara. But it seems, according to his own testimony (on YouTube), he was stranded in his hotel room for three days awaiting the next flight back to Addis Ababa. Why was he locked in his hotel? Was he ordered to stay there, or it was on his own choice? Judging from his earlier enthusiasm upon arrival in Asmara, we suspect the former.

The word "evangelist" used on three occasions in the quotation above, should actually read "Evangelical."

Let me say that I have mixed impressions about Suraphel. I have heard him say words that are worth pondering. And in a rather quiet context![1] But I have also heard him preach to a large audience with the kind of shouting and screaming which I find very difficult to understand and absorb. Regardless of the conclusions we may come to after reading the Awate article on him, it is quite clear that the movement known as Pentecostalism, in its different forms, has generated heated discussions as well as tensions of different magnitudes among religious groups and their members in Eritrea.

But what is Pentecostalism? What do the teachings of the Church on The Holy Spirit, from its earliest days, say about the possible sources of Pentecostalism? Can one provide some kind of sober presentation of its origins, traits, and impacts on the societies among which it takes root and grows with remarkable energy?

In the interest of the overall goal of the collection of articles in this book, I shall begin with a very brief glance at the history of The Church, as it relates to the Holy Spirit and the Spirit's role in the lives of congregations and individuals. I shall then continue with some tentative answers to these questions in the following articles under the title "Pentecostalism: Risk or Resource?"

The Church of the Centuries and Views on the Holy Spirit

As a mass movement, Pentecostalism is a relatively recent phenomenon. Its origins have been traced back to Charles Parham, a Methodist minister who started a Bible school in Topeka, Kansas in 1900, "with the intention of revitalizing the Christian experience."

What are we to say about views on the gifts of the Spirit in the Early Church and the later period leading to The Reformation? This is far too big a subject for me to take up in any detail in my limited project. But I must touch upon the subject so that I don't give the impression that the whole question of the gifts of The Spirit and the expressions that they took, started with Parham (and later his student, W. J. Seymour).

Montanus and Tertullian

An apocalyptic (End of Time) movement in the latter half of the 2nd century A.D. is associated with a person by the name of Montanus, in Phrygia (present day Turkey). The movement looked forward to a speedy outpouring of The Holy Spirit on the Church. The manifestation of this outpouring on prophets and prophetesses of the time (among whom we have the female figures of Prisca and Maximilia) strengthened the claims of the movement. A well-known Church Father in North Africa, Tertullian of Carthage (c. 160–c.225), joined the movement around 206. He has in fact been accused of having abandoned the Church of the Fathers. Montanism emphasized ascetic practices, forbade second marriages, condemned fasting regulations that it regarded as too lax, and forbade flight during persecution. Enthusiasm, ecstatic prophecy, which also appeared in primitive Christianity, were among the traits of the movement. Movements with similar traits in more modern times have been regarded as attempts to go back to the fervour of early Christianity, as a protest against the institutionalism and secularization of the Church.[2]

St. Symeon the New Theologian

Swedish Theologian, Peter Halldorf, who has studied and written on St. Symeon the New Theologian (994–1022), in his introduction to the Swedish translation of Symeon's *Ljusets Källa Tretton andliga hymner* (*The Source of the Light, Thirteen Spiritual Hymns*), writes:

> The appearance of a young spiritual revolutionary in the Eastern metropolis of the Christian world, in Byzantium, towards the end of the tenth century, became the beginning of a renewal whose rivulets have reached right up to our own day. Simeon the New Theologian witnesses about what can happen when a person surrenders his life to The Holy Spirit without reservation.[3]

Halldorf's reference to Symeon's far-reaching influence finds an echo in Pentecostalism in our day.

Wikipedia, a resource readily available to the ordinary reader, has the following entry on Symeon:

> *Discourses* are the central work of Symeon's life, and were written during his time as abbot at St. Mammas (980–998). One of Symeon's emphases is the power of the Holy Spirit to transform, and the profound mystical union with God that is the end result of a holy life. Symeon referred to this as the Baptism of the Holy Spirit, compared to the more ritualistic Baptism of water. Simeon [sic!] believed that Christianity had descended into formulae and church ritual, which for many people replaced the earlier emphasis on actual and direct experience of God. *The Discourses* express Symeon's strong conviction that the life of a Christian must be much more than mere observance of rules, and must include personal experience of the presence of the living Christ. Symeon describes his own conversion and mystical experience of the divine light.[4]

Montanus, Tertullian, and Symeon were all severely criticized by the leading elements in the mainline churches of their times. Symeon is reputed to be the father of a spiritual movement known as *Hesychiastic Mysticism* (which builds on the Geek word *hesychia* - quietness, silence), whose monks gave themselves to solitary contemplation. In the fourteenth century this movement flourished on Mount Athos, a mountain and peninsula in northeastern Greece and an important centre of Eastern Orthodox monasticism.[5]

According to Church Historian Kenneth Scott Latourette:

The Hesychasts claimed that by holding their breath, fixing their eyes on their navels, and making the spirit re-enter the soul, they could be enveloped by the light which shone around Christ at the time of the transfiguration on Mt. Tabor.[6]

Hesychasm resulted in a violent theological controversy. Latourette continues:

> In its [Hesychasm's] defence it was urged that the light was not the divine essence, for God Himself could never be seen by man, but that it was an operation or agency of God, divine grace. The critics contended that such a light could only be of the essence of God and that to separate the essence from the operation was to be guilty of falling into the error of believing in two Gods. The champion of the Hesychasts was Palamas, a monk on Mt. Athos, later (1349–c.1360) Archbishop of Thessalonica. The chief opponent was Barlaam, a native of Calabria, in Italy.[7]

Martin Luther

Let us move to the sixteenth century. What is one to say of Martin Luther, the "Father" of The Reformation? This too is far too big a subject for me to take up in any detail in my limited project. And I am afraid that I may be the target of some understandable criticism for venturing into this subject.[8] However, we must say something on our subject in connection with the Reformation.

An article in Swedish, entitled "Splittrad syn på Luthers karismatik" ("A Fragmented View of Luther's Charismatic Understanding of the Gifts of the Spirit"), by Tomas Nygren, a lecturer (Assistant Professor) at Johannelund School of Theology, in Uppsala, begins with the words:

> Luther is sometimes portrayed as one who fully embraces and operates within the realm of the gifts of The Spirit and sometimes as a devout follower of the teaching that the gifts of The Spirit disappeared after the last apostle.[9]

It is Nygren's view that one must understand the situation that prevailed at the time of the early stages of the Reformation if one is to understand why Luther acted and wrote the way he did on "charismatic phenomena." Besides the main furrow of the Reformation that followed Luther, there was a radical reformation with different representatives. This radical branch maintained that Luther hadn't gone far enough. Extreme representatives of this "charismatic" movement (like the "Zwickau" prophets and, later, Thomas Müntzer, 1490–1525) not only claimed revelations that bypassed the Bible but taught that one could speed up the advent of God's kingdom by killing the ungodly. Müntzer became one of the leaders of the Peasants' Revolt and was killed in battle.

For Luther, the adherents of the 'Radical Reformation' had abandoned Scripture and embraced a charismatic line that was characterized by individualism and fanaticism. To quote Nygren's words, Luther maintained: "If we want to share in the Spirit we should go to those places of meeting which the Scriptures have promised."[10]

According to Luther, the Spirit comes, in the first place, through the Word (The Scriptures) and The Sacraments (i.e., Baptism and Holy Communion). God's promises are linked to these places of meeting. In his *Sermon on the Fruit and Power of the Ascension of our Lord Jesus Christ*, 1527, Luther writes:

> Once, on Whitsunday, Christ gave the Holy Spirit visibly to the Apostles when there were seen sitting upon each of them cloven tongues like as of fire, and they spoke in many tongues, and exorcised devils and healed the sick. But now, and to the end of the world, He no longer gives the Holy Spirit and His gifts to His Christians as He did then, but invisibly and secretly.[11]

These words can easily give the impression that Luther's views on the discontinuation of the outer signs of the gifts imply the discontinuation or reduction of the gifts as such. However, he says clearly that Christ continues to give The Holy Spirit and His gifts *invisibly and secretly*. The implications of these italicized words must be studied seriously.

One cannot, nevertheless, deny that Luther does maintain that the outer signs of the gifts of The Spirit have ceased. It is therefore interesting to note that Nygren maintains that there are several examples, from Luther's writings and from his life, that show that he was not consistent in his caution or avoidance of what we call "charismatic" in our day. According to Nygren, Luther believed that God could speak through dreams, even though only time could prove that these dreams were from God. Luther believed in prophetic revelations and dreams but maintained that these needed to be tested by the standards of Scripture.

In Closing

A report by The Commission on Theology of The Lutheran Church—Missouri Synod, issued in April 1977, maintains:

> The Biblical teaching of the external Word as the instrument of the Holy Spirit, emphasized in our Lutheran heritage, rejects the subjectivism that seeks divine comfort and strength through "a personal experience" instead

of in the objective word of The Gospel. To make the former rather than the latter the basis of Christian certainty leads either to pride or despair instead of humble trust in the Gospel promises. (Augsburg Confession V; Formula of Concord Ep. II, 13.)[12]

A footnote to the text quoted above reads:

> Give serious consideration to the fact spectacular signs such as tongues, divine healing, and prophecy (in the neo-Pentecostal sense) may actually tend to draw attention away from the Gospel of forgiveness and centre it instead on physical healings, on unintelligible language, or on foretelling future events in one's life.[13]

This backward glance at the history of the Church, as far as the charismatic movement is concerned, is a very modest attempt to trace the course of development of a vital strain of Christian Theology and life. The *present* cannot be understood adequately without paying attention to the *past*. This statement applies also to Pentecostalism in our day.

Notes

1. See video message on *Presence TV Channel World Wide*, in late October 2019. Suraphel takes up the implications of the Nobel Peace Prize awarded to Prime Minister Abiy and the deep significance of the rapprochement between Ethiopia and Eritrea.
2. Entry on "Montanism" in *The Oxford Dictionary of the Christian Church* (2nd ed.), edited by F. L. Cross and E. A. Livingstone (Oxford, UK: Oxford University Press, 1974).
3. Introduction to Olof Andrén, *Ljusets Källa. Tretton andliga hymner / The Source of Light. Thirteen Spiritual Hymns* (Skellefteå, Sweden: Artos Publishers, 2005).
4. Entry on "Symeon the New Theologian" in *Wikipedia* (2019).
5. Mount Athos is home to 20 monasteries under the direct jurisdiction of the Ecumenical Patriarch of Constantinople.
6. K.S. Latourette, *A History of Christianity* (London: Eyre and Spottiswoode Limited, 1955), p. 570.
7. Latourette 1955, p. 570. For Pentecostalism in Ethiopia see, Serge Dewel, The Charismatic Movement in Ethiopia: Historical and Sociological Background for an Identity Problematic. 2014. Paris, L'Harmattan.
8. For a more recent treatment of Lutherans and the charismatic movement read *"The Lutheran Church and the Charismatic Movement* (St. Louis, Missouri.: Concordia Publishing House, 1977).
9. Nygren's article appeared in the periodical *Budbäraren* for June 21, 2017 (Uppsala, Sweden).
10. Nygren, op. cit.

11 Margarete Steiner & Percy Scott, *Day by Day We Magnify Thee. Daily Meditations from Luther's Writings Arranged According to The Year of the Church Year* (Philadelphia: Muhlenberg Press, 1946), p. 225.
12 Report by The Commission on Theology of The Lutheran Church—Missouri Synod, issued in April 1977 (St. Louis, Missouri: Concordia Publishing House, 1977), p. 7.
13 Ibid., p.14.

Year 2004 (2019)
Chapter 26

Pentecostalism:
Risk or Resource (II)

A Resource in Several Senses

It was Saturday, May 22, 2004.

"A string cannot bring two pieces of metal together," he said, as he sat beside me on the bus from Stockholm. "Only fire can."

He and I do not belong to a Pentecostal church, but we were coming back from a rousing charismatic conference. We were talking about bitter conflicts and inter-tribal factions in an African context. Metal, for my friend, is a picture of a hard, unbending heart. And fire represents the reconciling and uniting power of The Holy Spirit. That, I thought, was a Pentecostal way of putting things. My friend's language was, indeed, in season.

May 30 is the feast of Pentecost, ምራድ መንፈስ ቅዱስ ። (The Descent of the Holy Spirit), as the feast is called in Tigrinja. This festival is common to all Christians and this year it happens to fall on the same Sunday for all church traditions. This is one of the reasons for taking it up in a couple of reflections.

The designation "Pentecost" derives from The Greek *pentecosté*, meaning, "fiftieth" (implied: fiftieth *day*). Originally the feast fell on the fiftieth day after the feast of The Jewish Passover. To begin with, it was a rural holiday observed at the end of the harvest season and was the second of three Jewish feasts that involved pilgrimages.

It is general Christian belief that the Holy Spirit is a Person who speaks, guides, admonishes, warns, and can be grieved by the reactions and behaviour of Christians. He is not some type of neutral energy (like electricity or magnetism). The Holy Spirit is God's Spirit, His breath as it were. His role is that of Guide, Teacher, and Comforter. The term Paraclete (Comforter) in fact means "someone called to walk alongside of." The Holy Spirit has also been described as a Promoter of Christ, as a Pedagogue explaining who Christ is and what He did during His sojourn on earth (John 16:5–15).

The Book of Acts states that The Holy Spirit fell on the disciples on Pentecost (Acts, Chapter 2). The Day of Pentecost, in its New Testament variant, is associated with two events in The Old Testament. The first of these is mankind's intention to "make a name for ourselves" by building the so-called the Tower of Babel. This act of haughtiness provoked God's censure. God confused the language of mankind and scattered them over the face of the whole earth (Genesis 11:9). The Day of Pentecost, on which worshippers from different nationalities gathered in Jerusalem, heard "the wonders of God in our own tongues," in spite of barriers of language, is regarded as a reversal of God's censure at Babel and a re-gathering of scattered mankind (Acts 2:5–11).

The second Old Testament event associated with The Day of Pentecost in the New Testament is the granting of the Law to Moses on Mount Sinai. It will be remembered that this event was accompanied by, "thunder and lightning." Mount Sinai was covered with smoke, "because the Lord descended on it in fire." The whole mountain "trembled violently" (Genesis 19:16–18). These physical phenomena have similarities with the physical phenomena mentioned in connection with The Day of Pentecost.

The account in Acts 2 narrates how, suddenly, a sound like the blowing of a violent wind came from heaven and filled the whole house where they were sitting. They saw what seemed to be tongues of fire that separated and came to rest on each of them (Acts 2:2–3)

Just as the giving of The Law has something of an "inaugural" function in Israel's journey through the wilderness, Pentecost has something of an inaugural function in the earthly pilgrimage of the Christian Church. It has in fact been called the Birthday of The Church.

Why Write About Pentecostalism?

The Christian Church and its members constitute not only The Body of Christ, but also the Temple of the Holy Spirit (1 Corinthians 12:12-30; 1 Corinthians 3:16-17). In this respect, all churches have a claim to the workings of The Spirit. There is, however, one church tradition that regards itself as a church of The Holy Spirit *par excellence*. I am thinking of Pentecostalism, a movement possessed of such dynamics that no society or community can neglect it.[1] Pentecostalism is *the* branch of Christendom that is growing fastest in all parts of the world today.² It is a force to be reckoned with. In time, it may very well be such a force also in Eritrea!³

My acquaintance and association with Christians of Pentecostal conviction covers a period of 40 years. I have some very close Pentecostal friends both among Ethiopians and Eritreans. Still, I am now writing as an observer and a witness, not as an expert on this tradition of spirituality. Furthermore, I am fully aware of the fact that Pentecostalism is a movement with many faces and aspects, and that one cannot generalize in writing about it.

I do hope that my Pentecostal readers will bear this fact in mind. My writing about them at this time is my way of recognizing their importance on the religious maps of communities and nations. I have no intention whatsoever of trying to hang out Pentecostals for ridicule. Writing about them has become, for me in any case, a pedagogical challenge. As I have said on other occasions, ignorance is the mother of prejudice. However, any portrait of a movement must, by necessity, reflect both light and shadows. Both individuals and movements have strengths and weaknesses. This is also true of Pentecostalism.

Pentecostals in Eritrea

Refereeing the activities of highly motivated and potentially competitive religious groups in a small country like Eritrea cannot be easy. This is a young nation feeling its way forward in a context of fluid political, social, and religious developments. Let us face it: There are situations in which religion can constitute a real headache for the leadership of any nation. Northern Ireland, Nigeria, Pakistan, The Philippines, and Indonesia are examples of countries that have had or still have problems in this regard.

In spite of this fact, I think it is imperative that principle determine practice in the matter of freedom of religion, unless the religion itself is an obvious bearer of injustice and inhumanity. Religious rights denied or curtailed almost always become fuel for alienation and growing bitterness.

A Short History of Pentecostalism

There are movements that have the character of brush fires. They are propelled by an enormous amount of fervour and energy. Call these movements feast or frenzy, they sweep whole communities off their feet. And they don't stop until they have given or spent themselves by fulfilling their stated mission, by amalgamation, union, absorption, proliferation, fragmentation, old age, or dissipation. Such movements often meet a need or many needs. They fill a vacuum in the lives of people. They come as answers to obvious or implied questions. They appear as the fulfillment of overt or tacit longings. In the realm of the spirit, they are food to the hungry, drink to the thirsty. The law of demand and supply works also in the realm of emotions and the spirit. Formalism in excess, in services of worship, leads to a longing for spontaneity. Unbridled spontaneity on the other hand creates a craving for order and structure. Too much brain, too much rationality, leads to a hunger for more heart, more feelings! And too much heart, too much emotion, creates a longing for more brain, more thought-work. Life seems to seek its own equilibrium.

The eagerness with which Pentecostalism has been embraced all over the world suggests that it meets a need or many needs, that it fills a vacuum in the lives of people. As a mass movement, Pentecostalism is a relatively recent phenomenon. Its origins have been traced back to Charles Parham, a Methodist minister who started a Bible school in Topeka, Kansas in 1900 "with the intention of revitalizing the Christian experience." Parham opened a second school in Houston, Texas five years later. One of his students (welcomed half-heartedly!) was W. J. Seymour, a black minister. The Pentecostal revival as such caught fire some years later at Seymour's church, a simple but sturdy building at 312 Azusa Street in Los Angeles to which he had moved in 1906. From there, Pentecostalism was to initiate its worldwide campaign of spiritual conquest.

Since then, it has continued to attract unfailing attention.[4]

Pentecostalism reminds us of another world beyond the purely material and empirical. It actualizes the level of motives, the realm of that which Jesus calls "the heart." It calls attention to the forces that drive us or guide us on the inside. In this respect it is an ally of the principle that C. G. Jung underlines when he writes the following in the prologue to his *Memories, Dreams, Reflections*:

> I early arrived at the insight that when no answer comes from within to the problems and complexities of life, they ultimately mean very little.[5]

Leading scholars of Pentecostalism see unmistakable virtues in the movement. They tell us, in effect, that Pentecostals gathered for worship have the capacity to reach down to levels of emotional experience and language, that we others too would be able to reach, were we less inhibited, less tied by convention, less afraid to "Let go and Let God!" The sighs and laughter of Pentecostals gathered for worship are, according to these scholars, our suppressed sighs and laughter. Their tears are our suppressed tears. Their dances are our suppressed dances. Pentecostals are the doorkeepers, the gatemen to a world of memories, symbols, and emotions common to mankind. There is, according to these scholars, something deeply liberating and emotionally healthy about Pentecostal worship.

We cannot dismiss such an evaluation carelessly and characterize Pentecostal services as mere outbursts of infantile behaviour. We too have had moments when we have "let go" with cries of anguish or tears of uncontrollable joy or sorrow. We have had sudden stabs of inner inspiration. The utter abandon of a crowd at a football stadium can perhaps be taken as a secular example of aspects of the emotional world that Pentecostals experience at their services.

Marked by Solidarity

A certain kind of racist thinking has challenged Pentecostalism ever since its infancy. And even now there are Pentecostal churches where the colour line does play a role. The relations of the rank and file among Pentecostals are, however, marked by deep solidarity.[6] At its best, Pentecostalism is a "democratic" spirituality in the sense that anyone among its faithful can say, "Thus says the Lord," and be heard with attention. It is true that Pentecostalism has its leaders and its elite, and that certain types of Pentecostal leadership are autocratic. However, Pentecostalism is basically a religion of the people, a piety of the grassroots. It is, by and large, a spirituality marked by the absence (or near absence) of social boundaries. It is significant that the terms with which Pentecostals address each other are words like "Brother" and "Sister." Pentecostalism is, at its best, a movement of mutual concern, of generosity in giving of one's time, money, sympathy, and hospitality. It is a movement in which paying tithes has been restored to a place of honour.

Contrary to what is sometimes said about them, Pentecostals are basically patriotic and loyal citizens. They study hard, work hard, and are, for the most part, wisely frugal in their use of money. They are basically good examples to children and youth. Their productivity and frugality can be assets to the economies of the countries of which they are citizens.

Pentecostalism is a hopeful religion. It refuses to say that things are impossible. Many of its members pray, not with the qualifying words: "If it is your will?" but rather with assertions like, "Answer our prayer, O Lord, because we know that that is your will! You, who have given us the victory through our Lord Jesus Christ, prove your promises, show us your might!"

Spontaneity and a Personal Touch

Pentecostals take the spirit world seriously. Shepherds, leaders, and the faithful storm the gates of hell at the very beginning of their worship services. The Evil One (the devil) and his company are subjected to harsh commands to disappear. The invisible troops of the world of evil spirits are bound by words and voices filled with fervour and authority. The gathered army of the Lord sees to it that their meeting hall or church is cleansed from demons that may dare to disturb, intrude into, neutralize, or in any way weaken the worship and message of the day. Pentecostals challenge empty ritualism and formalism. They challenge other Christians to think of the relationships between the old and the new, tradition and innovation, hierarchy and churchly democracy. They actualize the issue of the relationship between logic and emotions in the realm of worship.

At its best, Pentecostalism is a spirituality in which "Deep" speaks unto "deep," a piety characterized by an encounter between God and the individual at the deepest level of the human spirit.[7]

Pentecostal meetings abound in sighs, hallelujahs, and cries of "Amen!"[8] The name of God or "The Lord" is repeated even in one-sentence prayers. Worship services are punctuated not only by short, vigorous exclamations, but also by long prayers and passionate petitions, reminiscent of long conversations with an intimate friend. From a purely human point of view, the raw material of Pentecostal piety is material common to the emotional and psychic equipment of mankind. This raw material is, according to my understanding, the stuff that Harvey Cox calls "primal religion."[9] This heritage of emotions, pictures, symbols, and figures held in common in the collective memory of mankind is believed to have been ignited by The Spirit of God and used in the service of The Church.[10]

It has been pointed out that the most important thing for a Pentecostal is *experience*, and not *creeds* or *dogma*. At the risk of some exaggeration, one can say that The Bible, for the Pentecostal, is primarily Holy History. It is a book of God's dealings with men and women and a reflection of their testimonies to God's dealings with their lives. For the Pentecostal, Theology is basically Narrative, not Philosophy or Theory. Written formulas and prayers, prearranged orders of worship are almost taboo among many members of the movement. An encounter with God is or should be as easy as gaining access to space, sunshine, and air.

When it is at its best, Pentecostalism is a religious movement characterized by joy, hope, confidence, and solidarity in the name and in the footsteps of the victorious Lord, Jesus Christ, and in the power of The Holy Spirit.

But only when Pentecostalism is at its best! And Pentecostalism is not always at its best.

In my following reflection, I shall try to point to some of the factors that make me believe that Pentecostalism also poses risks.

Chapter 26

God bless you, one and all!

Ezra Gebremedhin
May 22, 2004
Uppsala, Sweden

Notes

1. For an excellent presentation of the history and present state of Pentecostalism read Harvey Cox's fascinating book, *Fire from Heaven. The Rise of Pentecostal Spirituality and The Reshaping of Religion in The Twenty-First Century*. Cassell, Wellington House. London. 1996.) See also Fantini, Emanuele. "*Go Pente! The Charismatic Renewal of the Evangelical Movement in Ethiopia"*. In *Ficquet E., Prunier G. (eds), Understanding Contemporary Ethiopia: Monarchy, Revolution and the Legacy of Meles Zenawi*, 2015, and Father Kilian Mc Donald, *Presence, Power, Praise*. Documents on The Charismatic Renewal. Vol. II. Numbers 38–80, 1975–1979. The Liturgical Press, Collegeville, Minnesota, 1980.
2. It is believed that there are over 279 million Pentecostal Christians in the world (2019). Their number appears to be increasing, especially in the global south. Source: Pentecostalism. From Wikipedia, the free encyclopedia, 2019.
3. See Jörg Haustein's, *Pentecostal and Charismatic Christianity in Ethiopia. A Historical Introduction to a Largely Unexplored Movement,* in Hatem Elliesie (Ed.). Multidisciplinary Views on The Horn of Africa. Studien zum Horn von Afrika I, Köln. 2014.
4. Pentecostalism has become a subject of research, not only in the field of Theology and Mission, but also on a broader front. John P. Kildahl's book The Psychology of Speaking in Tongues (Harper and Row, 1972) is an example. Doctoral theses are being written on Pentecostalism and its missionary outreach. Only this year (2004), Gunilla Nyberg Oskarsson, a female Swedish scholar, defended a thesis (written in French) on the Pentecostal Movement in the south of Burundi, a work covering the period between 1935 and 1960.
5. C. G Jung, Memories, Dreams, Reflections. Ed. Aniela Jaffe. Flamingo. Fontana Paperbacks, 1977. p. 19.
6. There were and still are exceptions to this fact among Pentecostals. Parham, one of the pioneers of the movement, didn't really believe in racial equality. Pentecostals in South Africa allowed the policy of apartheid to determine their church policies.
7. Psalm 42:7.
8. Such interjections and cries in the course of Christian worship services are apparently not innovations, although orderly worship was strictly enjoined. St Paul writes, "If you are praising God with your spirit, how can one who finds himself among those who do not understand say "Amen" to your thanksgiving ... " 1 Corinthians 14:16.

9 Cox, 1996, pp. 99–122.
10 In the realm of Psychology, the designation for this common heritage is Archetypes.

Year 2004 (2020)
Chapter 27

Pentecostalism:

Risk or Resource (III)

Wheat Mixed with Tares

At its best, Pentecostalism is a living and dynamic branch of Christianity, characterized by a special emphasis on the gifts of The Holy Spirit. It is a promoter of genuine human feelings and fundamental modes of religious expression. Its strength lies, among other things, in its capacity to combine the spiritual and the human, the mental and the emotional, the spontaneous and the formal, the individual and the collective. This however does not mean that Pentecostalism does not have weaknesses.

Using But Not Giving Credit to the World

Without being in the least sacrilegious, we can say that many of the factors that create joy at Pentecostal meetings seem to be purely physical phenomena. That they can be and are often used for the praise and glory of God is another matter. However, we should realize that, in themselves, these experiences appear to be from below, not from above. They are available to believer and unbeliever alike. And there is absolutely nothing wrong in that. After all, God created matter and loves it. He created our emotions and pulses. He observed His creation and saw that it was good (Genesis 1: 4, 10, 12).

All good things are from God. But not all things are "spiritual" in the narrow sense in which many Pentecostals understand the term "spiritual." The quickening of the pulse and the throb of bodily rhythm created by drums, keyboards, and guitars at Pentecostal gatherings are identical to emotions and movements created by secular bands, orchestras, and artists. An outstanding theologian and warm friend of Pentecostalism, Harvey Cox, in fact sees a close relationship between Jazz and Pentecostalism.[1]

Where there is a basic Christian conviction and stance, all types of music and rhythm, all eating and drinking, all socializing can contribute to the glory of God and the edification of the individual. But let us be honest enough to admit that there are many, many occasions on which music, rhythm, and bodily movements, eating, drinking, and socializing can be sources of genuine joy, even though the name of God is not mentioned expressly. The activities I have mentioned are a part of the category of common, created gifts, like "sunshine and rain," that God grants to both the good and the evil (Matthew 5:45).

In their eagerness to be counted for God and God alone, many Pentecostals have a difficult time recognizing genuinely good things in what they call "the world." Hence their tendency to divide everyday life into two compartments—a spiritual one and a worldly one. Their attitude towards local culture (with its music, food and drink habits, folk-dances, literature, poetry, etc.) is ambivalent. They tend to be uncomfortable with traditional tales, stories, poems, proverbs, jokes, and melodies. Some Pentecostals are uncomfortable with conversations that don't insert the name of God or "The Lord" frequently. It doesn't seem to occur to them that activities and conversations that do not specifically mention the name of God can still be genuine and good.

Many Pentecostals must take a good second look at words like "world" and "worldly." What do these words mean? Aren't they references to the entire created order of feelings and bodily experiences? When does an emotion become worldly? When do food, drink, and music become worldly? When do our friends who live and work in the world but don't attend Pentecostal meetings become worldly? What does the word "Politics" mean? When is Politics worldly? Is there any Politics that is not worldly? What does the Bible say about the difference between the concepts of "body" and "flesh"? I think there is an enormous amount of difference between these two concepts. Read the eighth chapter of St. Paul's Epistle to the Romans! As our pastor put it in his sermon for Pentecost (May 30, 2004), "The term 'world' (in a biblical sense) does not refer to the created world, Cosmos, but to mankind, which has turned its back on God."

Tendency to Be Allergic to Order and Structure

There is a tendency among Pentecostals to be "allergic" (i.e., averse) to order, structure, and liturgy in worship. This, in spite of the fact that a somewhat vaguely outlined order of worship soon takes form in all Pentecostal groups! With time, all spontaneous ways of doing things tend to settle into some kind of order and structure. This is a rule of all of life. The fact remains, however, that no one is bound by the implied "order of worship" in many Pentecostal groups. The risk is that the leader of an assembly gathered for worship can "hijack" the meeting. If a leader is wise and balanced, however, the tone of the entire meeting can become wise and balanced.

A well-guided and soberly conducted Pentecostal meeting can be a tremendous source of joy and edification. But the quality of a service can stand and fall with the quality of the leader of the day. In general, Pentecostal services tend to be too wordy and too noisy for people who are used to "islands" of silence in a regular service of worship. Our old people belong to this category and, at least at the beginning, old people in our oriental traditions can feel completely lost in Pentecostal services. My feeling is that most Pentecostal churches that I am acquainted with break St. Paul's rules for the use of "tongues" during a common worship service. It doesn't seem to occur to many Pentecostals that St. Paul does not approve of one hundred or one thousand people speaking in tongues at the same time.[2] Tell me if I am wrong.

Whereas a "weak" Catholic or Lutheran or Anglican or Orthodox priest can be rescued by an already formulated liturgy, which he cannot do much to destroy, an over-confident and high-handed leader can almost ruin both worship and sermon in a Pentecostal service. Not least by endless repetitions of his (her) pet ideas or those of others! I know this from personal experience.

"Little Popes" and Fragmentation

I now pass over to those weaknesses that I regard as particularly serious. Pentecostalism's grassroots orientation, its tendency to shy away from hierarchy and from human authority in its churchly trappings, is both its strength and its weakness. Where there is no clear authority, embodied in structures and operating through a broad consensus, the risk of confusion and the misuse of authority is great. Pentecostal congregations run the risk of ending up under leaders with strong egos, claiming direct and unquestionable messages from The Spirit. This creates not only hotbeds of conflict and division, but also the loss of critical thinking and the blind acceptance of some of the most outrageous commands from self-appointed prophets.

At the risk of a drastic exaggeration, one can maintain that Pentecostal groups not only grow like mushrooms but also split at a galloping rate. Some scholars have maintained that even this trait has its advantages for Pentecostals. According to these scholars, this trait is an indication of how seriously Pentecostals take their freedom. It has also been pointed out that Pentecostalism has not suffered from its tendency to proliferate. It is a movement that thrives on divisions because even the breakaway Pentecostal groups grow. There may very well be some truth in this kind of reasoning, but the explanation provides hardly any comfort. In the first place, Pentecostal groups are not growing on all continents and in all countries. Some of them are decreasing in number. This is the case with Sweden.[3] Cox maintains that among white populations, the growth of Pentecostalism is clearly slowing down.[4] There is, however, an even more serious reason for worrying about the tendency of Pentecostal groups to proliferate. Separation and division can very well be signs of a tendency to flee from the difficult challenge of solving interpersonal problems in a religious community.

Flight from problems in a religious context can lead to flight from problems in a broader social context. And this, I think, is a very serious matter. I don't know if Pentecostals realize that the tendency to proliferate is a bad "testimony" to outsiders and poor public relations in the communities of which they are a part. But, of course, this criticism does not apply to all Pentecostal groups. And the right to separate is also part and parcel of religious freedom!

Tongues That Glorify or "Burn"!

The gift of "tongues" is, for most Pentecostals, at the vanguard, at the very front of all the gifts of The Spirit. This was the view of Seymour, the "father" of Pentecostalism, at least in the earlier part of his ministry. For many Pentecostals, "the gift of tongues" is the surest sign of one's baptism in or by The Spirit. It is underlined as the surest sign that one has received the second blessing, that one has experienced "the latter rain." This does not of course mean that Pentecostals neglect the other gifts. They don't all say that "the gift of tongues" is the most important gift. But most of them maintain that tongues *are* the surest sign that a Christian has received the second blessing.

Such a view is controversial, to say the least. In the first place, the Bible does not seem to teach that all people must or do receive the gift of tongues. This seems to be the implied teaching of St. Paul in 1 Corinthians 12: 11, and 29–31. That the Holy Spirit can and does mediate this "gift" is something that the majority of Christians accept.

However, scholars maintain that "speaking in tongues" (the phenomenon known as *Glossolalia* in Greek) is not exclusively Christian. The technique as such can apparently be both taught and learned. The sobering fact is that former believers have apparently claimed that they could speak in tongues fluently even after falling out of fellowship with the Lord. Many maintain that much speaking in tongues is the result of autosuggestion and outright mimicry.[5] That such views are open to debate is another matter.

The everyday implications of the concept of tongues (understood as speech and verbal communication) should engage our attention. Consider the expression "tongues of fire" mentioned in Acts Chapter 2. In the first place, the expression refers to the way the Spirit descended on the disciples on the Day of Pentecost. The Spirit is associated with fire and speech.

This gift of The Spirit is to be held in honour. St. Paul himself says clearly that one should not forbid "speaking in tongues" (I Corinthians 14:39). However, it is important to remember the tongue and its role in everyday life. It can be destructive. Here is what the Apostle James says on this subject:

> The tongue also is a fire, a world of evil among the parts of the body. It corrupts the whole person, sets the whole course of his life on fire, and is itself set on fire by hell. All kinds of animals, birds, reptiles and creatures of the sea are being tamed and have been tamed by man, but no man can tame the tongue. It is a restless evil, full of deadly poison. (James 3:6–8, New International Version)

The way one uses the tongue in everyday life is a good measure of a person's integrity and of the caliber of his or her spirituality. It is no wonder that the Psalmist prays:

> Set a guard over my mouth, O Lord;
> Keep watch over the door of my lips. (Psalms 141:3)

Rain Must Be Conserved

Pentecostalism is a religion that speaks of "the latter rain" (Joel 2:23), of the "second blessing," of the "filling" or "baptism" following salvation. The picture of rain is a telling one. In the first place, rain is a gift, pure and simple. However, once it has poured down, its effectiveness depends on what one does with it. Rain can be easily squandered. It can be wasted.

We have the Pentecostal saying: "The man with an experience is never at the mercy of the man with a doctrine." There is surely an important truth behind this statement. On one occasion, during the very infancy of the church, some of its missionaries stated their case before their adversaries in the words, "For we cannot help speaking about what we have heard and seen" (Acts 4:20, New International Version).

Nevertheless, even decisive experiences are recorded and described, sooner or later. If different types of experience are to help others, then one must decide in what sense they are to be *guidelines* or *norms*. Behind most marriages there is the experience known as falling in love. But if married life is to survive the ups and downs of everyday life, it must be based on consciously understood and mutually accepted principles of family life. The experience of initial love must lead to norms of behaviour willingly accepted.

In one sense, theology is recorded and interpreted experience. And that is why all religions have Scriptures and commentaries on or interpretations of these Scriptures. And in this sense, even Pentecostals must bear in mind that the man with an experience needs to try to understand the doctrine or doctrines that his experience reflects. One cannot flee from the responsibility of *thinking* about one's experience. Remembering is important, but not enough.

Rainwater needs canals if it is to move in a definite direction and carry out specific functions. Otherwise, it runs the risk of spreading thinly over a vast area and of evaporating or sinking into vast tracts of arid country. All revivals, but particularly Pentecostalism, need the preserving and conserving canals that at least some of the rich, common traditions of The Christian Church can provide. God is a God who works in and through history, in and through prescribed modes of action, even though He can and sometimes does act in ways that are unique and unprecedented. He is, after all, the God of Abraham, Isaac, and Jacob. He is the God of the Apostles and Martyrs of the Church. What He has said and done through them cannot be unimportant for Christians in our days. The commandment to honour father and mother (Exodus 20:32) also implies respecting all sound human tradition. Pentecostals have a lot to teach the other churches of Christendom through their uplifting and engaging forms of worship. But even they have a lot to learn in the matter of worship and the development of the spiritual life from the accumulated liturgical heritage of the church.

Is Pentecostalism Spirituality for the Successful?

Pentecostalism is a movement that holds forth faith, hope, joy, and a sense of victory. The death of Christ and His resurrection power, Pentecostals argue, have opened the way to well-being and success also in a purely material sense. Pentecostals have been accused of promoting the so-called "health-and-wealth-Gospel."[6] Accusing all Pentecostals of promoting such a teaching would not be fair. However, it is, I think, true that many Pentecostals have a difficult time answering the questions of people who have been subjected to life's bitter trials, those who have not succeeded in securing health and wealth.

How good is Pentecostalism at dealing with tragedy? There are thousands and thousands of people who have cried, prayed, fasted, struggled, and not been freed from sickness and anguish. What are we to say to such people? Is their faith lacking? Who is to give such a frightful verdict? How are we to explain their unanswered prayers? Pentecostalism tends to be an alternative for the strong, or for those who succeed. It tends to give precedence to "a theology of glory" over a "theology of the cross."

Catholic theology speaks of "offering up" one's sufferings to God. There is something deep about this teaching, a depth which logic does not fathom. Archbishop Fenelon writes:

> Love without the cross would be frenzy, and become an illusion, but the cross brings down all lofty ideas, all beautiful imaginations, all consoling fervors. One becomes very lowly under suffering.[7]

One recognizes something of Luther's "Theology of the Cross" in this statement. Suffering is an enemy. It can break the spirit of many a courageous man and woman. But it can be dealt with in faith. And it can shape sterling characters. History has many examples of this truth. A spirituality that sees very little meaning in suffering cannot go very far. Many shades of Pentecostalism run the risk of missing the mark in this respect. In some of its variants, Pentecostalism runs the risk of giving far too simple answers to difficult questions.

Group Pressure and "Elite Thinking"

Oswald Chamber writes:

> Never make a principle out of your experience; let God be as original with other people as He is with you.[8]

This is a rule that many Pentecostals break. Joy and a sense of having received something great easily tempt one to believe that he or she has the answers also to the questions of other people. Many Pentecostals want people to be blessed or visited by God in exactly the same way that they have been visited.

Pentecostalism is a movement in which group pressure is enormous. There is a tendency to promote uniformity, to resort to clichés in the use of language, to assume behaviour that is a result of imitation. In short, there is the risk of what one might call a "conveyor-belt spirituality," reminiscent of the chain-production of products of the same kind in factories. The danger of imitating others or of using "gimmicks" to get going, for instance in the matter of speaking in tongues, is great. One does not want to be left out.

There is a risk that Pentecostals, like all other religious people conscious of their virtues, fall prey to elite thinking. They consider themselves, after all, as the Spirit-filled, the Spirit-baptized. They have received not only salvation but also the "second blessing." They are not only saved but also equipped. They belong to the vanguard of The Lord's army. They are already equipped with the armor needed for the fight.

To be thankful to God for the gifts that one has received is one thing. To engage in a "we are better than you" thinking is, however, a completely different matter. People equipped with the gifts of The Spirit or other "spiritual" gifts, are easily tempted to look down on those who aren't or can't show that they are. Here we have a recurrence of the "spiritual" pride of the Pharisee in the parable of The Pharisee and The Publican, narrated by Jesus in Luke Chapter 8. And pride is the prince of all sins.

Risks Involved in the Spectacular

Signs have their significance in the proclamation of the Christian Gospel. Miracles and wonders have a powerful missionary function. We simply can't neglect the fact that healing and wonders were an important part of the ministry of Jesus. St. Paul, in his First Epistle to the Corinthians 2:4, writes:

> My message and my preaching were not with wise and persuasive words, but with a demonstration of the Spirit's power, so that your faith might not rest on men's wisdom, but on God's power.

However, signs, wonders, and miracles are not an absolute guarantee of authenticity in things spiritual. This is a truth that many Pentecostals rarely take up. Jesus himself has uttered some very pointed words in this regard. In Matthew 7:22–23, we read:

> Many will say to me on that day, 'Lord, Lord, did we not prophesy in your name and in your name drive out demons and perform many miracles?' Then I will tell them plainly, "I never knew you. Away from me, you evildoers.

It is an axiom of all sound spiritual guidance that the gifts of the Spirit and the fruit of The Spirit be regarded as inseparable. They are twin categories that condition one another. The category known as "the fruit of that Spirit" comprises a number of God-given virtues. These are "love, joy, peace, patience, kindness, goodness, faithfulness, gentleness, and self-control" (Galatians 5:22). The rule of thumb as far as the authenticity and use of the gifts of the Spirit are conceded is that *the fruit of the Spirit is the test of the gifts of the Spirit.*

Our Crucial Question

Does Pentecostalism pose a risk or is it a resource? Let me first try to reduce this question to a more general level. Does *religion* constitute a risk or a resource? I would say that it does both. History has taught us that religion is a plant that must be watched, for the simple reason that it makes such enormous claims on the lives and allegiances of people. It has been stated that the word "religion" itself conveys the idea of "re-linking," of "rejoining." At its best, religion can create unity and deep coherence in the life of a person.

However, this is only one part of the picture. Religion does also pose a danger. It can and has been exploited. This applies also to Pentecostalism. It is interesting to note that Harvey Cox, who has written a book highly appreciative of Pentecostalism, once wrote a book entitled *The Seduction of the Spirit: The Use and Misuse of People's Religions*. In it he states:

> The seduction of the spirit, in short, is the calculated twisting of people's natural and healthy religious instincts for purposes of control and domination. It is the cruelest abuse of religion because it slyly enlists people in their own manipulation.[9]

Unscrupulous religious leaders with strong egos can indeed enslave weak individuals. In this sense Pentecostalism too, with its tendency to place "Spirit-filled" individuals on a pedestal, poses serious risks.

As I write these words, the attention of the media in Sweden is riveted on a small village outside Uppsala, known as Knutby. The Pentecostal congregation in Knutby has been the focus of attention for over six months now. Very early in the morning on January 10th, a young woman, who had previously acted as a baby-sitter in a pastor's family, shot Alexandra Fossmo, the 23-year-old wife of Pastor Helge Fossmo, dead in cold blood.

Alexandra was the second wife to die in the pastor's home. Today, May 13, 2004, charges were brought against the pastor for allegedly engineering the death of both his wives. He is accused not only of having used the baby-sitter as a sex object but also of having ordered her to kill his second wife. The charges maintain that he did so in his capacity as a spiritual leader. The pastor, it is maintained, used Bible verses to manipulate the psychically unstable young baby-sitter. A verse from The Bible was allegedly used to legitimize the cold-blooded murder: "There is a time to kill and a time to heal" (Ecclesiastes 3:3).

Furthermore, the pastor is accused of having used the baby-sitter sexually by convincing her that sexual intercourse with her was an effective way of freeing him from the grip of demons! If these charges are indeed true, then they are examples of a ruthless misuse of the will of a brainwashed individual and the serious intent behind some difficult words of Scripture.[10]

Can One Simply Let Go?

The statement, "Let go and let God!" used by many preachers of revival, is indeed a deep statement. But it is also dangerous! It is a profound guideline. But it is also perilous! Much depends on what one lets go and which kind of god one lets into one's life. Such a slogan can lead to the realization of a person's deepest self. But it can also lead to the disintegration of a fragile personality, held together weakly by invisible threads of caution and reticence. Neither can we exclude the risk of a reduction of a person's life to that of a machine, an automaton, a spineless instrument at the mercy of ruthless "spiritual guides."

All fanaticism, be it political, religious, or otherwise, is a kind of possession. And all possession implies a being emptied and occupied in the name of a higher power. To be free is to be open, to dare to question prevalent ideas, to take intelligent risks, to be willing to learn and to change. But it is also to know and own oneself. It is to be able to stand one's ground. It is to have the courage to say "No!" To be a genuine human being is to practice deliberate, considered, unhurried choices. The alleged dependence on "The Spirit" and "Spirit-filled" people, taught uncritically by different religious movements, counteracts such mature behaviour in the lives of individuals.

Having said so, let me add that the statement "Let go and let God!" contains a deep truth, as long as we keep in mind that God has created us in His own image. He must have given us this honour, not to reduce us to robots or automatons, but to make us his junior "companions," individuals who are meant to use both body and soul, both brain and emotions to take care of ourselves and the rest of the created world.

I for one am open to a "Pentecostalism" informed by these sound premises.[11]

God bless you, one and all!

Ezra Gebremedhin
May 22, 2004
Uppsala, Sweden

Notes

1. H Cox, 1996, pp. 143–151. D. Hammarskjöld writes, "Spiritual liberation has its sensual component just as claustrophobia of the soul has its physical symbolism and physiological ground" (*Markings,* Vintage Books, 2006, p. 74). On "Tongues", C.S. Lewis writes, "Transposition occurs whenever the higher produces itself in the lower" (*Screwtape Proposes a Toast,* Collins, 1982, p. 84).
2. I Corinthians 14:26–40.
3. According to *Kyrkans Tidning* (The organ of The Church of Sweden) NR 21, 2004, The Pentecostal Church of Sweden lost 8835 members in 2002 and served 127, 245 members at the end of the current year.
4. Cox, 1996, p. 312.
5. John P Kildahl's book, The Psychology of Speaking in Tongues (Harper and Row, 1972) is very revealing in this regard. See especially the summary of his findings on pp. 76–86.
6. See Cox 1996, pp. 271 ff.
7. The Spiritual Letters of Archbishop Fenelon. Letters to Men. Rivingtons. Waterloo Place, London. MDCCCLXXX, p. 88.
8. Chambers, Oswald. My Utmost for His Highest. (Grand Rapids, Michigan: Discovery House, Classic Edition, 2017). Entry for June 13.
9. H. Cox. The Seduction of the Spirit. The Use and Misuse of People's Religions. Simon and Schuster, 1973, 16.
10. Such misuse of spiritual authority can have devastating consequences. It will be remembered that on November 19, 1978, 914 people committed suicide under the religious leadership of Pastor Jim Jones, in Jonestown, Guyana. At least 86 members of the sect of The Branch Dravidians, from Waco, Texas, committed collective suicide in 1993. On March 17, 2000, hundreds of members of the African movement for the Restoration of the Ten Commandments died in a suicidal conflagration at a village called Kananga, 230 kilometers south-west of Kampala, in Uganda.
11. A long time friend, Dr. Bereket Yebio, wrote the following words, particularly after pondering the more specifically theological treatments in my book: "I had hoped that you would give us a wider perspective of the Universal

Church, the Body of Christ. I am sorry to say that Pentecostalism is a too narrow perspective to deal with in such a book. Often the focus is more on the Preacher rather than the Message. We need to learn more about the different historical manifestations of the Witness of the Church. I know that you have the knowledge and experience that you could share with us. The Mystery of Incarnation, the Divine and Human nature of Christ, the Holy Trinity, the meaning of Baptism, the Sacraments, are issues I would love to discuss with you." These words constitute a meaningful challenge!

Year 2019
Chapter 28

Some Comments on my Articles on Pentecostalism:

An Interview with Dr. Agne Nordlander

First some words from our interviewee on September 11, 2019:

> It is easy to preach in Ethiopia because there, people are open for a Lutheran proclamation about sin and grace, a strong proclamation about what Christ has done for us and what Jesus has liberated us from. They are open for what The Holy Spirit can and will do in our lives; open for the kind of teaching that gives guidance on how to walk with Christ and how to win people for God.

Dr. Agne Nordlander, who turned 80 recently, uttered these words in an interview that has now been published in *Budbäraren* (*The Messenger*).[1] I prevailed upon him to comment on the articles that I had written on Pentecostalism in this book.

The opening words are based on Dr. Nordlander's first-hand contacts and research among members of The Ethiopian Evangelical Church Mekane Yesus (EECMY). His years of service as lecturer at The Theological Seminary of the EECMY have given him unique insights into the history and life of one of the fastest growing churches in the world. To take only one example, his book *Väckelse och växtvärk i Etiopien* (*Revival and Growing-Pains in Ethiopia*) is a brilliant survey, in Swedish, of the different kinds of revival that have been operative in Ethiopia, in those areas where both missionaries and Ethiopian proclaimers of the Gospel have laboured.[2]

He speaks of three types of revival. The first is the classical Lutheran revival in which a conscience awakened and shaken by the proclamation of the Law is comforted and uplifted by the balm of The Gospel, the Good News of salvation by grace through faith.

The second type of revival is the discovery, the experience that the proclamation of the Gospel leads to *freedom* from slavery under Satan and all forms of evil. Dr. Nordlander traces the occurrence of this experience among persons with Orthodox and other church backgrounds and in the missionary outreach of both Lutheran and non-Lutheran organizations. This is the freedom that Luther's Large Catechism holds forth as the fruit of the Lordship of Jesus Christ: being redeemed from sin, the devil, death, and evil of different kinds.

The third type of revival is the Charismatic Revival. Theologically, this tradition does not differ essentially from the tradition that emphasizes the role of Christ as Liberator. It does, however, place a greater emphasis on experiences related to The Holy Spirit and to the gifts of grace, not least the gifts of tongues, healing, and prophecy.

In a chapter entitled "What Can We Learn from The Mekane Yesus Church?" in his book, Dr. Nordlander identifies the following practices: Giving priority to Prayer, Trusting God's Word, A Christocentric proclamation on Conversion, The Evangelizing Vision, Openness to the Holy Spirit, and Suffering for the sake of Christ.

When we came to a consideration of my articles on Pentecostalism, in my interview, Dr. Nordlander pointed out that I should clarify the difference between the Charismatic Movement and the kind of Pentecostalism about which I had written. He had taken notice of some of my critical remarks in connection with Pentecostalism. His understanding is that the Charismatic Movement, which has found its place in a number of the so-called traditional or mainline churches, shouldn't be subjected to criticism without qualifications.

The Catholic, Anglican, Lutheran, Presbyterian, and Baptist churches have accommodated charismatic phenomena and modes of expression without rejecting their basic doctrinal positions and their understanding of worship. Laymen who are faithful to their 'mother-churches' take part in Charismatic movements. In Norway there are examples of developments in which the Charismatic Movement has been incorporated into churches and congregations of Lutheran persuasion. In Sweden we have what is known as the *Oasrörelsen* (The Oasis Movement). One can say that this movement is a High-Church movement within The Church of Sweden. It affirms the validity of the ministry of the Church and teaches that this ministry should be respected. The Eucharist (Holy Communion) is regarded with reverence in this movement.

Among Swedish representatives of this movement, he mentioned the names of Hans Weichbrodt and the female theologian Berit Simonsson. The movement recognizes and encourages the view that a Christian can be equipped with power bestowed by the Holy Spirit. The Spirit can and does give assurance of salvation, impart joy, and create eagerness to proclaim the Gospel. Worship services in which songs are used to give praise to God are encouraged. So is the teaching that God is waiting to give the Gifts of Grace. This line of theological thinking has been careful to avoid what has been called "Success Theology," which in Sweden has been associated with The Word of Life Movement, at least in the earlier stages of the life of the movement. "Success Theology" has been used as an example of the misuse of the concept of faith.

It was enlightening to hear Dr. Nordlander say that there are Pentecostal Christians (*Pingstvänner*) in Sweden who feel at home in the Oasis Movement, which has its spiritual home in The Church of Sweden. Their meeting-ground is a sober understanding of the work of the Spirit in the life of the Church and the individual Christian.

Our interview also touched upon the Lutheran Church–Missouri Synod, with its main base in the United States. I knew that this church either rejected or had strong reservations about the Charismatic Movement. What I found surprising was Dr. Nordlander's statement to the effect that Missouri Synod was also critical of Pietism, a tradition that I had always regarded as a self-evident part of the Lutheran spiritual tradition.

Pietism is a movement that arose within German Lutheranism in the 17th century. Its main proponent was Philipp Jakob Spener (1635–1705). Pietism tried to foster a living link between an emphasis on right doctrine and a genuine, personal faith. Pietism became an object of criticism because some of its proponents tended to regard the effectiveness and power of the Means of Grace (The Word and The Sacraments of Baptism and Holy Communion) as something dependent on the piety of the officiating pastor or priest. The hesitation of the Missouri Synod towards Pietism is related, partly, to this latter observation.

Nordlander expressed his appreciation of the fact that The Missouri Synod did underline the importance of the Second Article of the Creed, which highlights the person and work of Christ. He also appreciated the fact that The Missouri Synod emphasized mission outreach.

My mind went back to stories of revival in Western Wollega in Ethiopia, in the 1940s or even earlier. I remember the name of Qes (Pastor) Ashana in the earlier stages of the life of the church,(which later took the name Mekane Yesus), of stories of healing, of the casting out of demons through the biddings or rebukes of Qes Ashana in the west and by Qes Shamebo in the south.

Dr. Nordlander presented people like Qes Ashana and Qes Shamebo as pastors who built their teaching and pastoral acts on Jesus as the liberator from evil spirits, from fear and the witch doctors (ቃልቻች or *qalitchas*, the equivalent of the *shaman* in traditional Ethiopian religion). Jesus was proclaimed as the Healer from sickness and the Victor over the devil and death.

The fruit of the proclamation of persons like Qes Ashana and Qes Shamebo was seen in faith and liberation – not particularly in the signs of power mediated by the Spirit. Baptism in or by the Holy Spirit was taught by Scandinavian Pentecostal missionaries in Ethiopia from the very start, but these missionaries did not place their main emphasis on this teaching before 1966.

This teaching gained momentum with a Kenyan preacher by the name of Chacha Omahé, who began holding public rallies in Awasa, Ethiopia, in 1963 under the auspices of the Swedish Pentecostal Mission. Ethiopians connected with the Finnish Pentecostal Mission in Addis Ababa and later on Ethiopians connected with the Mennonite Mission in Nazareth were to receive teaching on baptism in the Holy Spirit. This teaching as well as the emphasis on sanctification by Chacha Omahé spread among Ethiopian believers. The Muluwengel Church was established in the mid-1960s. The concept and experience of being baptized in the Spirit is believed to have spread after this period. Dr. Nordlander did, however, narrate a story connected with one of the very first "charismatic" pastors of the Mekane Yesus Church, Pastor Tesfaye Dinegdé. He witnessed to remembering having received his baptism at three or four years of age! Tesfaye meant that he had experienced the touch of the Spirit at that tender age and that he was able to recognize the same touch of the Spirit later on, as an adult. Such a story was regarded with a special feeling of wonder when it was first heard.

The Ethiopian Evangelical Church Mekane Yesus (EECMY) is now a church with a total membership of about 9–10 million. It is difficult to arrive at the exact number of believers. What is more, EECMY is a thoroughly "charismatic" church, with all the possibilities and problems connected with such a designation. The church as a whole was hesitant to embrace the charismatic movement when the movement started gathering speed in Ethiopia, in the latter half of the 1960s. However, wise counsel by leaders in the church encouraged a careful opening of the doors for charismatic phenomena rather than issuing an uncompromising "No!" to the movement. Different sections of the church have shown different degrees of openness. The way in which the different gifts of the Spirit have been used in the church show both maturity and lack of depth. An unmistakable sign of the work of the Spirit is the eagerness of the faithful to witness and evangelize and the remarkable growth of the church.

At the time of writing, Dr. Agne Nordlander, a retired lecturer, and his wife Karin are back in Ethiopia, to give basic, biblical instruction to 20 pastors who have been in service for five to ten years.

Note

I am indebted to Dr. Tormod Engelsviken for the following survey of literature on Pentecostalism, mediated by Dr. Agne Nordlander:

Engelsviken, Tormod, "Gudina Tumsa, The EECMY and the Charismatic Movement," I: Church and Society, Lectures and Responses. Second Missiological Seminar 2003 on the Life and Ministry of Gudina Tumsa, edited by the Gudina Tumsa Foundation, Addis Ababa, Hamburg: WDL – Publishers, 2010, pp. 165–190, (The chapter contains a series of references to other works on the Pentecostal and Charismatic movements, the following, among others:

- McDonnell, Kilian (ed.): Presence, Power, Praise. Documents on the Charismatic Renewal, Vol. II, Collegeville, Minn. Liturgical Press, 1980, pp. 150–182. The document on Ethiopia contains a short description of the history of the charismatic movement in Ethiopia (pp. 150–153) and excerpts from the report from a seminar on The Holy Spirit and the charismatic movement, which was held at The Mekane Yesus Seminary in 1976 (pp. 153–182).
- Tormod Engelsviken, "Deliver Us From Evil: Evangelism, Spiritual Conflict, Signs and Wonders," I: Younghoon Lee Wonsuk Ma (eds.), Pentecostal Mission and Global Christianity: An Edinburgh Centenary Reader, Oxford: Regnum, 2018, pp. 193–206.
- Engelsviken, Tormod, Mulu Wongel: A Documentary History of the Ethiopian Independent Pentecostal Movement 1960–1975. Oslo: The Free Faculty of Theology, 1975 (Unpublished).

Comments by the Reverend Hans Lindholm, Uppsala

I think it would be informative for the reader if you could state that you are writing about observations made both within Church History and contemporary church life in Ethiopia, Eritrea and Sweden.

You write that Pentecostalism or the Charismatic Movement tends to be anchored more in the heart than in the mind. What applies among us (in the West?) is the opposite. When I asked a former Swedish missionary to

Ethiopia about what she had learnt about the Bible from African Christians she felt that she had no answer to that question. She said that the sermons were often weak. But she had learnt much about prayer. My conclusion was that many African Christians perhaps didn't analyze the Bible-text in detail, but that they lived close to it.

You write about the tendencies to proliferation and divisions. That is a Protestant malady, accentuated by Pentecostalism. In Lötenkyrkan (a congregation in Uppsala, Sweden) I was contacted, at different times, by at least three pastors from the same African country. They wanted to hold worship services in the church. At least two of them had come from the same congregation in their homeland.

We know that "*Livets Ord*" (Word of Life) propagated an American "Success-Theology" in Sweden in the Nineteen-eighties. But a couple of decades later I met one of their leaders at an Ecumenical gathering of pastors. He held a broken candle in his hands. He said, "Many people whom I meet are in this state. Even I often find myself in such a state!" A sign of humility!

The one who has seen something new and big can easily come to the conclusion that he or she is ahead of others. But, already at the Ecumenical Charisma Conference 1974, in Umeå, Sweden, a leading Pentecostal pastor said: "You may believe that we Pentecostals have a monopoly on The Spirit. That is not the case. Can't we all agree that we need more of The Spirit?"

You write about the tendency to divide the "spiritual" from the "earthly." I would like to say that revival movements often have a weak Theology of Creation and that they have become hyper-spiritual, in different ways. This tendency was very clear in the early stages of the "Faith-Movement," while many traditional churches pay less attention to the second and third articles of the Creed.

I too feel that you are completely right in your critical question as to whether one should really encourage mounting 'murmur' or 'buzz' in connection with speaking in tongues among a gathering of many people. This should be a subject of self-examination for Pentecostalism. As far as we Swedish Lutherans are concerned we should ask ourselves as to how speaking in tongues can be given place in our gatherings.

You write, rightly enough, that personality-related conflicts can arise between strong and self-appointed leaders. In the Church of Sweden, we tend to buy out the vicar if he or she happens to come into conflict with the chairman of the congregational council! In other words, we tend to seek too superficial solutions.

In Sweden the role of speaking in tongues as the natural or obvious point of entry for spiritual gifts has been toned down. I do not seem to hear about the division between so-called "ordinary" and "spiritual" Christians, any more. Such a distinction was noticeable at the beginning of the appearance of waves of the charismatic movement in the Nineteen-seventies. I am sure it is still found in some other places in the world.

It is easy to try to want to cling to 'peak experiences', and benefit from them in everyday life. But they can be decisive in the lives of individuals – perhaps a charismatic meeting or a youth-camp or a liturgical Communion service. Once again, we need balance between feasts and everyday life. After all, we are called to live as disciples of Jesus in such contexts.

I first heard about the picture of rain which comes with life but can develop into a swamp if it is not canalized, from Hugo Söderström, once a missionary in Zimbabwe. At the time the picture was used to describe a transition within a Christian student-movement from (in my opinion), a sound charismatic to a systematized and hyper-spiritual movement. The picture of the need for the canalization of rain is very fitting.

As far as the tragic case of Knutby was concerned, the Pentecostal congregation in Uppsala had tried to exert a stabilizing influence, in vain. It is perhaps not so easy to accept correction in a context where structures for the supervision of "prophets" who think that they know best, are lacking.

Note

After the dissolution of the congregation Philadelphia in Knutby in 2018, one of the pastors of the congregation, Urban Fält, confessed, "I beg all those that I have harmed for forgiveness, with deep regret." According to The News Section of *Dagen* for Friday, December, 27, 2019, court cases were expected to begin on January 14, 2020 and proceed over a period of three weeks. A long drawn-out court case on Knutby did result in verdicts on March 13, 2020. The newspaper *Dagen* for March 17, 2020 reports that three persons—Åsa Waldau (a female pastor), Peter Gembäck, and Urban Fält—were convicted and sentenced to community service and fines. The former main pastor of the Knutby Congregation, Pastor Helge Fossmo, is still in prison.

The April 28, 2020 issue of the Swedish daily, *Dagen*, had a two-page article on the novelist and playwright P.O. Enquist, who died on April 25, 2020. Commenting on Enquist's probably most celebrated book, *Lewis resa* (*Lewis' Journey*), which came out in 2001, one of the authors of the article, Joel Halldorf, writes the following in the Culture Section of *Dagen*:

> In *Lewis resa*, he explains, more clearly than anyone before him, the place of The Pentecostal Movement in Sweden. He describes the tension between spirituality and organization, between Pentecostalism and the

Folk Home (Sweden), between Lewi Pethrus and Per Albin Hansson. These were reflections of each other and Enquist explained how they fitted together. He wrote the Pentecostal Movement into Sweden's history.

Lewi Pethrus (1884–1974) was a famous Swedish Pentecostal leader. Per Albin Hansson (1885–1946) was, among other things, Sweden's Prime Minister (1932–1946) when he died. Halldorf's words in his article on P. O. Enquist remind us that Pentecostalism has left its mark on life in Sweden.

Notes

1   *Budbäraren*, # 8, 2019,
2   Agne Nordlander, Väckelse och växtvärk i Etiopien (Revival and Growing-Pains in Ethiopia), 1997, EFS-Förlag. See also Jörg Haustein's Pentecostal and Charismatic Christianity in Ethiopia: A Historical Introduction to a Largely Unexplored Movement, in Hatem Elliesie (ed.) Multidisciplinary Views on The Horn of Africa. Studien zum Horn von Afrika I, Köln 2014, pp. 109–127.

Year 2004–2005
Chapter 29

On the Seasons Around Uppsala (I):
The Call of Sweden's Seasons

I was born and brought up in Ethiopia, the land of "Thirteen Months of Sunshine," to use the language of the country's Tourist Organization. The number "thirteen" is a reference to the month known as *Pagumen*, a petty month consisting of five days (six days in leap years) that comes at the end of *Nähassé*, the Ethiopian month of August. What I remember about Ethiopia's seasons are the two obvious climate blocks—the long, basically dry and hot season that corresponds to the autumn, winter, and spring seasons in the Nordic countries; and the short but intensive rainy season that corresponds to summertime in the north of Europe. I do, however, remember something of the uniqueness of late summer and late autumn even in Ethiopia. The yellow, so-called *Mäsqäl*-flowers of late August and early September and trees that shed their leaves in plenty in late autumn come to mind! I can't, however, say that the seasons in Ethiopia had the colorful variety and the gradually unfolding character of the different faces of the seasons of Sweden.

Dag Hammarskjöld's Book *Castle Hill*

In 2004, the voices and faces of the seasons, especially in Uppsala County, made such a deep impression on me that I decided to keep a diary specifically on these seasons. My notes came to cover 2004 and 2005. Sometime in 2005 I came upon a small book entitled *Castle Hill*, an English translation of the book *Slottsbacken*, written in Swedish by Dag Hammarskjöld in New York and first published posthumously in 1962.[1]

The Uppsala Castle was the home of Dag Hammarskjöld during his youth and adolescence. His father, Hjalmar Hammarskjöld, was Governor of Uppsala County from 1907 until 1930.[2] The English version of *Castle Hill* was first published in 1971. The edition that I read was from 2000. *Castle Hill* was the last work that Hammarskjöld wrote and was published by Dag Hammarskjöld Foundation.

I wanted to use *Castle Hill* to reinforce my observations on the seasons in Uppsala County. I discovered, however, that Hammarskjöld's purpose was deeper, wider, and more far-reaching than the intention behind my diary-notes on the seasons.

Hammarskjöld's little book (only 12 pages of actual text!) consists of a series of reminiscences. A personal narrative, presented with a remarkable economy of words! Paul Tournier, a physician in Geneva (1898–1986), once wrote a book entitled *A Place for You: Psychology and Religion.*[3] He underlines the great importance of a *place* that a person can call his or her own. Castle Hill was indeed a *place*, in the deepest sense of the word, for Dag Hammarskjöld. His memory of Castle Hill is rich because it was a place that he remembered with joy.[4]

Castle Hill gives the impression that the seasons constitute not only meteorological phenomena to be described, measured and documented but also a drama in four acts: *Autumn*, the great "Painter" and also "Eraser"; *Winter*, the "Equalizer" before which no face or skin can claim special treatment; *Spring*, the great "Caterer" and "Toastmaster;" and *Summer*, the provider of "Breathing Space" for rich and poor alike. The seasons come in, unhindered, touch the thinking and feelings of mortal beings in numerous ways, and then move on, leaving both nostalgia and relief.

Hammarskjöld tells us how the birds longed for home to Sweden from warmer latitudes, even if the leafless trees (their places of rest and their sources of food) were not quite ready for them. Like human beings who long for home! We have flowers and birds, trees and moss cooperating in ushering in spring. And the song of a robin fills the bottomless globe of the sky.[5]

Winter is not only the introducer of darkness, cold, and withdrawals but also the wakeful guard and protector of the lofty honour of Caste Hill! Winter is personified and made into an actor of historic importance.[6]

Castle Hill is history, a description of life among high and low, glimpses backwards and forwards, across holidays and ordinary days, seen from Uppsala Castle as a vantage point. It is a panorama of church and society. The book gives us glimpses into the persons and doings of monarchs, men of might and means, of ordinary peasants, gardeners, and men of learning! In the book, the old and the young, men and women, autumn and winter, spring and summer pass in a cavalcade before us. It introduces the reader to the Church of the Fathers, Uppsala University, the main seat of learning of the nation, the ceremonies of the learned with the solemn conferment of doctors' degrees, the carefree feasts of the young.

And the seasons are interwoven into this rich narrative, with their sounds and colours, their chill and warmth. And their impact on the thinking and feelings of the County of Uppland!

Longing and Respect for the Seasons

In many ways, Swedish life is a witness to the deep desire and respect for the seasons. One senses this fact in the eagerness and anticipation with which almost all the seasons are expected, perhaps with some hesitation as far winter is concerned! Sweden is a country of iron mines, hydro-electric power, paper-pulp, and the like. It is a country of cars, aero-planes, and ships. Metal, wood, waterpower, and electrical energy are the sources of Swedish economic wealth. Sweden's life on a deeper level, its "quality life," is, however, dependent on Nature as a giver, as a mother to be protected. Swedes do protest about too low incomes or about certain types of medical care that do not reach the ailing as quickly as they should. But Swedes also protest, often with enthusiasm, against commercial plans to redirect rivers or build dams in areas that they believe should be preserved as national sanctuaries.

Glimpses of Spring

> On May Day the Botanical Gardens are opened for the official spring celebration. The air is sweet with the scent of maple. "Awakened are the meadows and bumble-bees and honey-bees." Music and singing resound up towards the Castle, which is again fleetingly joined to what was once the royal garden below the terraces, a Versailles of firs and granite from the time when Sweden dreamt of being a great power.[7]

These are words written by Dag Hammarskjöld, words about spring, which, for him, links past and present. Some of these words could also have been uttered by other Swedes. More or less! If we can take the liberty to say that autumn and winter here in Sweden are linked to each other, we can also venture to say that spring and summer too are linked to each other! I have the feeling that the seasons grow into each other. In this sense the four seasons belong to one and the same family. There is something merciful about this relationship. I would call this gift the mercy of continuity, the availability of time for adjustment to weather and wind, to cold and warmth, as the year progresses. Yes, everyday life, plants and birds, times of work and feasting, speeches and dances, the present and history keep each other company.

This interrelatedness of the seasons forms and enriches the emotions. It gives rise to the language of music and poetry, the language of painting and other forms of creativity. Yes, when embraced with openness and a sense of adventure, the seasons are enriching. This is particularly true of spring.

In Sweden there is both a meteorological definition of the seasons based on the temperature conditions, and a calendar definition in which spring extends from March to May, summer from June to August, autumn from September to November and winter from December to February.

But Sweden is an oblong country and there is a big difference between north and south as far as weather conditions are concerned. For example, summer can last for five whole months in the south whereas the length of summer in the north is hardly two months.

My diary notations take some freedom in adjusting the seasonal boundaries.

Autumn on the March

Something in me, perhaps the fact that the Julian New Year (ca. September 11) in both Ethiopia and Eritrea begins in the autumn, made me begin my observations of the seasons in Sweden with autumn. This also coincides with the academic year in Uppsala, which starts on September 1. Below are my own dairy notes on the autumn of 2004, in and around Uppsala.

> It is September 8, 2004 in Uppsala and autumn is on the march. A quiet, hesitant farewell to summer! This is a period in which sunshine is combined with chill. I see greenery still hanging onto trees slowly shifting colour. Yes, autumn is on the march, on a quiet, almost totally windless morning!

> It is 11.10 a.m. on September 9th. The trees remind me of cows dozing on their legs. There is a touch of darkness or semi-darkness in the air even though the time is only 11.10 a.m. It is remarkably quiet in the children's playground or park. The play-fixtures stand quiet, in their typical Swedish red, yellow, and yellow-brownish colours. And sand on the playground, not soil that can turn into mud when it rains! I see several rowanberry trees, richly loaded with clusters of red berries. Rich clusters of berries are supposed to be harbingers of a strong winter to come, according to tradition.

Chapter 29

Creation Shedding Its Garment

All visible creation around us seems to be waiting to shed its garment, to submit and hide. A season of cold, of hunger, of dieting and inactivity is on the march. Both plants and animals seem to be engaged in withdrawal. An approaching season of fasting and sleeping!

Looking at my surroundings, I get the impression that we have an invisible painter at work. A choosy, deliberative, meditative painter who takes out a palette and begins applying paint on a tableau of green! Not on canvas but on a bushy, greenish background of branches. A touch of yellow here, light pink there; the colour of maple leaves, reddish, yellowish! The colour of flames! A touch of light brown there! The prevailing tableau is a combination of yellow, light red, and shades of these. A temporary art exhibition, short-lived, intended to appear in a wealth of colours, shine in quick succession, and then disappear.

There was once a Swedish TV programme for children, entitled *Fablernas Värld* (*The World of Fables*). Its introducer used to intone the words "*Djur är också människor*! (Even animals are human beings!)" at the beginning of the programme. One could perhaps also say, "Even leaves are human beings!" The story of leaves in autumn is a parable of life, a parable of how our bodies behave in the dusk of our lives. The trunk of the birch tree that I looked at and studied was covered by whitish bark, cut or serrated by moss, yellow-green moss, beige-coloured swellings or undulations, areas with smoothened and rounded edges. The latter betrayed a place where a bigger branch had apparently been removed. What remained spoke of a process of healing in the midst of approaching death.

On September 14, 2004, I sat on a red park bench around a circular table in what is known as *Engelska Parken (*The English Park), in Uppsala. Around me were some impressive, gnarled trees. They were high and dignified. They formed a quiet guard of honour on either side of the broad earth alley, at the end (or almost the end) of which stands King Carl XIV Johan's bust.[8] The alley, literally arched by the top branches of these gnarled trees, ends at the back of Carolina Rediviva, the main library of Uppsala University.

The maple leaves, roots, stems, and branches are putting up a brave fight, still feasting in yellow. But they too are in different stages of defeat and decay. I saw a few rowanberry trees. They have lost all their leaves. But they still display their reddish rowanberries. In abundance! Trees clothed not in leaves but in berries. A little strange! Adam and Eve needed leaves to cover their private parts in their hour of shame. A fruit led to their fall; leaves came to their rescue.

The rowanberries! How stubborn, how tenacious, how steadfast they are. When all leaves have fallen, they keep vigil. Are they reminders of colour and nourishment in the midst of creeping death? Are they givers of hope in a winter wilderness? Are they providers of last-minute nourishment to birds on their way? Why are these rowanberries so stubborn? A red presence in a world of white!

The Movements of Birds

October 19, 2004. Autumn is marked not only by the pageant of colours of leaves and trees but also by the movement of birds—in companies, in droves, in colonies. One notices them at dusk, because that is when they gather to seek a place for the night. Their flight marks the advance of autumn, in two senses. Leaves can't fly long. They fly some meters from their home bases on branches and fall close by, on the ground. Birds fly on. They refuse to fall; they refuse to wilt. At least most of them! Birds fly in search of life. They save their lives by flight, by escaping, by a change of place.

October 20, 2004. Trees, shading their leaves and growing increasingly naked, are nevertheless busy, giving eleventh-hour hospitality to birds on the move southwards to warmer latitudes. These are birds fleeing from approaching winter. Trees, losing their vigour and bending their strength in the face of advancing autumn and approaching winter, make their last resources, the crumbs from their once rich tables, available to colonies of hungry birds on their pilgrim journeys southwards. What good hosts these trees are!

Once, in the early 1950s, a bird with a Swedish metal-plate tag identifying its place of origin was discovered in Ambo, Ethiopia, with the tag still attached to one of its legs. Swedes on a hike or a hunting expedition in the Ambo area found the bird. Imagine their surprise and the depth of their emotions.

October 26, 2004. Massive peeping outside, as I lie in bed. Waves of peeps! A thousand-headed choir tuning up or singing in early dawn. It was about 7.30 in the morning and I was already awake, though still half-asleep, and I recognized the noise and din again. The noise is a recurrent phenomenon in Sweden's succession of seasons. Birds in flight! A whole colony of them, performing their own air show as they flew in meandering, waving belts of advance, up and down, right and left, but always forward.

These birds had certainly spent the night crowding, jostling in the scantily clad trees in our neighbourhood in Uppsala. Now, at some strange signal, at some magisterial summons, at some mysterious "Go!" that must have sent vibrations into a whole flock fauna, the birds were on the move again.

Winter 2004–2005
The Church Year

Here are the winter-observations of an African, with only some decades of stay in the country!

The Church Year in the Church of Sweden begins with the First Sunday of Advent, at the gateway of winter, a colourful church festival marked by candlelight, music, singing, buns, and lussekatter, the saffron-buns eaten on Lucia Day (December 13th). We have the season of Christmas gliding gently into the season of Lent which in turn culminates in the Festivals of Easter and Whitsun. There are flowers for the different seasons. Amaryllis for Christmas, daffodils for Easter, to give but a couple of examples! Plants and flowers are the language of the Church Year too.

Today is November 28, 2004, the eve of the First Sunday of Advent, the four-week-long period that announces and prepares the faithful for the birth, the coming (advent) of Christ. It is 5:43 p.m. and I am sitting in Löten Church, our home-congregation in Uppsala. There is expectation in the well-lighted church, people filling the sanctuary. One hears the happy and expectant chatter of those who have already taken their places. It is still fifteen minutes before start time, but the church is almost full. A children's choir is still practicing. 5.58 p.m. The church is literally full but people are still coming in, now filling the annex. These concerts are of high quality and provide light and inner warmth in early winter.

Tomorrow, November 29, we shall be celebrating the First Sunday of Advent. We shall be moving on to the third *årgång* (an annual cycle of Bible-texts to be read in church). Sweden lives with two related cycles: a cycle of the seasons of the climatic year and a cycle of the Church Year, which also affects the life and traditions of the secularized.

There are families of light givers that help Swedes and dwellers in Sweden to ply through the approaching dusk of autumn and the thick darkness of winter. They are companions, escorts on the trek through winter. One such family goes by the name of candles, candles of all sizes, heights, thicknesses, colours, and shapes. Candles placed on stands of carved, sculptured glass, or candles atop graceful candle stands of ceramic, wood, or metal. Their flames dance, bow down, do courtesies, move side to side, stretch upwards and downwards.

The Nobel Feast

One of the events that create light and joy just before onset of calendar-winter is the "Nobel Feast" in honour of Alfred Nobel. The awarding of prizes and the traditional Nobel Dinner is always held on December 10th, the day on which Alfred Nobel died. A mighty tradition, a tradition embellished by colour, music, ceremony, entertainment, marching in, and walking out. Menus of the most elaborate nature and clothes of the most exquisite variety are a part of this Northern pageant, which representatives of the wise of the entire world attend.

This is a festival that mobilizes and recruits the young and the old, the royal family and the government, artists, Swedish culture, a building whose walls whisper of past glory. Here is a festival in honour of a son of this northern nation, who left his wealth from the production of dynamite, a warlike discovery, to people who would devote their energy to the search for truth and peace.

Here is a day and an occasion that lets light, colour, art, music, cuisine, and rhetoric shine. Here is a feast where royalty and young university students, republicans and monarchists, classical music and modern compositions jostle. This is the manger, the academic "Bethlehem" as it were, to which the wise men from countries in all directions of the compass come, bearing their gifts.

The Hurricane "Finn"

On December 22, 2004, the hurricane called "Finn" struck here in Sweden. One gives names to hurricanes, especially the names of females. "Finn" however, need not be feminine. I think it has a masculine ring. The weather didn't turn out to be the terror that it was feared it would be. But we had slush, snow mixed with rain and wind. Wet, wet, wet! Wet snow blowing into our eyes, ears, bicycle helmets, gloves, etc. There were reports of busses sliding off the road, talks of collisions and trees falling on electric lines. And, of course, warnings against wet snow, freezing and causing slippery roads and highways, the terror of holiday-time drivers!

A Snowless Christmas Eve

It is Christmas Eve, 2004, in Rinkeby, a suburb of Stockholm, the majority of whose residents are of "non-Swedish" origin. Our daughter Mimmi, a teacher, and her husband Ragnar, a lawyer, live here. From a window in their flat I can look out on a Christmas Eve bathed in sunshine. The sky is almost totally blue. The grass is greenish yellow or yellowish green.

The trees are naked, but I also see that one side of the pine trees is richly supplied with branches. There is a wooden fence separating the residential area from the local school. Sunshine plays through the cracks between the planks of the fences. Green grass with light playing on it!

New Year's Eve and the Aftermath of the *Tsunami*

Five minutes to midnight, New Year's Eve. Jan Malmsjö, a well-known Swedish actor, is reciting—nay, declaiming—Tennyson's "Nyårsklockan" (literally: "New Year's Bell") with great emotion.[9] This year, New Year's Eve was celebrated in the shadow of the *Tsunami*, the devastating flood caused by an earthquake in South East Asia, with one hundred thousand people, many from Sweden, dead. One line in Tennyson's poem reads, in Swedish, "*Ring den frusna tiden åter varm!*" ("Ring the frozen epoch back to warmth!").

Today is the 13th of January. The first two weeks of January 2005 have been characterized by weather reminiscent of autumn. The aftermath of the *Tsunami* has kept Sweden at a fever-pitch. It has shaken the whole county. The whirlpools, the ominous rings from the waves, were far away and yet so palpable, so audible. The powerful have been rendered powerless, the rich rendered poor, hope has turned into despair, joy into sorrow, laughter into tears. Last week, on the 6th or 7th of January, storm-winds in southern Sweden felled trees, destroyed electric and telephone cables, and made it impossible for thousands of families to get water and electricity. Many farm communities were suddenly cut off from people. Nature is showing its teeth. Nature growling or snarling or roaring!

Today, January 15th, reminds one of early spring or late autumn. The time doesn't quite have winter's usual garb—soft, white snow. Things were different in the 1970s, our first years in Sweden. Then we had sturdy, clean, challenging winters!

Notes

1   Dag Hammarskjöld, Castle Hill, Dag Hammarskjöld Foundation, 2000. See also Bengt Thelin's article: "Dag Hammarskjöld, Nature Landscape, Literature" in *development dialogue*, 2001, pp. 81–90.

2   Dag Hammarskjöld was born in 1905 and died in a plane-crash in 1961 while trying to solve the conflict in the Congo. For some unknown reason, possibly sabotage, his plane crashed near Ndola in Zimbabwe. He was The Secretary General of the United Nations from 1953-1961. He was a Member of the Swedish Academy from 1954 to 1961 and was awarded The Nobel Peace Prize in 1961.

3   Paul Tournier, *A Place for You: Psychology and Religion*. Harper and Row,

1968.
4 Dag Hammarskjöld, *Castle Hill*, 2000, pp. 5–6.
5 Dag Hammarskjöld, *Castle Hill*, 2000, p. 18.
6 Dag Hammarskjöld, *Castle Hill*, 2000, pp. 14–15.
7 Dag Hammarskjold, *Castle Hill,* 2000, 20.
8 Carl XIV Johan was Marshal Jean Baptiste Bernadotte, Prince of Ponte Corvo, and a former general of Napoleon Bonaparte. In 1810, he was elected as successor to the Swedish throne, to which he ascended in 1818.
9 The English equivalent to *Nyårsklockan* is Tennyson's poem *Out, Wild Bells*, published in 1850, and translated into Swedish by Eduard Fredin.

Year 2005 (2019)
Chapter 30

On the Seasons Around Uppsala (II):
Outbursts of Joy

We are already in meteorological spring. Next Sunday, March 20th, is Palm Sunday, according to the Gregorian Calendar, also *vårdagsjämningen*, the vernal (spring) equinox. Note that the word *vår* (spring) is used here.

It is the 22nd of March, 2005. The snow is melting, rivulets are on the go and pools growing in volume. Cars and bicycles slow down as they pass passengers separated from a speeding vehicle by a shallow pool. Spring seems to be on the way. I feel, but one never knows. *Dagens Nyheter*, one of Sweden's main daily papers, for Saturday, the 19th of March, had an article with the title: "*Den märkligaste våren sedan 1941* (The Most Remarkable Spring Since 1941)." The words are a quotation from an elderly woman who lives in Södra Virestad, in southern Sweden, not far from Malmö. An elderly woman, 91 years of age, had to have the help of her son-in-law because of the flooding of her garden and courtyard.

On Saturday, March 26th, at midnight, the clock was moved one hour ahead. Here is an accommodation of time to make it possible for people to enjoy longer stretches of daylight and sunshine. Positioning of oneself for spring and summer!

Sweden lives for spring. This is the gentle thesis, the soft slogan of my present essay. Swedes, old and young, native and naturalized, are either in a state of longing for the spring yet to come or in a state of nostalgia for the spring that has passed.

Spring is "hope fulfilled." It is waiting rewarded. There is an "At last!" about spring. That is what makes its special. Spring is the gentle invasion of northern time in which the grip of winter's cold and darkness is broken. Spring is the mother of summer. And as a parent it deserves to receive primacy of honour in the hall of the seasons.

A Special Welcome to Spring!

The celebration of May Day is indeed a way of underlining the importance of spring. Here follow some of my observations on the celebration of the eve of May Day in 2005. The celebration was held on the sloping ground leading up to Castle Hill and to Carolina Rediviva, the renowned library of Uppsala University.

At 3.00 p.m. on April 30, 2005, a sea of whitecaps surfaced from nowhere and filled the air. The waving of the symbol-saturated head cover, by excited arms, accompanied by innumerable acclamations, was followed by the placing of the student cap on thousands upon thousands of heads, male and female, youthful and grey, hairy and bald. The person, who led the time-honoured ritual was Bo Sundqvist, the Rektor Magnificus (Vice-Chancellor) of the University of Uppsala. A hum, a shout, a sound of jubilation surged through the crowd, consisting of individuals standing on slopes, hanging from trees, looking out of balconies. And someone took up the famous student song, "*Sjung om studentens lyckliga dag* (Sing of the Happy Student's Day)," composed by Prince Gustaf, Duke of Upland (1827–1852), the "Singer Prince" of Sweden, whose statue stands next to the library and is now surrounded by the jubilant crowd.

Valborgsmässoafton—the official welcoming of spring, at least among the students in Sweden, and in particular in Uppsala, where it is just as often called Last of April! Two propeller-driven planes of an older vintage flew a salute. This was the peak of a Swedish spring at a university town. The fact that there was a drizzle as the song was sung didn't seem to diminish the enthusiasm of the holidaymakers. The band and its leaders as well as the crowds were determined that this should be the ushering in of spring. Prior to the culminating ritual known as "The Putting On of the Cap," I had watched the *Forsränning* (floating competition) on the River Fyris.

It was striking to see what went into this celebration. In the first place we have the students themselves, with their imagination and fantasy. They had made the various water-going floats, constructed with a great deal of imagination and humour, for the short and often hilarious journeys on the only waterway that goes right through Uppsala, *Fyrisån* (the aforementioned River Fyris). The celebration gathered hundreds—nay, thousands—of spectators on both sides of the river. Water is an important part of life in

Sweden and water that begins to flow without reverting to ice, after being frozen during the winter, is a sign of spring.

The Song: Spring Has Come!

Prior to the arrival of the Rektor on the balcony of the university library, some ten minutes before 3:00 p.m., the "halo man" of the band called *Wijkmanska Blecket* led the crowd in singing a song in which the words "*Våren är kommen!* (Spring has come!)" were repeated, in spite of the fact that the weather was not optimal. This band started setting up its podium or platform on the stairs of the Carolina Rediviva Library around 1.45 p.m. The way the members of the band were dressed, the motley and utterly bohemian character of the group, betrayed an intentional minimization of the status of a group that is in fact made up of capable musicians. Together with the Rektor Magnificus on the elevated balcony of Carolina Rediviva were representatives of officialdom in its various categories.

What was even more impressive was the fact that the speaker of the Swedish Parliament, Björn von Sydow, was there with his wife. I saw Adjutant Bishop Ragnar Persenius, presumably a stand-in for Archbishop K. G. Hammar. I met Thomas Ekstrand, my colleague from the Theological Faculty, until recently Prefect but otherwise a Docent within the Department of *Tros- och livsåskådningsvetenskap* (Systematic Theology). I asked whether he was on his way to join the choir. No, he had been invited to a reception. He was the first one to give me the first-ever hint that there was an official reception on this occasion. I saw my friend Per Ström, Chief of Protocol at the University, offering a modest wave of the hand from the balcony. Slim of shape and always well dressed! I even caught sight of Anders Wall, a rich man who has donated millions of crowns to the University to promote important research. He has also provided financial help to the church at Vittinge, Uppland, that was once attended by his parents. Every summer he subsidizes concerts with high-quality music, held in the church where his parents once worshipped.

Icons of the Eve of the May Festival

There are some characteristic items (let us call them "icons") that are inseparable from spring and from *Valborgsmässoafton*. These icons are the beer bottle or can, the champagne glass or bottle, the cigarette, the plastic cup (sometimes dangling from the neck, at the end of a cord), and now even the mobile telephone.

The most distinguishing icon, however, is the student cap. Whether it is as white as snow or has turned yellow from the onslaught of weather or wind or from lack of sunshine, the cap is *the* thing. It is the mark of belonging. A landmark marking a transition, an initiation into adult life and spring!

Rektor Magnificus would actually come down to ground level, outside the entrance to Carolina Rediviva, to join the students who were dancing. At times the band played shabbily, poking fun at their art. They created an atmosphere in which the musical, the artistic was mixed with the clownish. There was indeed a mild drizzle during the putting on of the cap, the so-called *mösspåtagning*. For many a Swede, both native and naturalized, the overcast weather and the mild drizzle were tantamount to the loss of the golden lining of the festive atmosphere, the absence of the cream on top of the cake. But for Aboy Aregai Kibreab, my 90-year-old Eritrean friend, who was also out to witness the many-headed spectacle, the drizzle was TSäbäl(ጸበል , "holy water"), some kind of "chrism" (holy oil). A blessing! That is what an oriental culture can introduce into a more or less rational, cerebral Nordic way of looking at things.

Summer 2005—from My Diary
Midsommarafton (Midsummer Eve)

I have maintained that Swedes live for spring. But they also live for *summer!* They live for a chance to get back to their summer garden plots (their allotments), their summer cottages, with walls painted red and doors and windows painted white! Surely Swedes live for the celebration of *Midsommarafton* (Midsummer Eve), with its menu of dressed herring, fresh potatoes, *Janssons frestelse* (Jansson's Temptation, sliced herring, potatoes, and onions baked in cream), and strawberries with cream! Swedes live for summer vacation in July!

Those who have celebrated a sunny Swedish *Midsommarafton* (Midsummer Eve) with song and dance around the May Pole, in Leksand or Rättvik in the Province of Dalarna or even at *Disagården* here in Uppsala, surely know the heights to which Swedish feelings can rise. And how easily newcomers to Sweden can be drawn into the jovialities around the May Pole!

Today is June 21, 2005. About a quarter of an hour ago, ca. 8:30 a. m., I heard the morning news in which the weatherman said: "At 8:46 the summer solstice will have been a fact. It is now 8:58. Twelve minutes have passed since the magic point of time called 'the summer solstice'."

On the occasion of the celebration of Sweden's newly promulgated National Day, June 6, 2005, the question *"What is Sweden?"* appeared on the editorial page of one of Sweden's evening papers, *Expressen*. Some of the journalists at the paper came up with the following replies: "*A Map ... No one knows ... Shyness ... One thing ... An idea ... Weather.*" They then elaborated on these replies. The journalist who contributed the very last reply, Tommy Hammarström, complained bitterly about "hellish rains, devilish patronization, north-westerly breezes and local tax offices." He then continued: "But then the sun comes out and the lake, adorned in its garland of deciduous woods, begins to glitter. And nowhere in the world does one have a better view as one does here. That is Sweden for you, the best motherland on the earth."

Hymns and the Seasons

The hymnbook of the Church of Sweden has a section entitled "*Årstiderna* (The Seasons of the Year)." Under it there is a hymn by the famous Danish theologian and hymn writer, N. F. S. Grundtvig, which builds on the theme of spring. On April 24, 2005, we sang the hymn that begins with the words, "*Likt vårdagssol i morgonglöd* (Like the springtime sun in the glow of morning ...)*,*" written in 1846 and set to music by Archbishop Nathan Söderblom in 1915. The hymn weaves spring beautifully into the theological subject of the Resurrection of Christ. No joy without sorrow. No fruit without pruning. So too in life!

There are hymns for summer too. The famous hymn, written, according to tradition, by Israel Kolmodin in the late 17th century, which begins with the words "*Den blomstertid nu kommer* (The time of flowers has now come ...)" embraces both spring and summer in four of its five verses. Flowers, cultivated fields, trees, birds, and harvests are held forth as subjects for thanksgiving. Another hymn, which begins with the words "*Härlig är Jorden,*" has been translated into an English hymn that begins with the words "Beautiful Saviour, king of creation." It has a touch of Christmas about it.

Glimpses from a Summer at the Monastery of Östanbäck

June 22, 2005. Two days before *Midsommarafton* (Midsummer Eve). It is 5:07 p.m. and only some minutes before Vespers (The Evening Prayer). I am back at the Monastery of Östanbäck, a place to which I first came in the early 1970s. My place of refuge, spiritually and physically!

It is a cool summer evening or dusk, if one can at all speak in these terms about Nordic summer evenings! I am sitting in the monastery garden. This is a simple garden, the work of monks who have so much to do in other areas of their lives that they can give such a place only rudimentary care. Only white, common flowers around me, flowers whose names I don't know. And the chirping of birds and flute music coming from somewhere. We also have an evening sun playing hide and seek with gentle clouds. Someone has painted the veranda and doors on the front side of the guesthouse. A piece of paper posted on the door reads "*Nymålat* (Newly painted!)."

A massive juniper tree towers above me on the right. Brother Paul has just come out, dressed in his habit for Vespers, having taken off his working-gown, preparing for the 5.30 p.m. Vespers. Yes, I am back at the monastery. I hear a door banging shut. Perhaps at the workshop where the brothers make candles. Saw a brother hurrying away, surely to Vespers, in which I too am planning to participate.

It is clear that I have been away from the monastery for a long time. At my place in the dining room the little slip of paper bearing my name is now gone. I got a serviette all right but not in a serviette holder but rather in an ornamented (wooden) ring, a nice handiwork, one reminiscent of products from the province of Dalarna. Something related to the famous *Dalahäst* (Dala horse). The new dining room is a new creation, in wood panel. There is now a pulpit-like enclosure, from which Father Caesarius addressed us at the end of the evening meal.

The monastery is a place where all the seasons of the year are compressed into a day and a night, a twenty-four-hour period. Here, in the hours of prayer, spring, autumn, winter, and summer are accommodated. In the stations of prayer known as *Vigilia, Matutin, Ters, Sext, Non, Vespers,* and *Completorium,* one experiences the seasons of the year, the seasons of life. And these times of prayer at a monastery are a challenge to Nature, a harnessing of Nature, a way of transcending Nature itself. Here one doesn't have to wait for the shifting of the seasons. In one and the same Eucharistic service, there is, as it were, the death of winter, the resurrection of spring, the fruition of summer, the ageing of autumn. Be it cold or hot, dark or light, truth, life and experience are compressed into worship. And thus one experiences something of life at its best. One has time, solitude, quiet, and a proven tradition of spiritual guidance at one's disposal. Here the telephone, the radio, the TV, or advertisements are not allowed to reign. Even meals are almost always eaten in silence, to the accompaniment of reading at lunchtime and music in the evening. Neither spring nor high summer is worshipped as if they were gods in their own right. Worship, the summons of the King, the *leitourgia* (the lay peoples' work for the king), have precedence over the warm rays of the sun.

Chapter 30

Comments Related to Experiences around the Seasons:
Midsummer in Northern Sweden, 2019

My wife Gennet and I, as well as two relatives from Atlanta, Georgia, Samuel Awalom and Awotash Kefela, were in northern Sweden at Midsummer time in 2019. We were guests at the lovely farmstead home of former Swedish missionaries to Eritrea, Aina and Bertil Holmgren, in Tuvan, not far from Skellefteå. On the wall in the small bathroom upstairs I saw a poster entitled, "*Några av Sveriges vanligaste fåglar* (Some of Sweden's Most Common Birds)." The poster showed 14 varieties of birds. I read the short descriptions under each picture. There was one recurring theme in a number of these descriptions. The theme of migration!

The *Gräsand* (mallard, a kind of wild duck) is described as a migratory bird that moves southwards to Western Europe during winter. The male and female *kråka* (crow) keep together throughout their lifetime, and some of them fly to Denmark in wintertime. Most *fiskmås* (gulls) move to Western Europe during the autumn. The birds known as *tofsvipa* (lapwing, peewit) return to Sweden already in the month of March.[1] Some weeks later, Aina and Bertil wrote the following words to us:

> During our years in Eritrea we were fascinated, on many occasions, by the migratory birds which we could see both there (Eritrea) and in the northern part of Sweden where we live. The places which have given us most of our reminiscences of wagtails and swallows are Tuvan outside of Skellefteå and Kunama (or Gash Barka) in Eritrea's western lowland. Here, in Sweden, and in Eritrea, the wagtails trip around (with mincing steps) and the swallows crisscross the air, hunting for insects, in different places and at different times of the year.[2] This fact reminds us of the fact that we human beings, in different parts of God's creation, are indeed united, in spite of all that separates us. Seen from God's point of view, Eritrea and Sweden belong together. The flight of the birds, fascinating as it is, triggers, as it were, also our human thoughts on the inscrutable implications of the, often, highly risky flight of human beings between different parts of God's creation.

They certainly had in mind also Eritreans and Ethiopians who had come to Sweden either voluntarily or as refugees in flight (like the birds) from the "winters" of war and other forms of unbearable circumstances.

Comments on My Articles on the Seasons in Uppsala County

Maria Nygren, a medical doctor, writes:

> I like your descriptions of autumn and all the fantastic colours best. The descriptions are captivating and vivid, and one feels that you yourself like autumns very much!? The invisible painter is active, but at the same time a process of dying, of being stripped, is in progress. I myself like autumn more than any of the other seasons. Let everything that is unnecessary disappear! Let me miss all flowers! Let me see only that which is important! That which is left! *"When the trees lose their leaves, one sees farther away from our kitchen."* This is the title of one of Tomas Sjödins's books.[3] Wonderful!

With a friendly greeting

Maria Nygren

Notes

1 According to Longman's Dictionary, the lapwing is a small black and white European bird with raised feathers on its head.

2 According to Longman's Dictionary, the wagtail is a small European bird that moves its tail quickly up and down when it walks!

3 Tomas Sjödin is a well-known pastor and author here in Sweden. The trials that he and his family have experienced, have equipped him to speak to people faced by trying circumstances.

Year 2005
Chapter 31
Glimpses from Eritrea's Battlefields (I):

Reflections on Nakfa—The Town on the Rock

Places are quiet storytellers. And in that role, they outlive generations. Such places are sources of inspiration and dearly acquired lessons. Names of battlefields like Hastings (1066), Waterloo (1815), Adwa (1896), El Alamein (1942), and Dunkirk (1944) awaken both pride and pain, among victor and vanquished. On March 22, 1977, the town of Nakfa, in northern Eritrea, fell into the hands of *tägadälti* (ተጋዳልቲ—literally, "strugglers" or "contenders"). It is twenty-eight years [i.e., at the time that this article first came out!] since this event—with such far-reaching consequences for the emergence of Eritrea as a nation—took place. Two and a half decades are long enough for a child to be born, grow up, be educated, acquire a profession, establish a family, and start producing children. But this is also long enough for people to begin forgetting events with deep symbolic value.

Those who regard war from a safe, poetic distance are tempted to glorify it and sing its praises. I have no intention of joining such a company. However, I do believe that something can be salvaged from the ruins of war. After all, roses grow in the midst of thorns. And war does, sometimes, bring out some of the best qualities in human beings. There are many instances of human concern, courage, and selflessness displayed in the midst of the horrors of battle. And there is one virtue associated with Nakfa, the quality of *Tsin'At* (ጽንዓት — Tenacity). Hence its well-earned epithet, "The Town on the Rock."

To Keren and Onwards

Permit me to share my impressions of Nakfa with you, from a trip undertaken to "The Town on The Rock" just over a year ago. The date was February 24, 2004. My hosts from the Eritrean War Disabled Fighters Association (EWDFVA) and I started from Asmara roughly around 5:30 in the morning in our Toyota Land Cruiser. The car was something of a bulldog, perfectly fitted for the terrain on which we were going to travel. We passed Imbaderho, Serejeqa, and Deqemhare (እምባ-ደርሆ ፡ ሰረጀቃ ፡ ደቀምሓረ) in quick succession. In the dim light of dawn, we could see some early risers, hurrying on their sandal-clad feet, canes in hand. Some raised their hands prayerfully, entreating the driver to stop and give them a mercy ride. At 6:30 we passed Addi Tekelezan (ዓዲ ተከሌዛን), the home of my wife's parents and their ancestors. I could see her uncle's humble "snack bar" to the right of "the main highway in town," still shrouded in receding darkness.

On we drove, along a road with endless curves, ascents, and descents. News and music from the radio and fold after fold of rugged hill country kept us company. We climbed or descended on a road twisting perilously, snake-like, as we leaned in towards the protective feet of many a slope and tried to keep away from the edges of yawning precipices. For me, a passenger from the tamed highways of Sweden, the hill-hugging, cliff-skirting road to Keren was a nightmare. Our driver, a former *tägadalai* (ተጋዳላይ—guerilla fighter), was however in perfect control of his vehicle. On to *Ilaber'Id* (ዒላ በርዒድ) and *Keren*, whose distant hills were enveloped in morning mist.

In Keren we ate *shehanfool* (ሸሓን ፉል) for breakfast at Geza´ee Haile's Breakfast Café (ገዛእ ሃይለ ቤት-ቁርሲ). This was the first time I had eaten this morning meal (with a Sudanese ring to it!), a combination of a spiced, sauce-like vegetable dish and breakfast food. I enjoyed it thoroughly. After our pause in Keren, with some of its ambitious buildings (which included an imposing Catholic cathedral), we drove on through more sparsely populated regions. We advanced through simple checkpoints marked by pieces of cloth flapping in the wind, sleepy villages with humble huts, and small towns that boasted a shop and an eating place. There was an arid beauty about the countryside through which we drove, with its mountain ranges and bush-dotted valleys. We drove past Ad-Shrom (ዓድ-ሽሮም) and its carcass of "enemy" tanks. We crossed dry riverbeds, waving to many a camel or goat owner, often with an axe balanced on a shoulder. Bareheaded or turbaned, these children of the Eritrean wilderness seemed neither hurried nor worried.

The Climb

At 10:30 a.m., our Toyota Land Cruiser started climbing the road up to the Rock. The vehicle must have started using its entire horsepower, as it roared and whined on, slowly, respectfully but stubbornly. Symbolically, the vehicle, clad in metal and moving on sturdy tires, was evidently doing what strugglers (ተጋደልት) had done over two decades ago, slowly, laboriously, in khaki shorts and on feet covered by simple rubber-bottomed sandals. All around us, valleys kept opening and disappearing in rugged curtains, as we left them both behind and below us. We stopped by a ridge and looked down on former trenches, once occupied by Ethiopian and Eritrean soldiers, alternately. I have read accounts of how cold it can be at night on these heights. But we were travelling in a comfortable car, in good sunny weather.

The terrain awakened in me some of the pictures painted in the words of the late Ethiopian journalist and author Be'alu Girma in his Amharic novel, *Oromai* (meaning *Too Late*):

> Sahel is cursed ground, filled with mountains, linked like chains and speeding out of sight, from horizon to horizon; like skyscrapers piercing the space heavenwards, these sharp, stony elevations; like the open mouths of hell and the yawning jaws of Sheol. ... The mountains provide neither paths for the feet nor crags for one's toes to dig into. Not even monkeys (leave alone human beings) can find this terrain hospitable! ...
>
> Some mountains are shrouded in fog, up to their shoulders, resembling proud highwaymen, standing wrapped in their gowns, contemptuous of the world. This is the natural fortress that the enemy has chosen to give battle.[1]

We climbed on, negotiating one curve after another. This was movement to higher ground, physically and emotionally. Those who once scaled these heights must have done so at the cost of blood, sweat, and many an uncertain moment. And surely, for those who had to climb down, the descent must have felt dark and depressing. Our ascent up the Rock was far less dramatic, far less demanding. Our guide continued his narrative about the quiet secrets that these rocky slopes harboured. There is a saying in

Tigrinja: "To narrate about these events is easy!" (ክትዛረቦ ቀሊል እዩ), the implication being that words can never do justice to events.

At last we a saw the sign, "Welcome to the Land of Tenacity!" (እንቋዕ ዓዲ ጽንዓት ኣቶኹም), a name of honour given to Nakfa. We were now approaching the outskirts of The Town on The Rock. A training centre was the first building complex that met our eyes. Finally, we drove into the mystical town, unchallenged.

The Town on the Rock

We were welcomed by some local representatives of the Eritrean War-Disabled Fighters Association (EWDFA) at their offices, a building with a commanding view over Nakfa town. We then went out to look at the historic place. Our eyes took in the skyline with the help of a pair of binoculars. A mosque or two were in evidence, as was the local Orthodox church, located on elevated ground at one edge of town. We visited some government offices (manned meagerly that day because of a religious festival), we saw the signs of a cemetery in the midst of town, paused at Nakfa's town square, and looked into some shops, cafés, and simple eating places. And, of course, took pictures.

The local Orthodox church was celebrating the yearly festival (*nigdet* – ንግደት ኪዳነ ምህረት) of *Kidane Mihret* (The Covenant of Mercy), a commemoration of The Virgin Mary. A former fighter received us in his home. After some time, his pious wife returned from church, clothed in white, with her baby strapped on her back. She and her helpers gave us a delicious, vegetarian meal, appropriate to the season of Lent. I noticed that her husband had only one (healthy) eye and only one (natural) leg. He had paid for the soil on which he stood with the currency of those limbs!

Following a leisurely meal, we drove in the direction of the trenches of Denden. The sight of bullet, grenade, and mortar shells still dotting the rocky ground told the story of grim struggles. There were evidently battles in which flying metal filled the air. I saw the tattered remains of a military uniform. I even picked up a small, rusty medallion with some fading *Ge'ez* letters!

A Thumb Rendered Limp!

We moved on to some stony, jagged lookouts, perched on elevated terrain. These rocky posts reminded me of tall, lean, reckless individuals, balancing precariously on the edge of an ominous precipice. The highest of these lookouts had the intriguing name of *The Globe*. I climbed, at times literally crawled, up the rock. Our guide, a former fighter, had reached The

Globe well ahead of us. I soon learned that he, who had hopped from rock to rock with the nimbleness of a goat, had only one leg of flesh and blood. His other leg was of wood, a so-called *bamboulla*!²

The word *Wardia* (ዋርድያ – literally, "guard") was neatly painted on a metal-plate at the highest point of this part of The Rock. For a moment I was caught between the excitement of having arrived and the apprehension of losing my foothold. To my embarrassment, I succeeded in dislocating the *Wardia*-sign as I nervously reached out with one hand for some support! My right hand shot to the ground in an attempt to keep my feet steady.

It was then that it happened. I struck my thumb against a hard object. The pain was so intense that for a while I thought that I had broken my thumb. But no, I had only knocked it against a piece of rock. I did manage to straighten up, encouraged by the loud reassurances of my more sure-footed companions. But I was already dizzy from both the height and the pain. And I noticed that my thumb had become an aching, limp appendage. My right hand was hardly able to keep the other fingers together in a respectable grip! But this little incident was a trifling reminder of what those who were not tourists once experienced on this Rock! A reminder that one cannot pretend to play the part of those who experienced real pain and real heroism!

Or did my aching thumb perhaps have an even deeper significance? Was it an analogy for the absolute necessity of co-operation between a healthy thumb – *'Abbai 'Abäyto* – ዓባይ ዓባይቶ) and healthy fingers (ኣጻብዕ) if a hand (*id* – ኢድ) is to function well? Was The Rock in fact saying something to me about the challenges facing present-day Eritrea?

Honour to Whom Honour Is Due

His name was Erwin Rommel (1891–1944). The German general, a Field Marshal, had the respect of his German compatriots already before he took command of the German Africa Corps in North Africa during Second World War. But Rommel also won the respect of his foes among the Allied Forces. And that is the point I want to make in the following section of my reflection. Though the Allied Forces under Field-Marshal Bernard Montgomery (1887–1976) finally defeated Rommel's troops decisively at The Second Battle of El Alamein (in Egypt) in 1942, both friends and foes continued to refer to Rommel admiringly as *The Desert Fox*. He was a model of military brilliance and tenacity (ጽንዓት).

Above all, Rommel was a gentleman in war. It is interesting to note that though he was a general in the German Defense Forces (the *Wehrmacht*); he was not a member of the Nazi Party. When Lucie-Maria Rommel and Fritz Bayerlein came together and published Rommel's personal papers and notes in 1950, they chose the striking title *Krieg ohne Hass* (*War Without Hatred*) for their publication.³ A British officer (whose name I don't remember now), captured by Rommel during the North Africa Campaign and kept in prison for some time under him, later wrote a highly appreciative biography of his former captor!

Tenacity Among One's Foes

Honour to whom honour is due! Permit me to mention an unsung soldier who fell just outside Nakfa in 1977. I first read about Mammo in a book written by an Eritrean surgeon, Dr. Tekeste Fekadu, author of the fascinating account, *Journey from Nakfa to Nakfa. Back to Square One. 1976–1979.*⁴ When a young combatant handed Dr. Fekadu a letter from the Eritrean Commander of the front line at *Emba 'luqo* on March 18, 1977, only four days before the fall of Nakfa, Dr. Fekadu said to himself, "The days of Mammo are numbered."⁵

And I wondered who this Mammo was, named only by his first name. I later found out that his title and full name was Major *Mammo Temtimé* and that he was commander of the 15ᵗʰ battalion of Ethiopia's army in Eritrea. Already on the next page, Dr. Tekeste describes Mammo as "the staunch and tough commander inside Nakfa." The surgeon then adds:

> Mammo commanded the different units in the camps within Nakfa. He was tough, decisive, and cool, and had never been intimidated by the many surprise attacks we had launched during the past months. Most admitted that he was a real soldier. Although there was no hope for the Derg to hold Nakfa, Mammo was determined to fight to the last bullet. I witnessed two surprise night attacks ሁጁም (*hujum*) by our combatants from the compound-post. I was very impressed by the way he was encouraging his soldiers.⁶

Describing the events after the fall of Nakfa, Dr. Tekeste continues:

> Many (Eritrean) combatants were eager to know what had become of Mammo. He was found dead. He had allegedly shot himself just outside of Nakfa in the place where the few Ethiopian soldiers fled towards Afabet. It was a desperate attempt to escape at the last hour. Alas, he did not get credit for bravery and was labeled a traitor after Nakfa and Afabet fell into our hands. Even we combatants felt sorry that he was labeled a traitor.⁷

Honour to Dr. Tekeste Fekadu and his like, for magnanimity in the midst of war! For, indeed, honour should be given to whom honour is due! I know that cruelty and blind injustice, in war or in-peacetime, can create deep bitterness. I have full understanding for such reactions, although I cannot condone them. However, sustained and cultivated hatred is poison, both for those who nurse it and those who are targets of it. And a soldier who only hates and is intent on solely pouring contempt on his or her foes cannot be a good combatant!

Honour to whom honour is due! That too is a message from Nakfa. Such a generous attitude may very well contribute, in the long run, to the cause of mutual understanding and respect among people in conflict. Men and women of genuine courage and a true sense of justice somehow find each other, even across the chasm of bitter conflict. Be'alu Girma, author of *Oromai*, was a first-hand witness of the Derg's highly-trumpeted Red Star Campaign in Eritrea in 1982. He writes the following words, in Amharic, about an Eritrean fighter by the name of *Si'ilay BeraKhi* (ስእላይ በራኺ), one of the characters in his novel:

መቸም ጠላትም ቢሆን ጀግና ይከበራል (A hero is worthy of respect, even if he is an enemy!)[8]

Be'alu's novel describes incidents that exemplify the maxim that honour should be given to whom honour is due, regardless of the camp to which such a person belongs. It is to be remembered that Be'alu later disappeared under mysterious circumstances. From what I understand, his car was found abandoned on the outskirts of Addis Ababa. One can only speculate about his fate, but my guess is that he was liquidated, not only because he had challenged persons in the Ethiopian military, but also because he had implicitly questioned a prejudice, the prejudice that one's foes should be painted black, at all costs!

Honour to Ethiopians like Be'alu Girma and Eritreans like Dr. Tekeste Fekadu, who give credit where credit is due! This too is a lesson from the town on The Rock.

The "We" of Solidarity

Her name was Berhana.[9] She could just as well have been a Miniya or a Zeineb or a Rayet. I am not writing about Berhana because I have evidence that she was more heroic than other male and female Eritreans who fought by her side or hundreds of kilometers away. I am writing about her because of a question that she put to Dr. Tekeste Fekadu and because of the circumstances under which she asked the question. She was assisting the surgeon at an operation at the field medical unit at Tenas, in late March of 1977. Dr. Tekeste had returned from Emba'luqo clinic in the vicinity of Nakfa without carrying out the emergency operation that he had been summoned to perform. Later on, he understood that he had been called to treat a head wound to Berhe Tsa'ida (በርሀ ጻዕዳ), the Commander of Battalion 3, a senior cadre who had died two hours after he was wounded at Nakfa.

For some days, the wounded had been coming into Tenas, in a steady stream, on donkeys, on the backs of comrades, on stretchers carried by fellow fighters. They were being brought in and sorted out according to the type and intensity of their wounds. Berhana had waited anxiously during Dr. Tekeste's absence. When he came, she could no longer hold back her question. While they were attending to a patient on the primitive operation table, she asked Dr. Tekeste: "By the way, where are we now? I mean, how far had our comrades reached when you left Emba'luqo?"[10]

I cannot pride myself with knowledge of the details of the Eritrean struggle. I am sure that, as is the case with all armed struggles, there are both noble and not-so-noble aspects to this struggle. Human beings and human achievements should not be idolized. I must, however, honestly admit that when I first read Berhana's question to Dr. Tekeste, I felt electrified by it.

For me, Berhana's question reflected solidarity at its deepest and most authentic level.[11] For weeks, she and her companions had slept little, eaten frugally, rested only intermittently and worried about the gigantic challenges that faced a field medical unit not far from a blazing war front. Uncertainty was their lot during a good part of the siege of Nakfa. And yet Berhana's primary concern was not personal. There was no sign of self-pity in her question. The words, "By the way, where are we now?" was a veiled cry. Here was the quiver of the expectations of a whole people, expressed in one voice!

In Closing

Tegadelti (ተጋደልቲ – literally, "strugglers") took possession of the top of The Rock on March 22, 1977. Their arrival implied the end of trails of sweat and blood. Having visited Nakfa, crawled into some of the trenches around it, and heard some first-hand accounts of its story, I too am inclined to say, "Honour to whom honour is due!"

But to have ascended The Rock is, or should be, to realize that one has also been carried by The Rock. The valleys around Nakfa were there before valour echoed in their rugged corridors. The cliffs were there, waiting, before the climbers arrived. The terrain was there before the trenches were dug into its sides. In its immensity, variety, and durability, The Rock is a reminder of the generosity of a quiet, elderly host. Nakfa is a witness to the fact that Eritrea is an heir to allies of hidden rocks and ravines, crags and crevices, springs and streams. Moreover, the rocky-ascents and descents around Nakfa are, or should be, reminders to Eritreans of the ups and downs of fortune that any community is bound to encounter along the path of its history. To be aware of these facts and let them form one's thinking is to be wise in a quiet and lasting way. It is to listen to the voice that summons one to gratitude and humility.

"By the way, where are we now?" This was Berhana's question to Dr. Tekeste, almost on the eve of the fall of The Town on The Rock. Let us face it: Without the "we" of this question and all that it implies in terms of a common vision, a common commitment, and a common forging ahead, a small, struggling country like Eritrea would be in a sad shape. Without this "we," this inner cement, this substratum of solidarity, rooted, nurtured, and promoted consciously, along the length and breadth of the country, Eritrea runs the risk of squandering its hard-won gains. It has no greater resource, no better weapon. To say so is not to indulge in self-worship, demagogy or belligerence. It is simply to pay homage to the aspirations of generations of Eritreans, old and young, who longed and paid dearly for the preservation of their self-respect.

Peace and blessings

Ezra Gebremedhin
March 22, 2005
Uppsala

First published by *dehai.org* in March of 2005 and republished in March of 2012.

Notes

1. B. Girma, *Oromai*. August, 1991, p. 291, Kuraz Publishing Agency. Addis Ababa.
2. He was an *akale sinkul* (a war disabled person), a member of that remarkable breed of Eritreans with whom I was to spend some weeks, bouncing or cruising on roads of varying qualities and peering into trenches or looking into simple restaurants, coffee shops, bakeries and enormous baking ovens!
3. Lucie-Maria Rommel and Fritz Bayerlein, *Krieg ohne Hass* (War Without Hatred), Published by Heidenheimer Zeitung, Heidenheim. 1950.
4. Tekeste Fekadu, *Journey from NaQfa to NaQfa. Back To Square One 1976–1979*, 2002, by Sabur Printing Services, Asmara.
5. Tekeste Fekadu, p. 89.

6 Tekeste Fekadu, p. 91.
7 Tekeste Fekadu, p. 97.
8 Tekeste Fekadu, p. 65.
9 At a house of mourning here in Uppsala, in February 2005, an Eritrean woman told me that Berhana was still alive and that she was now a medical doctor in Eritrea!
10 Tekeste Fekadu, p. 96.
11 Tekeste Fekadu, p. 96.

Year 2005 (2019)
Chapter 32

Glimpses from Eritrea's Battlefields (II):

Nakfa and Nadew Commands as Remembered by Ethiopian Generals

> If what we know about Sha'ebia [EPLF] so far is to be taken for granted, it follows that, if and when it loses a battle or sustains damage, it interrupts its fighting and considers the weaknesses and strengths displayed in the battle in which it had engaged. It corrects its weak traits promptly, and takes steps to strengthen its strong traits even more. It makes efforts to gather detailed information on its enemy. On the basis of the information that it had acquired, it studies the weak and strong traits of the enemy. It then launches an irreversible attack and never comes back without accomplishing its goal.[1]

After reading the book in Amharic, *On the Battlefield* (የጦር ሜዳ ውሎ – *Yä Tor-Meda Wullo*), by General Tesfaye Habtemariam, described as one the most distinguished Generals of Ethiopia, often described simply as an Airborne Soldier, Commander of a Battalion of Special Forces, especially in Eritrea, until the end of the Battle of Nakfa in 1991, I felt that I had met an officer of unusual stature both as a person and as a military leader. His story can perhaps contribute to a measure of humility among Eritrean war heroes from Nakfa. There is a ring of authenticity in what General Tesfaye narrates in his book.

Ali Said Abdella as a Witness from Nakfa

On Sunday August 28, 2005, *awate.com* published an obituary on Ali Said Abdella, the Foreign Minister of Eritrea. He had died at home of a heart attack. By the time I read this news, I had gone halfway through my reading of Brigadier General Tesfaye Habtemariam's book, *Yä Tor Meda Wullo*. The book deals, among other subjects, with the siege of Nakfa. A strange coincidence, I thought. Tesfaye and Ali Said had a lot to do with each other, as far as Nakfa was concerned. They both survived the bitter siege, but now Ali Said was dead, not from one or two of the thousands of bullets that must have gone above, under, and past him, but from a heart attack. *Awate.com* had the following to say on the death of the Foreign Minister:

> While with the EPLF, he had several responsibilities, including that of Commander of the Nakfa Front in 1976, emerging triumphant over Ethiopia's six-month offensive. ... His role in 2001 was foreshadowed in an interview he gave *Hwyet* magazine in 1996, where he seemed to miss the days of the revolution and lamented his new life as a civilian. Here are his words,

> The field work was relatively easy because your agenda and your vision is one: the enemy. But now, the mission to reconstruct the demolished, to organize a large population; to deal with the individual who had high expectations and is faced with a diminished reality; to correct wrong attitudes – the transition is like the difference between a small lake and a wide river. It is a different life. Here, one cannot even have sovereignty over oneself. The current situation is difficult and stress-inducing. However, whether you like it or not, you have to live it! But life in the field was a different experience: there was a spirit of oneness. You are, simultaneously, a leader and a follower. You give orders; you take orders. Life is ordinary. And because you have had this life for a long portion of your life, it is hard.

Ethiopian Military Leadership

The more I read about the Ethio-Eritrean struggle in and around Nakfa, the more I feel that what tipped the balance in the various military confrontations and battles in favour of Eritrea might have been the collapse of morale, conviction, cohesion, and efficiency on the part of large sections of the Ethiopian army and not solely the tenacity and courage of Eritreans in battle. In any case, this is the impression one gets from reading Brigadier General Tesfaye's book. One wonders how things would have developed

Chapter 32

on the Eritrean war scene had Ethiopia had five generals of the calibre of Brigadier General Tesfaye.

We have the Amharic saying: "Bread that satisfies can be recognized already from the baking pan or clay-oven on which it lies!" (የሚያጠግብ እንጀራ ከምጣዱ ያስታውቃል) I feel that the saying applies to General Tesfaye. In his person we have a seed planted in the simplicity and rustic integrity of Chebbo-Guragé, in Ethiopia. He was brought up in the context of an environment with mothers who love without getting in the way of firm fathers, and fathers who give order without becoming cruel. A child brought up in the simple idyllic atmosphere of country life.

Tesfaye writes:

> Like any other child from the countryside, I grew up in the village of my birth with my age peers, fighting water-fights, mixing mud, wrestling, riding saddle-less on the back of a mule and swimming in rivers.[2]

To this simple, rustic beginning, in an environment free from malice, were added an education in agriculture, close to the soil and, lo and behold, a continuation with a military education in the context of dry, arid fields, craggy hills and mountains—yes, an education in the bosom of an arid motherland. His was an education in survival, a quiet, calm, down-to-earth, intelligent survival, partly under Russian military trainers.

The book holds forth a series of life dramas. It is a scene, a stage, where deep human tales are told and struggles exemplified. I remember the tantalizing, tricky questions that Roman officials asked in ancient days or the offers they made to convince stubborn, potential Christian martyrs to relent, to come to their senses. One sees a parallel in the wooing of besieged Ethiopian soldiers by means of the loudspeakers of the EPLF. This comes forth rather clearly in Tesfaye's book.

My mind goes to the Eritrean Dr. Tekeste Fekadu, author of *Journey from Nakfa to Nakfa. Back to Square One. 1976–1979*, about whom I have written in my *Reflections on The Rock*, in this book. He and Brigadier General Tesfaye Habtemariam are profiles in courage, inventiveness, tenacity—under extreme circumstances. These people could have led countries because of their sober common sense, their good nerves, and their practical disposition. They are the kind of people which the Bible calls "the quiet in the land" (Psalm 35:20). Tesfaye could hold the spirit of a beleaguered fort from sagging, from collapsing. But he could also administer a chaotic Keren successfully.

These two, an Eritrean and an Ethiopian, are also storytellers. Their books cover the same period, the same terrain, the same vicissitudes, the same ups and downs in the conflict between Ethiopia and Eritrea. They narrate about the same battles, skirmishes, ambushes, victories and defeats, advances and retreats, with their language lapses. The two have experienced the same events but in different capacities, as different actors. They were great survivors and mediators of survival. They are owners of that great gift of tenacity, whose other name is stamina. Both had left their families behind. They were driven by a higher or deeper cause, a lofty calling.

And my suspicion is that they both come from good families, close to the earth, children of farmer stock with simple standards of honesty and integrity. These indications or indices seep forth into the stories of their backgrounds. Their qualities were cultivated in simple, country villages, with simple virtuous mothers and fathers. These simple things are the bricks, the building blocks, from which countries are built. Not loud platforms. Not parades. Not demagogy.

I think of people like Brigadier General Tariku Ayné (1931–1980 [Eth. Cal.]), Head of Nadew Command. Tesfaye mentions him. He was appointed head of the Nadew Command, with his base at Af'abet, at the end of 1979 (Eth. Cal.) Why was he summoned to Asmara on February 6, 1980 (Eth. Cal.) and executed the following day in Addi Gua'idad (ዓዲ ጓዳይ), not far from Asmara, by order of Mengistu Hailemariam? What had he said, what had he done? If he did challenge Mengistu, wasn't that in itself a reflection of something deeply wrong in the conduct of the campaign in Eritrea?

Mengistu Hailemariam had come to Eritrea in early February, 1980 (Eth, Cal.) on a crisis visit to the top leadership of the Ethiopian army. One of the persons he met was Brigadier General Tariku Ayné. His daughter Mäqdäla Tariku Ayné, in her book about her father, *Hero Like Tewodros, Decisive Like Petros!* (ጀግና እንደ ፡ ቴዎድሮስ ፡ ቆራጥ ፡ እንደ ጴጥሮስ ፡), maintains:

> The truth that he spoke at that time made it perfectly clear that the militia-army that the government of the Derg had organized could in no way defeat the team of Shaebia and Jebha, trained as they were in guerrilla fighting. After stating clearly that there was no military capacity that could win a victory and maintain its superiority, he underlined, unequivocally, that one must create an army trained in military skills that can lead to victory and maintain the army's superiority ....

> Writers of history have witnessed to the fact that the courage of the general and his frank description of the state of military weakness at the time caused Colonel Mengistu enormous frustration. The fact that rumours of a conspiracy, aimed at unseating the government, were afoot at the time in the northern region, a development that had already become a source of worry for Mengistu, further enflamed the Chairman's worry.

Mäqdäla believes that her father's appointment was the result of ill will and something of a death sentence by officers who were against him. She quotes a certain General Amsalu to the effect that:

> Even if Tariku hadn't been executed, The Nadew Command would have been smashed. General Tariku should be admired for arguing that no military option would provide a way out and for urging that we should chose a peaceful solution. [3]

Mäqdäla maintains that, soon after the execution of Tariku:

> Shaebia (EPLF) rained its thunder on Nadew Command. The command which was equipped with more than forty tanks and more than sixty artillery-pieces and was far-better trained was completely dismantled after a three-day battle.
>
> According to Professor Gebru Tareqä, 18,000 (eighteen thousand) wounded and dead were registered after the Battle of Af'abet, which was fought after the killing of General Tariku on February 6, 1980 (Eth. Cal.) It is estimated that Nadew Command had a total of 22,000 (Twenty-two thousand) military personnel.[4]

In an article entitled *"Let the Eyewitness Speak! A Voice from Beyond the Grave,"* published, I believe, on *dehai.org* on June 12, 1999, Professor Habtamu Bihonilign quotes the following words from the reporter Tsegaye Hailemariam, on General Tariku Ayné's decision to withdraw from Hill 1702: "…supposedly the precarious gateway to Nacfa." The quotation is taken from Be'alu Girma's book *Oromai*:

> I was sitting in the shade of a magnificent boulder looking over the pages of my notes. All of a sudden, I heard a deafening volley of heavy artillery from the right flank of Hill 1702. I had a rush of adrenalin thinking this has to be the beginning of the final push. To my chagrin, Col. Tariku, the commander of the Ethiopian forces, sent a messenger urging me to go back and see him immediately. I followed the messenger to the Colonel's bunker. I did not like the look on his face.
>
> "What is going on?" I screamed in excitement.
> "We have to evacuate" he said. "at exactly 1800 hours!"
> "You must be joking!"
> "This is my order," he punctuated.
> "But why? What has happened?" I screamed, even more loudly.
>
> He explained calmly that the enemy has regrouped and moved its B-10 anti-tank, 120 and 82 mm mortars forward. Moreover, using canons and mortars from a distance, the enemy has recaptured another strategic

outpost, Hill 1755. Because our forces are dangerously exposed on the left flank, and due to the delay in the arrival of reinforcements, defending our position has become out of the question .... Since the enemy has good intelligence and is well aware of all our movements and manoeuvres, the only choice we now have is either to evacuate or suffer encirclement and annihilation.

Professor Habtamu comments:

Unfortunately, what Tsegaye Haiemariam was forced to witness was the debacle of one of the largest military campaigns in the annals of African history.[5]

Let us go back to Brig. General Tesfaye's narrative on besieged Nakfa. What he says about Colonel Mammo, an Ethiopian officer remembered with respect for his leadership in Nakfa and about Mammo's last words, is worthy of our attention. So is the story of the remarkable escape of a soldier who had been left for dead on the flight from Nakfa, and the last-minute escape of Tesfaye himself! The story of the officer who, though wounded and bleeding, led his troops until he collapsed because of loss of blood, is a reminder of the truth that courage and dedication is to be found also among those whom we regard as enemies.

General Tesfaye is of the opinion that the outcome of the battle for Nakfa did hang on a thread. According to him, a greater degree of alertness on the part of Ethiopian soldiers at Afabet, "not relaxing," as Tesfaye implies, and perhaps a quicker move on Nakfa itself would have tipped the balance. For the reader of Tesfaye's book, these innuendos add drama to the whole story around Nakfa.

My one-armed Eritrean friend here in Sweden, a person who is quite active in our Swedish Chapter of the Eritrean War–Disabled Fighters Association (EWDFVA), spoke in tears as he remembered Ali Said. He said:

I knew Ali Said personally. The siege of Nakfa dragged for months. Nakfa was cold and we were often hungry. We combatants said: "How long are we going to wait under these circumstances? ንሁጸም (Shouldn't we attack) by day and get it done with?"

Ali Said, who was a quiet, calm person, is reported to have replied. "Be patient! Things will come!"

The speaker wept as he pleaded with his audience, Eritreans now divided into different factions," How can we forget all that we have gone through!

Chapter 32

Dr. Tekeste on Tenacity Among One's Foes

Permit me to mention an unsung soldier who fell just outside Nakfa in 1977. I first read about Mammo in a book written by an Eritrean surgeon, Dr. Tekeste Fekadu, author of the fascinating account, *Journey from Nakfa To Nakfa. Back To Square One. 1976–1979.*[6] When a young combatant handed Dr. Tekeste a letter from the Eritrean Commander of the front line at Emba' Luqo on March 18, 1977, only four days before the fall of Nakfa, Dr. Tekeste said to himself, "The days of Mammo are numbered."[7] And I wondered who this Mammo was, named only by his first name.

Already on the next page, Dr. Tekeste describes Mammo as "the staunch and tough commander inside Nakfa." The surgeon then adds:

> Mamo commanded the different units in the camps within Nakfa. He was tough, decisive, and cool, and had never been intimidated by the many surprise attacks we had launched during the past months. Most admitted that he was a real soldier, although there was no hope for the Derg to hold Nakfa, Mamo was determined to fight to the last bullet. I witnessed two surprise night attacks (hujum) by our combatants from the compound post. I was very impressed by the way he was encouraging his soldiers.[8]

Describing the events after the fall of Nakfa, Dr. Tekeste continues:

> Many (Eritrean) combatants were interested in learning what became of Mamo. He was found dead. He allegedly shot himself just outside of Nakfa in the place where the few Ethiopian soldiers fled towards Afabet. It was a desperate attempt to escape at the last hour. Alas, he did not get credit for bravery and was labelled a traitor after Nakfa and Afabet fell into our hands. Even we combatants felt sorry for him being labelled traitor.[9]

It is good to be able to piece things together. Today (September 2, 2005), I finished reading the *Yetor Meda Wullo*, the Amharic version of *On the Battlefield* by Brigadier General Tesfaye Habtemariam (1997, Addis Ababa). He writes, among things, about the same battles about which Dr. Tekeste writes. We get more facts about Mammo in this account by an Ethiopian officer who had come to Mammo's rescue under dramatic circumstances and fought by his side at Nakfa to the very end. Tesfaye reproduces the text of a telegram message sent to the entire Ethiopian army on 7/2/69 from Major (later Lieutenant Colonel) Mammo Temtimé, commander of the 15th division *shaleqa* (ሻለቃ) in Nakfa. Here is part of the text (taken from the latest English version of his book):

> Two hundred of us have fought as hard as we can, day and night, for one whole month against separatists with much greater numbers and weapons. We intend to keep fighting until our last breath. Over 60 of our wounded men are suffering, rotting in the trenches. Our concern is not for our lives. We are concerned about having the weapons and equipment in our possession taken by the enemy. And, defiling the good name and reputation of our country. Since we have not received the aid we requested from our comrades while fighting all this time, we are beginning to doubt that we have a government that we can rely on and in which we can have faith. If we do have such a government and comrades who are concerned about our country and their fellow soldiers, we should be given immediate help. Not with words of support, but by action. This telegram is our final message.[10]

What Dr. Tekeste wasn't aware of, perhaps, is that, towards the end, Mammo had a courageous inventive and tireless actor by his side. This was the leader of an Ethiopian airborne unit that was dropped from unusually dangerous heights and came, against all expectations, to the assistance of Mammo and his beleaguered group in Nakfa. This fascinating story is narrated in chapters 8 and 9 of General Tesfaye's book.

After the successful completion of his parachute mission, Colonel Tesfaye meets Mammo in Nakfa. Their meeting is a mild echo of the dramatic encounter of Henry Morton Stanley (1841-1904) and David Livingstone (1813-1873) in Ujiji, Tanganyika in 1871. Tesfaye writes:

> I had not yet met Major Mammo. Major Mammo Temtem was a short, stocky man of middle age, strong and active. Later I learned that he had been transferred as an NCO from the regular army to the bodyguard unit where he had attained the rank of officer. By 1976, he'd attained the rank of major. When I arrived, he greeted me warmly.

> Good evening Captain Tesfaye. Thinking you would come, we had arranged a sleeping place for you. Why didn't you come?

> "I thought it would be better for me to stay with my troops," I replied.

> "You could easily coordinate their activities from here," he went on.

> "I could, but in airborne units we prefer for the commander to be with his troops."[11]

This was typical of Tesfaye.

Here are some of his words on the last, dramatic minutes in Nakfa. Tesfaye writes:

With our machine guns placed in the middle of our formation, we lined up and advanced towards the enemy, in a north-easterly direction. We approached enemy-trenches and started firing. We then drew our lances forward and rushed into enemy trenches. Shaebia soldiers jumped out of the trenches and fled, head over heels.

We got an opportunity that we hadn't even dreamt of, an opening that was free from the enemy. The soldiers hurried on in the direction of Afabet, without awaiting any orders! Major Mammo said, "I can't move any further. If you come out alive, give this letter to my family."[12]

With these words he handed his testament to a trusted soldier. He then added, "Listen, child! If you get into a situation in which your life is in danger, hand the letter on to someone else, with the same message that you received from me. Let him do the same, in his turn." Having said so, he turned to the left of the road and went away. After some minutes a shot was heard. Those who were with him said, "We have assumed that he had fallen after having 'drunk' his pistol," as the Amharic expression has it.[13]

Notes

1. *Yä Tor-Meda Wullo. p. 173.* [On The Battle Field], Commercial Printing Press, Addis Ababa, 1997 (Ethiopian Calendar).
2. Tesfaye Habtemariam *Yä Tor-Meda Wullo*, p. 1.
3. Mäqdäla Tariku Ayné, *Jägna endä Tewodros, QoraT 'endä Petros!* (Hero like Tewodros, Decisive like Petros!), Alfa Printers, Addis Ababa, 2007 (Ethiopian Calendar), p. 190.
4. Mäqdäla Tariku Ayné. p. 166.
5. Mäqdäla Tariku Ayné. p. 165.
6. Professor Habtamu Bihonilign, Let the Eyewitness Speak! A Voice from Beyond the Grave", p. 2. dehai.org, June 12, 1999.
7. Tekeste Fekadu, *Journey from Nakfa to Nakfa. Back to Square One 1976–1979*. Printed in 2002 by Sabur Printing Services, Asmara. See also his The Roads to Asmara, 1984–1991. Hidri Publishers, Asmara, 2015..
8. Tekeste Fekadu. p. 89.
9. Tekeste Fekadu, p. 91.
10. Tekeste Fekadu, p. 97.
11. Tesfaye Habtemariam, *On The Battlefield: A Memoir of an Airborne Soldier*. (Translated by Sahlesellssie Berhanemariam), 2018, pp. 71–72.
12. Tesfaye Habtemariam, p. 100.
13. Tesfaye Habtemariam, YeTor Meda Wullo, 1997, p. 179.

Year 2019
Chapter 33

Glimpses from Eritrea's Battlefields (III):

Göran Assbring (1950–1983), a Swede Who Gave His Life for Eritrea

This book is a collection of reflections on Sweden, Ethiopia, and Eritrea. And for good reasons! The involvement of Swedish missionaries in the area now known as Eritrea goes back to 1866. The first Swedish missionary came to Addis Ababa, Ethiopia, in 1904. There is a rich history and ample documentation on Swedish missionary activity in what is now Eritrea. Swedish archives and libraries are also well-supplied with documentation on Ethiopia.

One can say that direct Swedish missionary impacts on Ethiopia began, in earnest, in 1904, with the arrival of Carl Cederqvist in Addis Ababa, almost 40 years after the arrival of the first missionaries in Massawa. However, in time, Sweden's ties with Ethiopia became far stronger than her links with Eritrea. Permit me to quote from my book *"May This Reach Monsieur Stjärne. War-Time Correspondence between Emperor Haile Sellassie I, and A Swedish Missionary"*:

> The Emperor was so impressed by the quality of services given by Swedish missionaries in the fields of education and medical care that he had Swedes recruited to serve in The Ministry of Foreign Affairs and within the military establishment. He makes it a point not only to include accounts of the specific assignments given to these Swedes but also to lift forth the appreciation with which their labours were regarded.[1]

There were Swedes who played prominent roles in Ethiopia's hour of trial when Mussolini invaded the county in 1935. Among these were Dr. Fride Hylander, head of the Swedish Red Cross Ambulance and the pilot, Carl Gustaf von Rosen, both of whom visited the Emperor during his time of exile in Bath, Great Britain between 1936 and 1940.

What are we to say of Eritrea's struggle for self-determination and the involvement of Swedes in this struggle? In general, Swedes are champions of Ethiopia's historical claims and admirers of its royal past. The claims of Eritreans to self-determination and independence were and are often regarded with skepticism and, by some, as an expression of outright rebellion. However, this does not mean that there were no individual Swedes who took Eritrea's ambitions and dreams seriously. A significant minority did, even though they did not buy all the arguments that the Eritreans used in the propagation of their goals.

In 1987, Lars Bondestam, Philip Gottlieb, and Gunnar Stensson from EGIS (Eritrea Groups in Sweden) were invited to attend the second congress of the EPLF (The Eritrean Peoples' Liberation Front) near the town of Nakfa. About two years later, in December 1989, Lars was killed when his car hit a mine at the Sudanese border on his way back from a research tip to Tigrai. The organization known as *Afrikagrupperna* (The Africa Groups), established in 1968, did pay attention to the plight of Eritreans, although its main concern was fighting *Apartheid* in South Africa.

How I Came to Write on Göran Assbring

I had planned to write about battle literature on the Eritrean struggle for self-determination, as a contribution to the collection of writings in this book. One morning I woke up with a new idea. I thought of the book in Swedish, *I Eritrea* (*In Eritrea*) by the Swede, Göran Assbring.

The book had been published posthumously by *Bildförlaget Öppna Ögon* (The Open Eyes Picture Publishers) and *Fotograficentrums förlag* (The Photo-Center's Publishers) in 1986.[2] The copyright holders are Kalle, Lisa, and Malin Assbring. I now know that they are the children of Ingela and Göran, the author of the impressive and vivid picture-and-text book on war-time Eritrea. In fact, I did talk to Lisa some months ago to ask her if I could use one of the photos in said book. She was very kind and forthcoming. At the time I only thought that I would use a photo from the book. Now I want to write about Göran, the father of Lisa, Kalle, and Malin. This is a Swedish family that has experienced deep sorrow for the sake of Eritrea.

Under the title *Resorna* (*The Journeys*), the very last text in the book, *I Eritrea* (page 86) reads:

Chapter 33

1983. The fifth and last journey. This time too he visits The EPLF. Besides, he also visits the so-called *Betengruppen* in ELF.[3] He had plans to enter Tigray in Ethiopia, after having travelled with the EPLF. On a trip with a column of vehicles Göran is shot in an ambush.

Another source specifies that Göran (1950–1983) was in fact shot in the chest and that his body was found in a dried-out furrow of a river, somewhere on the Eritrean countryside.

I don't remember when and where I got my copy of the book *I Eritrea*. I had had it for some time. Nothing is written in it. No name. No date. On the morning of September 25, 2019, I decided to write this article.

Let me say that the book consists of a selection of texts and pictures. Håkan Pieniowski, who wrote the forward to the book, concludes with the words:

> He left behind him a large amount of material from his journeys; meticulously recorded diary notes and records of many interviews and tape recordings. We have collected the texts and pictures with which Göran was satisfied. The book has attained the status of a big report, rich in details.[4]

In the same forward, Pieniowski writes:

> Göran had a rich store of experiences on Eritrea, primarily because of his many journeys to the country, but also because of the concern he had for the liberation-struggle of the people of Eritrea. He was totally captivated by what he had experienced in a country to which he first came almost by coincidence. The friendship and warmth which Göran found in Eritrea drove him, again and again, to the country. He developed from the young adventurer that he was at the beginning to someone who arrived at an unusually deep knowledge of a subject with which very few were acquainted.

Göran began "documenting" Eritrea in 1974. It is interesting to note that it is the well-known British journalist, Basil Davidson (1914–2010), who wrote the introduction to the book *In Eritrea*.[5] These are some of his words on Göran:

> What Assbring's proficiency and dedication gave us, year after year until death took him, was a living testimony to the humanness and creativity that characterized these people either by remaining defiant in the midst of their suffering and want or by remaining assured of their ability to create a better existence, for themselves as well as for their neighbours.[6]

This is a witness to the respect that Göran and the people of Eritrea had won. The diary notes to which I have access are an illustration of the "Showers" and "Rain-Drops" that I was hoping the reader would experience in this collection of articles. Reflections in depth, expressed in a whole series of paragraphs and reflections as flashes of insight, presented in shorter texts! Most of Göran's diary notes are "Rain-Drops." His wonderful pictures on war-time Eritrea, which combine variations of austere landscape and human faces with eyes full of warmth and engaged presence, are also "Rain-Drops."[7] I have found "Showers" in his presentation of individual guerilla fighters like Aicha, Sebhat Efrem, Haile, and Goitom and in his thorough analysis of the position of women in both traditional and war-time Eritrea.[8] It has struck me that Göran, a young man from a Nordic country, far from the Horn of Africa, could develop such a hunger and thirst after knowledge about a people engaged in a seemingly impossible struggle for self-determination.

From Göran's Third Journey to Eritrea

Göran had graduated from Christer Strömholm's Photo School in Stockholm in 1974, after a two-year course. With his camera hanging from his shoulder, he made his first trip to Eritrea. I don't know how much previous knowledge he had about the country or if some person had encouraged him to undertake his first journey. But reading the following words from his diary entry for New Year's Eve, 1979, in Eritrea, moved me deeply:

> I woke up because "my father" Gerezgiher sat on my bed. A warm reunion after three years! In the evening I saw my "family" again. It was a joyful experience to be with them again and to see that they had managed to come out of the war unscathed. I was expecting to hear the worst but all stood there before me: Father (pappa), the mother Mihret and the children, fully alive, as I too was. Wonderful!
>
> The only hen at their home was "necked" (had its neck cut off) in my honour. They said that they had talked about me three days earlier and had wondered how I was doing in Sweden. They said that I had promised to send pictures and to appear in person some day. And now I was there! "It must be God's will!" Many, many hugs! A good end of the year, and of the Nineteen-seventies!"[9]

Love had taken root among the members of a simple family from the Eritrean countryside and a young Swede, born and brought up with the skills of a photographer, in an urban centre far away in the North. A meeting of hearts across barriers of geography, language, and culture!

Aicha—A Child Exposed to the Terrors of War

Göran shared not only Chicken Sauce (ጸባሒ ፡ ደርሁ) with Eritrean families but also the pains of war, separation, bomb attacks, bleeding, and death. In a section of his book entitled "Fronten" (The Front) Göran has the female name *Aicha* as a subtitle. He writes:

> The flames cast their weak light on the walls of the mountain, way down in the long valley. Close to the flames sits little Aicha and watches the kettle which is placed at the centre of the fire, blackened by soot. The chill of the night leaves her naked feet slowly, she feels how sleep creeps up her toes, advances through her legs, up her back until it reaches her dark eyes, which become heavier and heavier…They [the family] had been on the road all night. Pushed their way forward with the help of the stars, through the entire labyrinthine valleys…Aicha had already fallen asleep when the sun rises over the sharp mountain-crests and spreads its soft light over the valley.
>
> Before anyone could react, hell broke loose! Out of the sun, two pairs of silver-bright wings shoot out and release their eggs. Within some seconds the entire valley is filled by thousands of small steel-bullets which bore their way into the mountain, tear off flesh from human bodies and quench all life. Before Aicha manages to get on her feet, the two Soviet Mig-planes are back. They come in waves, with their roaring engines accompanied by the choppy bullet-sounds. Faster than sound! Again bodies are torn to bits and the sand becomes increasingly red because of blood. The planes disappear into the sun gain, as fast as they had come. Silence descends over the valley again. The two pilots have accomplished their duties. A guerilla-nest has been purged. Soon the pilots are going to sit in their mess-room, sipping away at their beer calmly, and joking with their colleagues.
>
> Aicha rises slowly, brushes the dust from her face and looks around. Her mother lies nearby, dead. In her hand she holds an unopened bundle. A little further away Aicha sees her father, lying on his stomach. The shirt is stained with blood on the back side. He too is dead. Everywhere dead camels! Aicha is alone. [10]

Indeed, Aicha is alone. What potent words! What a pregnant statement! What we meet in Göran's words is the instantaneous collapse of the world of a small girl. Loneliness, confusion, terror, poverty, and want are multiplied to the 'Nth' degree in a matter of seconds. This is the face of war encountered at first hand.

We who hear or read about war at a distance often cannot grasp a fraction of its implications for people of flesh and blood. The cost paid by thousands of simple Eritrean families in the war for self-determination is incalculable. Not only in terms of people killed but also in terms of those who are wounded, incapacitated, and separated from home and hearth! Having worked with an association for Eritrean war-disabled here in Sweden and in Eritrea, I have some idea of what the struggle for self-determination has meant for Eritreans. Not even girls like Aicha were exempted from the ordeal!

Göran's book has helped me to get rid of my naivety on the "glories" of war.

Meeting Sebhat Efrem—A Leading Fighter

There is one more experience for which I am grateful to Göran. He gave me a chance to meet a person by the name of Sebhat Efrem on the pages of his short book—Sebhat as he was about 36 years ago. Here are Göran's words:

> Hundreds of feet lift and touch the ground, with measured, rhythmic steps, on the loose sand, sand which lies like mist over the long valley. Breathing accelerates for every step. The sweat runs down young faces when they pass their leader's scrutinizing look. Hands tighten their grips around their Kalashnikovs. Suddenly the echo of a command is heard, "Zet bel!" [Attention!]. Young soldiers stand at attention and wait. A new command and the soldiers rush for shelter under the trees.
>
> We are no longer fighting against a purely African army but against a military power which is entirely administered and manned by Soviet officers."
>
> The accusation comes from Sebhat Efrem, a member of EPLF's politburo, at a lunch in his underground office, deep among the mountains in Eritrea. High above us an Antonov-plane is on a reconnaissance for guerilla troop movements,
>
> 'It has been so for a long time. At night the reconnaissance planes buzz about and then the attack planes take over. For the Ethiopians everything which moves is an enemy, a 'bandit'. Even the goats which move on the slopes of the mountains! The tent of a nomad can be suspected of being a hideout for bandits', says Sebhat Efrem.

Göran continues:

> And the Ethiopians are perfectly right. Eritrea is enemy country. For them, every living thing, human beings, animals, yes even the stones which can be suspected to hide a guerilla soldier are, are enemies. Three months ago the Ethiopian Military Junta set in motion the so-called Red

> Star Campaign in Eritrea. According to the leader of the junta, Colonel Mengistu, the goal of the campaign was to give the highest priority to the rebuilding of his "province", Eritrea. The propaganda machinery has been at work at high pressure for months. Now was the time to bring about peace, once and for all. But there was one problem which the Ethiopians must solve, once and for all. The "Bandits" in Eritrea must be removed ….
>
> Now, three months later I am sitting in the company of the "Leader of bandits", Sebhat Efrem, once sentenced to death.

To go back to Göran's words:

> The first time I met Sebhat was on a morning in the month of May, 1982, when he came into my room at the guest-house of the guerilla. He was dressed in a worn-out uniform. Around his waist hanged a cluster of hand grenades and on his head he carried his trophy, an Ethiopian floppy hat of military model. He was very polite, poured out tea with ginger and he asked me if I was hungry and tired.
>
> I was indeed tired. I had arrived at dawn after a journey of fifteen hours from Sudan, through a glowing-hot desert, up winding roads among the mountains to then arrive, fully exhausted, at the base-area of the EPLF. … Before me sat a skinny man of my age, with a mouth wounded by gunshot. A man who, together with his comrades, had rendered the Ethiopian army and its allies check-mates! He told me that the strength of Eritreans was different.

Sebhat comments:

> Lack of material is compensated by discipline and goal-consciousness, and by the certainty that the struggle is a just one, in spite of the fact it has demanded big sacrifices. This is the difference between occupation and defence.

Göran continues:

> When he gets up to go I ask him what his main task within the EPLF is.
>
> "I am a fighter", he says, in so many words.
>
> "Yes, yes!" I say. "All people here call themselves fighters. What do you do between Monday and Friday, so to say?"
>
> "I am a simple member of the politburo."[11]

What would Göran say if he were to know that Sebhat Efrem, who had come out alive from Eritrea's armed struggle, was the subject of an assassination attempt in liberated Eritrea on February 13, 2019?

Civil War Among Eritreans

There were surely a number of experiences that contributed to joy and hope in Göran's relationships to the liberation movements in Eritrea. He visited both movements and had friends in both camps. The armed conflict that finally broke out between them must have caused him deep sorrow. That he does not dwell long on the subject in the written material that we have in his book *In Eritrea* suggests that the subject was too painful for him to grapple with during his strenuous journeys in Eritrea. I am only guessing. But back to our narrative. Göran has a fighter by the name of Goitom saying:

> Sometimes our way is crossed by nomads. Their camels are fully loaded with Kalashnikovs and magazines of bullets. They pick up weapons here and there, where soldiers have fallen. And they give them to us. That is how we get our weapons.

And Göran takes over:

> At last we approach the village of Hal-Hal, which consists of some mud-huts in a long valley somewhere in Eritrea. This is the village about which Haile had narrated for us earlier. The men of the village come towards us, tell us about the battle that had taken place earlier, thank Allah for the help provided by The EPLF and offer us tea with cinnamon. Some men came forward with a cow. A sign of gratitude! This evening all are going to eat until they are fully satisfied.
>
> As the cow was being cut into bits I started wandering around the houses. For some reason, the village feels very familiar. Suddenly I saw, between the burnt-down houses, the fruit-garden where I had eaten six years earlier. At that time *Hal-Hal* was a part of ELF's stronghold. ELF is the second Eritrean liberation movement. I ate with people who were later killed or had to flee in the civil-war which was caused by political and traditional conflicts between ELF and EPLF. ELF was crushed militarily. The tragedy, the frightful waste in human life, was not only a result of fighting with Ethiopia. The tragedy was also directed inwards. In the shadow of the fruit-garden, the meat from the slaughtered cow had a different taste! I don't say anything to Goitom. Here there is no point in digging deeper into a wound which has not even begun to heal! [12]

Göran's last sentence looks short and light, but its emotional content is heavy. These words cover the darker, uglier side of Eritrea's struggle for self-determination. The ELF-EPLF conflict is a crack, a schism that has torn apart families, siblings, fellow religionists and former school mates. Those who regard war, a liberation struggle, from a safe, poetic distance are tempted to glorify it and sing its praises. Göran must have seen and pondered the fact that there are both noble and not-so-noble sides to all just struggles.

Women and Children—Hope of a Nation

Göran's engagement in Eritrea's future expressed itself not only in his documentation of the political and military aspects of the struggle for self-determination but also in his concern for people in the context of everyday life, marked by fear and instability. He writes:

> I have now, in the course of a period of ten years, had the privilege of following these people in their long and difficult struggle – a struggle which is certainly not free from mistakes and difficult miscalculations. But mistakes are, at the same time, a dialectic necessity. The decisive issue is to learn from one's mistakes and to draw the right conclusions. For me, personally, the Eritrean women are, in many senses, a strong proof of this fact, a truly living synthesis in a process full of birth-pains. To travel to Eritrea, to a land in revolution, is to land in a hurricane from which no one can escape. And in the midst of this hurricane we find the Eritrean woman in constant growth as far as numbers are concerned. I found her lying under a lorry, repairing a universal (cardan) joint, in the shadow of a tree with some nomad women, in the operating-rooms, in the classrooms and in the trenches on the front.
>
> Sara, Ghinet and little Aicha are some of these women who have raised themselves by their own efforts and made themselves visible.[13]

Before coming to the conclusions that he has expressed above, Göran had done his homework. He had observed and studied the situation of women in Eritrea and in the context of the liberation struggle.

Ghinet (the name was presumably "Gennet") was 25 years old and was working as a nurse anesthetist at the EPLF hospital when Göran met her. All night she had taken care of a patient whose head had been hit by a bullet. She took Göran down to the underground hospital where her patient lay. The poor man suffered an epileptic attack every tenth minute. Göran noticed that the patient had a T-shirt with words that glorified the struggle for the rights of women, observed on March 8.

Göran writes:

In the evening, as we sat and drank tea before the fire, and I mentioned what I had seen, she laughed at me and said: "What is remarkable about that? That is the way things should be. Here we are all comrades, men and women who fight side by side. Why shouldn't he wear a T-shirt with a message about the fight for the rights of women on his chest?" [14]

Göran knew that Eritrea's cultural attitudes towards women among both Christians and Muslims were not as bright as Ghinet had implied. He writes:

> In traditional Eritrea, marriage was and is, above all, an economic transaction among men. The men establish economic and friendship bonds with each other through their children. Marriage traditions are economically conditioned and are in the hands of male parents .... Love is an unknown concept and divorce is unthinkable .... [15]

Göran holds forth a tradition that didn't give women the right to inherit, a privilege that only sons had. He also writes about circumcision, "a thousand-year old ritual which has come to stand for an extreme example of the oppression of women." A woman who was not circumcised was regarded as a prostitute and was excluded from full membership in society.[16]

But Göran also adds:

> What is happening in Eritrea today is that thousands of young women have come to terms with their social heritage, left the kind of life in which their role had been already determined for them for centuries and cast themselves into a process whose consequences can hardly be foreseen. This is a process which has prevailed for a whole generation. With their backgrounds and, not least, in view of the enormously bloody and brutal situation, they find no patterns that they can follow. Every new step must therefore be taken with extreme care and consciousness.[17]

He was saying, in effect, that the armed struggle had provided women in Eritrea a measure of escape from the cruel restraints of tradition and culture. Closely connected with the fortunes of women are the fortunes of children. Göran has Ghinet saying:

> Children know everything about death before they have learnt to know life.[18]

This is a sobering statement and I presume that specialists in the study and treatment of traumas would grow somber in the face of such assertions. Ghinet had a child whom she and her husband tried to meet as often as possible. Their child was supplied with food and clothing by EPLF. However, she underlined the fact that it was important for her to avoid pregnancy. There were more than 3,000 children at the Revolution School at the time when she met Göran. To provide food, clothes, medicine, and schoolbooks to so many children was a headache even for a movement whose motto was "Never kneel down!"

I have often thought of the consequences of conflicts like the Vietnam War on parents and children, both in Vietnam and in the USA. Ghinet tells Göran:

> The war has been on for such a long time that no one really knows what it means to live in peace. Now, I am fighting so that my child can grow without being anxious about Soviet Mig-planes. I shall perhaps never experience that moment, but I know that it will come.[19]

Göran too must have lived with that hope, until an ambush and a bullet ended his life in Eritrea sometime in October of 1983.

Note on "*Betengruppen*"

In reply to a question from me, Professor Tesfatsion Medhanie wrote the following explanation on "*Betengruppen*," which Göran visited on his last trip to Eritrea, in 1983:

"Bettin" is a Tigrigna word which means "scatter" or "split". The infinitive verb is "mibitan" (to scatter or divide). What came to be known as Bettin was a faction that emerged in the ELF when the latter retreated to the Sudan following the EPLF-TPLF offensive. There was a crisis in the ELF. There was disagreement within the leadership and between the bases and the leadership. When Abdullah Idris and his followers left the Sudan and went back to Eritrea to restart armed struggle, the ELF forces in Sudan became increasingly embroiled in accusations and counteraccusations. Big sections of the bases or the masses of ordinary fighters and cadres demanded the resignation of the whole leadership and its replacement by a new one. The ELF in Sudan was thus divided into two - one comprising mainly the former leaders (but including some from the bases), and another comprising mainly the bases (but including a few from among former leaders, notably Ibrahim Idris Toteel). In the course of exchanging accusations, the two groups gave "names" to each other. The bases called the leadership group "Tiar-am", an Arabic phrase meaning "general tendency"; and the leadership group called the bases "Bettin" indicating that the latter was divisive and destructive. Bettin later assumed the name "Saghim" and joined the EPLF. But many of them became disappointed; they abandoned the EPLF and went to Tigray where they were accommodated by the TPLF and assumed a new name again. They are very small and still based in Tigray.

Notes

1. Ezra Gebremedhin (Editor: Martin Nilsson): *May This Reach Monsieur Stjärne. War-Time Correspondence between Emperor Haile Sellassie I, and A Swedish Missionary* (Uppsala: EFS Budbäraren, 2017), p. 49.
2. Göran Assbring, *I Eritrea* (In Eritrea), published by *Bildförlaget Öppna Ögon* (The Open Eyes Picture Publishers, and *Fotograficentrums förlag* (The Photo-Center's Publishers), 1986.
3. On the meaning of "Betengruppen", see note at the very end of this chapter.
4. Göran Assbring, p. 7.
5. In 1988 Davidson made an arduous journey into Eritrea, after which he wrote with great engagement in defence of the right of Eritreans to independence from Ethiopia.
6. Göran Assbring, p.10.
7. Göran Assbring, pp. 13–59.
8. Göran Assbring, pp.63–68, 69–75.
9. Göran Assbring, p. 11.
10. Göran Assbring, p. 63.
11. Göran Assbring, pp. 63–64.
12. Göran Assbring, p. 68.
13. Göran Assbring, p. 70.
14. Göran Assbring, p. 69.
15. Göran Assbring, p. 69.
16. Göran Assbring, p. 70.
17. Göran Assbring, p. 70.
18. Göran Assbring, p. 75.
19. Göran Assbring, p. 75.

Year 2005
Chapter 34

Michela Wrong:
A British Journalist's Narrative on Eritrea's Struggles

Dear Michela!

I have now read two books by you: *"In the Footseps of Mr. Kurtz"* and *"I Didn't Do it For You,"* which I finished this morning.[1] I finished the latter book with a mixture of soft sorrow, yes grief, but also a flicker of hope. Your last paragraph, where your character tells the West … "Don't push us away," is a beautiful appeal to the world, and gathers into a few words, the pleas and prayers of numerous Eritreans. The fact that the person, who uttered these words, too lives in Sweden, makes me happy. I too am a resident, indeed a citizen, of Sweden.

You have not given up on us. And that makes me happy. And the rebuilding of the Asmara-Massawa railway perhaps augurs well for Eritrea. May we begin again, by God's grace!

And I want to thank you for two beautiful and poignant pieces of work. Your book on Mobutu's Congo is heavy in its ruthlessly thorough and honest reporting. You are no less thorough and honest in your reporting on Eritrea, though your story on her is far more uplifting. You have educated us. You have worked hard. I want to say it again. "You have worked hard!" With your legs, hands, brains, emotions, pens and, surely, computers! It is very clear that you are a person capable of being involved with a primitive kind of dedication to a task, a vision undertaken. Thank you for being involved and making our story yours.

I know that some Eritrean reviewers have given you far more twigs (i.e. lashes) than roses, as the Swedes would put it. In some cases, their criticisms are justified. You could indeed have interviewed and commented on the views of more Muslims. You could have interviewed refugees in the Sudan. Perhaps you have done that. In that case we would have liked to hear some of their stories. But I feel that some of those compatriots, who have reviewed your work, could have been far more generous in recognizing the downright hard work, the sweat and anguish involved in producing such an admirably researched and lyrically written work.

Thank you for a job well done.
Ezra Gebremedhin
May 2005
Uppsala, Sweden

Reply received by e-mail:
Date: Sat, 28 May 2005 05:12:56 EDT
Subject: from michela wrong
To: Ezra Gebremedhin

Dear Pastor Ezra
Thank you for your wonderful letter, which put a spring in my step and lifted my spirits. It was especially welcome as I had just received an email tirade from one of the PFDJ militants we have here in London, who managed to inject an extraordinary amount of vindictive loathing into every word. As long as I get the occasional letter from Eritreans like yourself, I can brush off the other stuff.

Yes, the book did involve a lot of hard work. I made a fundamental mistake in setting out to cover too much of Eritrea's history, and the effort to do that only became clear to me when it was too late and the project just got longer and longer and longer. You and other Eritreans have asked, quite reasonably, why I didn't include certain things. Firstly, the book would probably have become too hefty to a general and non-Eritrean reader to ever think of picking up in a bookshop (and that is an audience that I do want to reach). Secondly, I would probably have had to spend another year doing the research and I had simply reached the stage where I wanted to complete the thing and get it out. May be I am being too idealistic, but I do hope this book will have a small, helpful impact on the border issue by increasing international understanding of Eritrea's position and history, so the sooner it entered the domain of public domain the better.

Have you thought of publishing your thoughts on my book? I often suggest to people who send me letters that they think of calling up the amazon websites (*www.amazon.co.uk* for Britain, *www.amazon.com* for the United States) and continue to the "readers comments" section. It is very easy to do and quite satisfying if you like seeing your name in print. The PFDJ guys have cottoned into this a long time ago, so I am always keen to see alternative voices on those websites. But maybe you prefer to keep your correspondence private.

Once again, thank you for a very kind and cheering letter. By the way, if you see specific mistakes in the book, please let me know. Some I have already corrected for the paperback, but there is always room for improvement.

Best wishes
Michela Wrong

My Comment, 2019: No, I didn't publish my thoughts on Michela's book. Was my caution due to cowardice? One thing is clear to me: Michela Wrong's work is a vital contribution to the Eritrean narrative. The more Eritreans read it, the better.

Notes

1   The full title of Michela's book reads: "I Didn't Di it for You: How the World Betrayed a Small African Nation. Harper." 2005.

Year 2005
Chapter 35

Water

I am not a swimmer. My siblings and I never had the opportunity to learn to swim in Ethiopia. After my decades in Sweden, I can keep somewhat afloat for about thirty meters, until I am suddenly reduced to a frothy confusion of panicky limbs.

In and around the Addis Ababa of our childhood, the bodies of water with which we were acquainted were either wells or muddy, torrential rivers which, fed by "summertime" rains, thundered away, mainly past the outskirts of town or under what seemed to be ominously high bridges. Unfortunately, our well-meaning environment inculcated in us not only respect for but also fear of water. Our children and grandchildren here in Sweden have a completely different attitude to water. After overcoming their initial fears of water and its intentions, they regard water basically as a playmate, not as a host with evil intentions.

Recurring TV news about hurricanes and floods in all parts of the world and the sight of flood-frightened men, women, and children, clinging to roofs and trees, have recently shaken me into making some effort to revive and augment the minimal swimming skills that I have. I go to *Svettis*, the main Gymnastics Centre of the University of Uppsala. I have literally said to myself: "Wouldn't it be irresponsible of me to die (terrible thought!) for lack of being able to swim thirty, sixty, or a hundred meters under the tumultuous circumstances that floods can create?"

At the same time, my clumsy swimming practices have reminded me once again of man's relationship to water and water's relationship to man. The interesting thing is that the calmer and the more relaxed one is in water, the friendlier and more supportive water appears to become. It seems as if it is those who are most relaxed who float most easily. I have seen accomplished swimmers lying on their backs on water, with the palms of their hands cupped under their heads, pedaling gently with their toes and keeping afloat. With a minimum amount of effort! Water seems to be a friend of those who trust it.

I have also experienced, on many occasions, that water appears to become aggressive towards those who become nervous and panicky. As soon as I lose my composure and start kicking and splashing, water invades my body, by way of my nose, my mouth, my eyes, my ears. The nervous and panicky swimmer becomes the victim of a relentless, liquid invader.

Swimming has become a matter of survival. A must! But my little story also contains a parable for life. Swimming is a picture of life. Water is a picture of the circumstances which surround us—our successes and failures, our joys and sorrows, our hopes and fears, our certainties and doubts.

Would it be wrong to say that the more quietly and calmly we tackle the issues of life, the better?

With sincere greetings,
Ezra

Year 2005 (2019)
Chapter 36

A Nordic Perspective on Ethiopia and Eritrea

Today is May 17, 2005. I started looking at a TV programme broadcast by NRK (Norsk Rikskringkasting, Norwegian Broadcasting Corporation) at 9:45 a.m. It is 1:25 p.m. and I have just taken a break. I shall try to narrate something of the sum total of my impressions. In the first place, the programme was a feast in the true sense of the word, a celebration. Not a demonstration. No sharp edges. No bitterness, no heated feelings or words spilling over. The occasion was the commemoration of the separation of Norway from Sweden one hundred years ago. May 17th is the celebration of Norway's acquisition of the charter (*grunnlov* in Norwegian) that gave a large measure of autonomy to Norway and which became the basis for its claim to complete independence from Sweden on June 6, 1905.

This year, the 17th of May (the Norwegian festival known as *syttende mai*) is being celebrated in conjunction with Norway's gaining of independence from Sweden on June 1905. A festive aura rests on both events.

Forced solutions to conflicts between two countries are never healthy solutions, unless such moves have the character of indisputable and weighty verdicts, with the weight of an international tribunal behind them. Norway and Sweden were on the brink of war in 1905. People in both the government and the military were tempted to play it tough around the issue of Norway's demands. There was a dangerous stalemate; but sense, good judgment, and a readiness to compromise won the day. The prime ministers of the two countries arrived at a compromise solution, surely an expression of a widespread public opinion.

In the city of Karlstad in Sweden, where the key negotiations were held during the years of high tension, there is a statue commemorating this sober solution—a woman with the sections of a broken sword in her hands! The avenue on which the hours-long school parades are held on May 17th every year, has been named Karl Johan Gata. It starts at the Railway Station of Oslo and climbs up to the Royal Palace. The other end of the avenue is marked by a statue of Karl Johan on horseback. Karl Johan was a symbol. He was king of both Sweden and Norway. His roots go back to the France of Napoleonic days.

The camera that I was following covered Norway from North to South, from East to West. It gave me glimpses of Norwegians and their descendants celebrating their history in the USA, Spain, Nepal, Singapore, and Australia, to name some countries. It was moving to witness how closely attached these Norwegians were to their country and their history.

I also saw how Swedes joined their Norwegian neighbours in the celebrations of May 17th, both in Norway and in the USA. Individual Swedes, school delegations, and representatives of Swedish business were present in different parts of Norway, sharing the pride and joy of the Norwegians. A Swedish girl who was interviewed said that her group was going to sing the Swedish National Anthem in connection with the celebrations that were in progress. Swedish involvement in these Norwegian festivities was, for me, an impressive witness to the capacity to forget and overcome past disappointments and pains in national relations.

I was touched by a couple of things that Liv Ullman, a Norwegian actress and once a life partner to the famous Swedish dramatist Ingmar Bergman, said as she was preparing to lead the May 17th parade in Trondheim, Norway. In the first place she said that she could sing the Swedish National Anthem, *Du gamla, du fria* ("You Old One, You Free One"), and Norway's National Anthem, *Ja, vi elsker dette landet* ("Yes, We Love This Country") with equal dedication and commitment. She also said, "It is good to have roots and the sort of air with which one can feel at home, without being a nationalist in an exaggerated way."

I recall the role that certain leading Norwegian literary figures had played in bringing about the molding and maturation of Norway's national ambitions. Henrik Wergeland (1808–1845), poet and the "king" of May17th; Björnstjerne Björnson (1832–1910), author and politician; Edvard Grieg (1843–1907), composer; and Henrik Ibsen (1828–1906), author, come to mind.

H. Arnold Barton's book, *Sweden and Visions of Norway: Politics and Culture, 1814–1905*,[1] gives the definite impression that some prominent Swedes, especially writers and politicians of the more radical camp, supported the ambitions and struggles of Norwegians who were bent on asserting their autonomy in their relations to Sweden.

Svinesund Bridge—Amicable Encounter at the Border

The Swedish newspaper *Upsala Nya Tidning* for June 10, 2005 contained a picture and a short notice on the inauguration of the new Svinesund Bridge between Sweden and Norway, officiated by Carl XVI Gustaf and Norway's King Harald. A part of the text reads:

> Thousands of spectators applauded in the sunshine but were a little shaken by the chilly wind. The ceremony was given a golden lining by the robust presence of royalty. Besides the two royal couples, Princess Victoria and Norway's Crown Prince Haakon and his wife Mette-Marit played their part.

The ceremony is a continuation of the conciliatory spirit of 1905 between Sweden and Norway. May this chapter be a reminder, a lesson, that Ethiopia and Eritrea would embrace and foster![2]

Notes

1 Arnold Barton, *Sweden and Visions of Norway. Politics and Culture, 1814-1905*. Carbondale: Southern Illinois University Press. 2003.

2 Permit me to quote some words from my friend Dr Bereket Yebio: Your cross-cultural experience and ability to integrate and become part of the different societies enable you to make comparative analysis. Comparing the historical relations of Norway and Sweden, for example, makes it easier for people in the Nordic countries to understand what the conflicting relationship between Eritrea and Ethiopia is all about. I was once explaining to educators from Namibia that the relationship between Eritrea and Ethiopia was like that of Namibia and South Africa.

Year 2010
Chapter 37

The Cough That Was Permitted

We were in Löten Church, Uppsala, Sweden, on February 12, 2010, for the memorial service of Rigmor Arén, the widow of Gustav Arén, author of the two well-known books *Evangelical Pioneers in Ethiopia* (1978) and *Envoys of the Gospel in Ethiopia* (1999), books that are also histories of Eritrea. Rigmor had died at the age of 91, twelve years after the death of her husband. After the well-known musical piece on the theme "The Lord Is My Shepherd" by G. Nordqvist, the officiating pastor began the service with the words, "We are gathered here today to bid farewell to Rigmor Arén and to commit her into God's hands."

The ceremony continued with the quiet dignity of a funeral service in The Church of Sweden. The relatives of the deceased sat in front, on the right side of the row of church pews. Most of the relatives of Rigmor had come from different parts of Sweden. Some relatives had come from Germany, where the first-born of the Arén family, Gunilla, and her family lived. The rest of the congregation was made up, in no small measure, of Swedes, Ethiopians, and Eritreans with mission connections.

People were dressed in dark. Close relatives among the men wore dark suits and white ties. And mourners had brought flowers to place on the coffin at the time of taking farewell. A quiet, sad, but colorful scene, with "black" as a reminder of why we were gathered in church that day.

The service was in progress when my first cough came. I coughed as gently as possible into the fold (joint) of my right arm, thinking of the risk of infecting people in these times of swine influenza. How I wished that I wouldn't cough on such a solemn occasion! But there were more coughs to come. One, and two, and three, and four!

It was then that my thoughts started rolling. The cough that was permitted! Not a single person looked back to see who was coughing. Not a twitch of the back, not a tilting of the neck, not a raising of the shoulders in the seats ahead of me. No one seemed to have entertained the slightest thought that what I was doing was wrong. It was taken for granted that a person who needed to cough would and could cough. Even at a memorial service for the dead! My coughing was an expression of a human right in the deepest sense of the term. An ageless and universal privilege! Nature's sovereign demand, recognized by the rank and file and by men of power in Sweden, Ethiopia, and Eritrea.

My cough, this outburst of embarrassing noise, was not one-tenth as melodious as the musical number that the organist had played at the beginning of the funeral service. And yet, the cough was permitted and understood, with a good measure of unspoken sympathy.

Coughing is only one kind of reaction. In everyday life we are overcome by sneezing, sighs, cries, and tears—bodily reactions related to our needs and the needs of others. But there is also an inner, human, emotional, and existential dimension to such external, physical reactions. We live in a turbulent world. Our insides remember, with pain, those who have left home and hearth at a tender age. Our thoughts go to the hungry and thirsty, the naked, the sick, the imprisoned, and the tortured.

If coughing is given such an obvious recognition in our human relations, why aren't the pains of our hearts for fellow human beings given the same kind of respect and recognition? Please tell me why. Is your cry of anguish over a fellow human being, now in prison, less important than your cough at a funeral?

Stay well!

Ezra Gebremedhin
February 13, 2010
Uppsala, Sweden

Year 2012
Chapter 38

Aboy Aregai Kibreab:
A Person Who Helped Me Discover Eritrea in Sweden

I am reminded of the commandment in the Bible, "Honor your father and your mother, so that you may live long in the land the Lord your God is giving you" (Exodus 20:12, New International Version).

We honour our parents also by remembering them and speaking about them. My intention is to narrate, as simply and as naturally as possible, the story of a man whose age and bearing gave him the role of a father among both Eritreans and Ethiopians in Sweden.[1] I want to pay him homage personally as someone who was very closely associated with him. I know that he would have approved of what I am doing. And that, for me, is the most valid form of authorization for the writing of this article.

Let me add right away that Aboy Aregai was one of those parents who sacrificed their children (four sons, in his case) for the cause of Eritrea. In this sense, his story is intimately connected with Eritrea's struggle for self-determination and with the general tenor of this book.

This article is by no means an exhaustive treatment of the life and family history of Aboy Aregai. My knowledge of his large family is limited and stems mainly from what he narrated for me in our many, informal meetings. I do hope that members of his family will understand this limited perspective out of which I have written. I do hope that this short story of his life will be to the benefit of coming generations in his family and among Eritreans in general.

I have one more reason for writing about Aboy Aregai in this collection of articles. He was an African and, more specifically, an Eritrean who lived far from home, in a historical and cultural milieu that was in stark contrast to the place of his origin. The way he tried to adjust to his Swedish surroundings while keeping faithful to his own background is, in my opinion, worthy of respect. He was a quiet bridge, a calm link between North and South. In this sense he is a role model. He was a person who helped me discover Eritrea here in Sweden.

I knew him well, having associated closely with him for several years here in Uppsala. He belonged to the inner skyline of this town of universities, of a cathedral which has the status of a national shrine, and of many other historical sites. A familiar figure, the short, impressive person was greeted by people with their gentle smiles on the streets and sidewalks of Uppsala.

He used to call me several times a week. He often began in a low tone, both vocally and emotionally. He cheered up, however, after having uttered some sentences and ventilated his feelings. He had a good sense of humour. He used to spice his speech with popular Eritrean sayings like "Be that as it may, see to it that you take care of me!" (ዝኾነ ኾይኑ ንኣይ ተኸናኸኑ). He always ended our conversation with the words "Don't forget me in your prayers!" (ብጸሎትኩም ኣይትጋደፉና).

He used two Tigrinya words repeatedly. One was *Habbo* (ሓበ), meaning "courage." The other word was *mitsmam* (ምጽማም), which carried the senses of "patient silence," "quiet determination," and "waiting hope-fully."

He was orderly and careful. He weighed his words, like my own father, Ato Gebremedhin Habte-Egzy. On more than one occasion he advised me: "Father Ezra! Be careful about what you say. People usually add to what one says!" (ኣቦይ ቀሺ ኣብ ዘረባ ተጠንቀቑ ፡ሰብ ወሲኹ እዩ ዝዛረብ).

There were times when I could not come and keep him company, due to other engagements. He never complained. He usually answered: "Don't hesitate, don't drag your feet, before an assigned task! [In other words,] Concentrate on what you are doing!" (ኣብ ቅድሚ ስራሕ ኣይትጽናሕ,). He had been industrious throughout his life.

How old was he? His Swedish identity card put his date of birth at August 27, 1914. He was not happy about this date. He was convinced that he was older. Towards the end of his years in Sweden he said repeatedly that he had already turned a hundred. His children, grandchildren, and great-grandchildren celebrated his hundredth year for him in *Deqemharä* (ደቀምሓረ), *Akälä Guzai* (ኣከለ ጉዛይ), Eritrea, on July 24, 2012—an anniversary that appears to have been a compromise between the date on his passport and Aregai's claim that he was older! In connection with the celebration of his 100th year of life, he appeared on Eritrea's TV. A very good gesture, I felt. His age and life experience qualified him for such an appearance.

Aregai and His Parental Background

This is how Aboy Aregai narrated his own story:

> I was born in Addi Samra, in Qolla Serayé. My Father's name was Kibreab Habteab. There were three brothers in my father's family and they were known as 'Deqqi SibHat' [The sons of SibHat]. My father walked to Jerusalem on foot to become a monk. The monks at the Ethiopian monastery in Jerusalem told him, however, that he couldn't become a monk. For twenty years he was their Treasurer. At last they advised him "You are called to produce seed," meaning "You are called to marry and give birth to children."

Kibreab had, furthermore, developed a lung ailment and was advised to return to his country, to "change air" as the expression goes. Kibreab had no other choice but to return. Aregai adds:

> As soon as he had climbed up to the cross that had been erected at the very entrance of the compound of the monastery of Debre Bizen, he spat something out of his lungs and he became healthy.

Kibreab then married a pious girl who had close family connections with the Debre Bizen. Aregai often spoke about his mother with great warmth. Here are his words:

> Her name was Hiddegga Medhané. She was literate. She said her morning prayers very early before starting her daily duties. She recited her Dawit (meaning the Psalms of David). She was an angel and displayed great humility and patience in her behaviour towards my father. Among my siblings are four sisters and one brother. The names of the sisters are Zewdi, Awotash, Jenber, and Imouna. My brother, the father of Binyam, was called Gebre-Yesus. I had many brothers and sisters but they all died.
>
> My first wife was called Abrihet Gebrihet [Gebre-Hiywet]. She was the daughter of Beramberas Gebrihet, from Addi Aboun in Tigrai. One of her brothers was known as Qegnazmatch Beyin. She was an efficient, industrious person. No man was her equal. A brother of hers, by the name of Asmelash, a driver, died in an accident on the way to Asäb. He was buried at the place of his death, temporarily. However, I saw to it personally that his remains were moved to Dammo.

Aregai's wife was, according to her husband, a capable, warm-hearted, tolerant, and generous woman. Often the very mention of her name almost drove him to tears. Aregai lost four sons during the years of Eritrea's struggle for self-determination. Their names are Kibrom, Halefom, Haileab, and Habteab. Kibrom attacked a tank and met his death in Qolla Serayé. Another son, Tekle, was wounded during the war. He survived and now lives in DeqemHarä, in the town and house where Aregai lived before he left for Sudan.

"They were fair-minded," he said of his four martyred sons. "They had a strong sense of justice. They couldn't stand and watch idly if they saw someone being mistreated. They would jump in and punish the evildoer. We were able to give them a good education. They were intelligent. But they all died in the struggle for Eritrea's self-determination."

Of their mother and his wife, Woizero Abrihet, he used to say, "She went before witnessing evil things!" (ከፉእ ከይረኣየት ከይዳ).

Aregai—The Sick Boy Who Became Healthy

There are a couple of things that Aboy Aregai narrated for me on several occasions about his early youth. At around the age of twelve, he suffered from an ailment that caused his stomach to swell. Since he was short of stature, the swollen stomach must have made him look somewhat grotesque, as is common with children who suffer from severe malnutrition! In Aregai's case, however, the cause of the ailment was not poverty or lack of food. His parents were relatively well-to-do. His mother had a simple "food joint" (ቤት-ብልዒ). The young and ailing Aregai hung around and guests who came to eat noticed him. There was, however, no self-pity in Aregai. He took life as it came. In time, a certain client saw the boy's state and commented, *"Iwai*! What has happened to this poor boy?"

Aregai's mother answered in tears, "We have tried everything. And now he must be operated [on]."

"Don't let him be operated [on]!" pleaded the guest. "Take him to *Takhita* (ታኽታ) [a place near *Tera-Imni*, Mendefera (ተራ-እምኒ : መንደፈራ)] instead, to a certain *Abba* [a monk] who applies local medicine on his patients. The boy will get well."

I don't remember the name of the monk in question. And so Aregai was taken to *Takhita* by a horse-drawn wagon, which stopped at various stations (ጣቢ). In the course of his treatment, he was suspended in such a way that medicine could drop into his mouth and his seat was placed in such a position that he could dispose of excrement without difficulty. He used to tell me jokingly, "The medicine came in at the top and the worms came out under!"

I have often wondered if his problem didn't have to do with worms which had found their way into his digestive system, a condition which many of us experienced as children! Be that as it may, the treatment given by the local doctor, the monk, was successful. Aregai's weeping grandmother and mother were relieved. Their prayers had been heard. The boy became a sturdy, healthy young man and was to maintain his health to the very end of his life. Aregai adds, "We children used to play war. We ran naked in the rain. There was no talk of *Polmonito* [pneumonia] or *Bronchito* [bronchitis] among us! I was good at running and wrestling."

Aregai had his religious scruples on how meat should be acquired and prepared. He had his periods of fasting, which he observed stringently. Otherwise, he was not choosy about food. "My mother used to feed me with food made only with butter, not water," he added.

He ate all kinds of food without difficulty—pork and meat from fowl excluded! About Eritrea he said, repeatedly, "In the entire world there is no other country which has two *Kiremti* [rainy seasons]!"

He was thinking of the rainy seasons on the coast and on the highlands of Eritrea.

Aregai's Education

Aregai had been educated up to the 4th grade at the *Scuola Vittorio Emanuelle Terzo*, as he expressed it (i.e., The Vittorio Emanuelle III School). He told me on several occasions about a visit by Duca D'Aosta (The Duke of Aosta) in Asmara. In fact, Aregai seems to have taken part in the reception ceremony for the duke in some way. It will be remembered that Amadeo D'Aosta, a so-called "enlightened" member of the Italian nobility who were to serve under Mussolini, had arrived in Massawa on December 27, 1937. A couple of days later he was installed as new Viceroy in Addis Ababa, after the recall of the gruesome Rodolfo Graziani to Italy. It is very likely that Duca D'Aosta appeared in an official capacity in Asmara before proceeding to Addis Ababa.

Aregai was an orderly person and kept records of his financial and other paper-related transactions. I used to help him fill out forms. On such occasions he would remind me, politely, not to hurry, lest I should make a mistake. He quoted an Amharic proverb, "One can arrive at all goals without rushing!" (ሳይቸኩሉ ይደረሳል ተሁሉ).

Aregai—The Young Butcher

Aregai was short of stature. One day he was helping his father, who also worked as a butcher of the traditional Eritrean type. The two were dividing the limbs of an ox that had been slaughtered the same morning and which had to be portioned into piles of more or less the same size and weight. The particular system of portioning meat from slaughtered cattle was known as *goozzi*. In spite of his age, Aregai was skillful at dividing the meat into equitable portions. Aregai adds, "When Dedjatch Beyene was judge in Abba Shawl, we used to slaughter seven oxen per week."

The meat was laid out on a mat of dried reeds (ተንክበት), and placed on the ground. Italian authorities had, however, objected to this practice, which they felt was not hygienic. The meat ran the risk of being exposed to dust and other types of contamination from the ground. The family was ordered to place the meat on a table. However, since Aregai was short of stature, a footstool was provided for him to stand on. A passerby, a long, well-built person, stopped to admire the efficiency of a boy who did his work from his elevated position. In his innocence, the onlooker uttered, "Just imagine a young boy doing this!"

Aregai's father, evidently a person with temperament, felt that the stranger's commentary was an intrusion. He therefore cast himself upon the admirer and pulled him down to the ground. Aregai, who felt that a fight was in the offing and that his father could fare badly (the stranger was tall and well-built) picked up a sizeable rock and slung it on one of the legs of the innocent admirer. The man fell on the ground, agonizing in pain.

To make matters short, the victim went to court and opened a case against Kibreab, Aregai's father. The incident took place in Asmara and the judge was *Degiat* (ደጊያት) Beyene Berakhi. Kibreab and the plaintiff were summoned to court.

The judge asked the plaintiff, "Who is your witness?"

The plaintiff answered, "The boy is my witness. He saw what happened."

The judge, who felt that the testimony of someone below the age of discretion wouldn't be acceptable, told the plaintiff to bring an adult as a witness.

The plaintiff insisted: "The boy is my witness." Therefore, Aregai was summoned to court. He was asked by the judge: "Who started the whole thing?"

Aregai answered, "My father did. He was the one who pushed this man, simply for admiring my performance. But I was afraid that my father would fare badly if he were to be left at the mercy of this man. I therefore came to my father's aid by casting a piece of rock at the man's leg."

The judge accepted Aregai's testimony. Kibreab was found guilty and was ordered to pay a penalty of 50 *Batera* (ባጤራ – Maria Theresa dollars). True to tradition, the plaintiff declined to receive the *kaHsa* (ካሕሳ – com-

Chapter 38

pensation). In traditional Eritrean society, to receive ("eat") a compensation resulting from a court case was regarded as a disgrace.

"No," the plaintiff said: "I won't take any compensation. This boy's testimony is enough of a compensation for me!"

However, the same Eritrean tradition which frowns upon the acceptance of compensation approves of a voluntary gift to the victim of a quarrel or a fight. Aregai adds, "We took a sheep, some butter, honey and other things to soothe the pain experienced by the victim and to speed up the healing of his wounds. Times were good! (ጊዜ ጽቡቅ ነይሩ)," Aregai concluded.

He used this expression on many other occasions. Surely not all "times" in the past were good. Many of the occasions about which he narrated for me were, however, indeed "good."

Aregai the Driver

Aregai was often on the road. In his long life, he was able to see a number of countries. He knew them inside out, he claimed. He had travelled to many parts of Eritrea, Ethiopia, Sudan, Egypt, and, finally, Sweden. He was once the driver for the Italian head of the Municipality in Asmara, the *podesta* ("bodesta") as Aregai pronounced the word. In Fascist Italy, the word meant the "mayor" of a town or the chief magistrate of a commune.

In his function as a driver, Aregai wore a uniform and a hat. He made it a point to tell me that whenever his car came to a stop, he used to hasten from his driver's seat to open the door of the vehicle nearest the seat where the head of the municipality sat. On a couple of occasions, he told me, half-jokingly, that he should really claim a pension from Italy for the services that he had rendered as a driver:

> It was a relative who persuaded me to go into driving. I became his assistant (*ayutanti*). At the beginning I was hesitant. However, he continued pleading with me, and I gave in. After working for some years as an ayutanti I started on my own.
>
> I was always well-equipped. I was also a driver for the monastery of Debre Bizen. I used to drive passengers to Himbirti and other places. I used to take food and food-ingredients with me on my long trips. My considerate wife (She was efficient and loyal!) used to provide me with all the things needed to make food. I had my own primus-stove and could make food. I slept in my lorry. Gondar was my favourite stop as a long-distance chauffer. I was respected. I was generous to those who needed a ride. I became acquainted with the family of Getatchew Abate. Their forbears were Eritreans. There, in Begemdir, they had settled and

multiplied. They were respected. Robbers respected me and left me alone because of my connections with people like Abate Abraha.

I helped other drivers on our long journeys. They used to wait for me. They said: Let us wait for Aregai! He can help us to ford the river. I used to pull them out of the river if they fastened while trying to cross. My advice to them was to take it slowly when crossing rivers. When the noise of the engine disappeared, they used to go into panic and accelerate. That is when the engine disappeared. I used to tell them: Even if the sound disappears or becomes subdued, don't accelerate. Keep the accelerator pressed to the bottom.

If they did fasten in mud, I used to take out my metal chain and pull them out.

I was away from home, driving in the dry-season, and came home for the rainy season. I returned with a lorry richly loaded with gifts of grain and clothing for my family and for relatives near and far. My sister Imouna used to sing and dance in honour of my return for the ክረምት – the rainy season.

Aregai must have been a technically gifted person. To take one further example, he was also into farming during a shorter period in his life. He drove tractors at a farm owned by Degiat Abraha.

How did Aregai end up outside of Eritrea? He left Eritrea during the reign of the so-called "Derg," Ethiopia's Marxist military regime. His intention was to accompany some of his children out of Eritrea into the Sudan and then return home. He managed to get the children out. However, while he was still in the Sudan, he was warned not to return.

In his old age, Aregai still spoke of trucks. He had one truck "suspended" at a garage in Deqemharé, without its tires, he said. He wished that the truck would be put to use.

Aregai and His "Swedish" Family

I have already said that this article does not intend to cover the whole spectrum of Aregai's life. However, since the title of this article is *Aboy Aregai Kibreab – A Person Who Helped Me to Discover Eritrea in Sweden*, I would like to take the liberty of saying some words about his immediate family in Sweden. His wife is called Berhana Woldeabzgi. The marriage resulted in five lovely children: two sons by the names of Bekuretsion and Zikrom and three daughters by the names of Kibra, Selamawit, and Semhar. The love shared by an elderly father and especially the young daughters was impressive. When they met their father in downtown Uppsala, the daughters hugged and kissed him in such a touching manner that even passersby paused to look on. They were moved. If the daughters happened to be in the company of their Swedish friends, these female friends too got their shares of hugs from Aregai. I was a witness to such touching encounters.

Aregai and Ethiopia

Like many Eritreans of his age, Aregai had a sober view of the relationship between Eritrea and Ethiopia. I have already stated that Gondar was his favourite stop as a long-distance chauffer. He was respected in Gondar and its vicinity.

Aboy Aregai told me that there was a period when he devoted his time, money, and truck to the cause of union with Ethiopia. He told me that he was proud of the fact that he had met Emperor Haile Selassie. The Emperor had given him a pistol and said: "He shall not be prevented from access to any place!" (የትም ፡ እንዳይከለሉ) However, Aregai was also well acquainted and on friendly terms with Eritreans of the "independence" or "nationalist" camp, persons like *Degiat* Abraha and *Ra'isi* Tessema. When it was time to assert Eritrea's right to self-determination, Aregai was ready. He had no doubt as to what his choice would be. He had, after all, given the best that he had to the Eritrean struggle—four sons. And I know that at least one of his daughters, Gennet, had devoted a part of her life to the struggle for the independence of Eritrea, in active field-service. It is very likely that other children too had had their shares in this regard.

Aregai and His Faith

Aregai tried to live as a pious Orthodox Christian. He loved the Virgin Mary and mentioned her often. I was impressed by the fact that three "female" figures occupied special places in his heart and mind: The Virgin Mary, his mother Woizero Hiddegga, and his first wife, Woizero Abrihet. The monastery of Debre Bizen was an important part of his parents' lives as well as his own.

He accepted my role as a pastor (*Qeshi*) fully, though he knew that I was "Kenisha" (Evangelical Lutheran). Whenever we met, he kissed my hand in a typically Orthodox Tewahdo manner. Had I been an Orthodox priest, I would have offered him my hand-cross. However, since I don't carry such a cross, he had to be satisfied with the back (upper side) of my right hand. Swedes on many a street or side-street in central Uppsala used to look on enthralled, as an old man kissed the hand of a much younger person! I used to respond with a warm hug and the words, "*Birukh! Birukh!*" (ብሩኽ ብሩኽ , ብሩኽ ብሩኽ), meaning "Blessed! Blessed!"

We usually went to the café *Güntherska hovkonditoriet* (Günther's Patisserie, Purveyors to The Royal Family), almost on the bank of the Fyris River, which traverses Uppsala. On Wednesdays and Fridays, he didn't take any bread or cookies with his coffee, for fear that he would come in touch with milk products or eggs on these days of fasting. After tasting any kind of food or drink, he would say, in good Eritrean fashion, "*Ti'Um!*" (How tasty!). I should have perhaps told the Swedish waitresses at the counter about Aboy Aregai's many words of appreciation in this regard. I certainly didn't cook the coffee that he drank with relish at *Güntherska*!

Aregai and Life's Sunset

Aboy Aregai and I kept close contact with each other until he left for Eritrea on February 29, 2010. By then, he was a tired man, with some signs of confusion. The short giant had started becoming shaky. He showed, however, occasional flashes of his former vigour and alertness. He had a cane. Previously the cane was more of a decoration than a means of support. I urged him to use his cane, especially while descending stairs. I noticed that he tended to repeat things and to forget what he had done or said. He longed for many hours of chatting. He had looked forward to a life in the company of age peers who shared the same past and who would enjoy talking about it. The clock, the almanac, the time-steered agenda that dominated life in a Nordic country, was not for him. That was one of the sorrows of life in exile (ስደት).

I felt that he was slowly entering a twilight land, the approaching sunset of life. His family (both in Uppsala and in Stockholm) noticed these changes even more, since they took care of him during his last months in Sweden. It was time for him to return to his homeland.

He did so early in the morning of February 29, 2010. Some of his daughters, Abäba, Gennet and Feben too, were were present at Arlanda Airport, near Stockholm. So was Jimmy, a grandson and an upcoming salesman! Abäba was to accompany Aregai on his homeward journey. He bowed his head and kissed my hand. His final farewell here in Sweden! He did the same with his grandson Jimmy, who was deeply moved by such a gesture.

Aregai loved Sweden and praised its generosity, as well as its concern and respect for young and old, rich and poor, sick and healthy!

"This country is heaven on earth. But people are not happy. People don't smile," he used to say.

But now it was his time to leave, to return to the land that had produced his father Kibreab and his mother Hiddegga. A land where the sun shone longer hours and where people smiled more often!

When he died on September 12, 2012, Aregai was in DeqemHarä, at the home of his son Tekle, who had taken care of a father who was no longer the energetic "butcher" or driver, or family father. May his memory remain alive! May he rest in peace!

Ezra Gebremedhin
September 19, 2012
Uppsala, Sweden

Notes

1 I felt encouraged by the following comment from Professor Mussie Msghina: I enjoyed mostly the narrative approach of highlighting the possibilities and difficulties of integration. I enjoyed specially Aboy Aregai's story which was told with great warmth and empathy.

Year 2013
Chapter 39

Words Along the Way

እንቋዕ ኣሓጎሰና , roughly translated, means "God be praised that joy has become our lot!"

I was walking when my mobile phone rang. I recognized the voice of an Eritrean woman.

Today (at the time of the writing of this message) is Eritrea's 22nd birthday. Tomorrow, May 25, 2013, Eritreans in Uppsala will be celebrating the event officially. The woman who called knows me well as a pastor. I told the woman on the phone that I was coming to the celebration but that I couldn't stay long.

Not unexpectedly she answered: "The flag will be hoisted at 16 hours [4 p.m.]. Your presence, though short, and your words of advice, would be appreciated."

A man, a good friend, to whom I had talked on the phone the day before, had commented, "It does not matter that your stay with us must be short. It is enough that you give us your blessing!"

Here were two Eritreans, a man and a woman, representatives of a people traditionally known for their respect for age and grey hair, echoing the longings of thousands upon thousands of Eritreans! One feels small in the face of such expectations.

Now back to the telephone which rang on my way home. I had been in town with it. There was something wrong with the phone. I couldn't recharge the battery. In spite of vigorous efforts to plug my charger into an electric socket, there was no sign of pulsating current moving into my phone. I was afraid that my small communication device would soon be lifeless. I had to go to a repair shop for mobile phones. The proprietor asked where I had bought the phone and if I had the receipt from the purchase of my phone, two years earlier.

I didn't have the receipt. I couldn't even remember where I had placed it. The man couldn't repair my phone. That was it. The price of neglect or carelessness in small things!

But a simple, non-functional telephone awakened weighty thoughts in me, suddenly and unexpectedly. As I was waiting in line to be served at the Tele2 repair shop at the Central Station of Uppsala, the following thoughts, which have occupied me for many years, emerged once more:

1. Don't live a lie. Be truthful.
2. Don't speak or act hastily. Haste makes waste. (Say that to me again!).
3. Don't flee from life's challenges. Cowardice is degrading.

I thought to myself: If I do get an occasion to address my Eritrean brothers and sisters, sons and daughters, in Uppsala at the celebration of Eritrea's 22nd birthday on May 25, I shall recite these pieces of advice for them.

On my way home with my unrepaired telephone, I came upon a further piece of advice:

4. Remain committed to Eritrea.

And why? Because there were genuine dreams and ideals—ideals compatible with sober self-respect—behind Eritrea's emergence as a nation. And much has been paid for her existence, much of the stuff that resides in heart and mind, much of life and limb, much of sighs and tears, much of hope against the seemingly impossible.

My older brother, Naigzy, had once quoted for me the saying: ኣብ ዉራይካ ኣይትጋየሽ ("Don't consider yourself a stranger at a feast [undertaking] which is irrevocably yours!"). And Eritrea is our ዉራይ ("undertaking"), through thick and thin!

I know that my four pieces of advice are tall orders. And I don't enumerate them with the pride of someone who has observed them. But they deserve to be held forth by a person of grey hair. If I am to believe my brothers and sisters, my sons and daughters in Uppsala! Honour to many an Eritrean, in the past and in the present, for truthfulness, for a sense of sober judgment, and for courage in matters that touch upon an embattled homeland. Virtues still knocking on the doors of our hearts as we celebrate Eritrea's 22nd birthday!

And what about my mobile phone, whose battery risked running dry? Perhaps it too wants to put in a word, a greeting to Eritreans far and wide. Who knows? Would it be wrong to suggest that we all need a "recharging of our inner batteries"—a renewed and reinforced vision, a new pulse as it were—as we move into the future with Eritrea, all Eritreans and all our neighbors? God grant us such a recharging!

Peace and blessings.

Ezra Gebremedhin
May 24, 2013
Uppsala

Published on *dehai.org* on May 27, 2013.

Year 1993 (2020)
Chapter 40

Our Way to the Referendum on Eritrea (April 17, 1993, Uppsala, Sweden)

It is the 14th of May, 2020 as I write these words. I woke up to a sunny but chilly morning in our flat in Uppsala. My immediate impulse was to work more on the introduction to this chapter.

I don't remember the details of the day when we voted for Eritrea's independence. I even had to ask my wife if we voted in Uppsala or in Stockholm.

"Uppsala," she answered. "Don't you remember? At a school close to the shopping centre known as Migo!"

What is more, later on during the day, my wife discovered, among my papers, a Certificate of Participation (ወረቶት ምስክር ተሳታፍነት) in the preparations and registrations around The Referendum. The certificate was issued in Asmara on July 26, 1993 and signed by Ali Said Abdella, Secretary of the Interior!

I had forgotten, all these details! Well, I hope that I shall be forgiven. It is over 27 years since the Referendum took place (on April 17, 1993) and I am well into my eighties. I looked at my Eritrean identity paper (ኤርትራዊ ወረቶት መንነት), issued by The Eritrean Embassy in Stockholm on December 1, 1993. My profession is registered as that of a *Mämhir* (መምህር), a Teacher. I hope that what I write in this chapter can reflect the spirit of a teacher seeking to bring about a greater measure of mutual understanding on a sensitive subject.

I know that there was a festive spirit both in Eritrea and abroad, in the Diaspora, on the day when the Referednum was held. I remember a picture of my uncle, Ato Woldeab Woldemariam, walking towards a voting center in Asmara, surely one of the very first Eritreans to vote. He was dressed in a white *Ijjä Täbbab* (እጀ ጠባብ), a traditional Ethiopian and Eritrean costume.

In *Säné* (ሰኔ) 2003 (June 2011), i.e., eighteen years after the Referendum of 1993, Daniel Täfära J. published a biography on President Negaso Gidada, entitled *Dandi. Negaso's Way* (ዳንዲ የነጋሶ መንገድ), in the form of an interview. The book has a chapter entitled "Yä Ertra Referendum" (የኤርትራ ሪፈረንደም), "Eritrea's Referendum." To the question, "By the way, how was the referendum conducted?" Dr. Negaso answers:

> What I remember is that the referendum, which was based on the decision of the peace conference, was coordinated by The United Nations, and that I went to Eritrea as the leader of the parliamentary team that had been invited to act as observers. At the time I was Minister of Information.
>
> Our team, divided into groups, was able to observe the progress of the referendum in southern Eritrea, right up to the border of ትግራይ Tegrai. I was able to travel to ደቀምሓረ Deqemhará, Massawa and the environs of Asmara. I even travelled up to ሳሆ Saho in the north.
>
> The referendum was peaceful. People in the various regions not only came out to vote but also prepared feasts in which coffee, ፈንዲሻ fendisha – pop corn, bread and ጠላ *tälla* (traditional beer) were served. When the people saw us they embraced us and said: 'We are brothers. We shall never be separated from each other. We have no enmity towards the people of Ethiopia.'

Here in Uppsala I remember that we experienced both joy and sorrow within our extended family, a family that embraces both Ethiopians and Eritreans. After all, casting a "yes" vote at the Referendum was introducing something of a painful split in a family. I was told that one member of our extended family wept when he heard that my wife Gennet and I had cast "yes" votes. I hope that sharing a narrative from the heart can lead to a healing of hearts, even some decades after the Referendum on Eritrea.

I shall begin with a translation into English of a letter, written originally in Amharic, to Ato Emmanuel Abraham, a former president of The Ethiopian Evangelical Church Mekane Yesus, and a "father" to me and my wife Gennet Awalom. I shall then reproduce a translation, into English, of the reply that Ato Emmanuel wrote to us.

April 17, 1993, Uppsala, Sweden

Chapter 40

To our dear Father Ato Emmanuel Abraham,

May the peace of the Lord be with you and your family! Even though geographical distance and the passage of years have separated us, we have not ceased to consider you as a father and counsellor.

Occasions which require that a person make major decisions are not few. Choosing an academic discipline for one's education and choosing a life-partner are examples of such major choices. A country, however, is a gift which is bestowed by virtue of birth. It is not a subject of choice. The situation in which Gennet and I find ourselves now has, however, placed us before a very difficult choice.

The reason for this state of things is the fact that we have deeply rooted family relationships on two sides, namely Ethiopia and Eritrea. Only we who are caught in the present situation can understand the burden related to our circumstances. There were times when we said to ourselves,

Fortunate are those who don't have to make the difficult choice before which we stand!

The love we have for Ethiopia is still deep. To say so is not only to be true to our feelings but also to obey the dictates of our conscience. It is a Christian duty to give honour and express gratitude where these are due. For both Gennet and me, Ethiopia is the land where we received life both physically and spiritually, where our personalities were molded, where we found comrades and made friends, where we experienced joy, love and honor. Ethiopia is a land which enriched our emotional life through narratives about her beauty and expanse. To us she is a benefactor, not a debtor.

Having said so, we must add that one side of our being has been bleeding for over thirty years, due to the armed conflict and devastation which have been plaguing Eritrea, where our parents were born and where we still have many blood relatives. Since this conflict has also quenched the lives of thousands of Ethiopians, it is proper for us to say that we have been bleeding on two sides. We have been forced to come to the conclusion that instead of being a wound which could be healed, the conflict between Ethiopia and Eritrea has developed into 'gangrene' – a condition which demands that some part of the body be subjected to surgery, if the entire body is to be saved. It is true that there can be situations in which one can maintain that surgery is only a temporary solution. We know nothing about the future. After having undergone intense inner pain, which involved our emotions and consciences, we have come to the conclusion that we cannot only look on at a time when Eritrea and her population, indeed when the birthplace of our parents, its people and The Evangelical Church of Eritrea, are engaged in determining their future.

Even though the choice is heavy and we are unsure about the end results of our choice, we have arrived at the decision that we should vote on Eritrea's future. Today we gave our voices on Eritrea. We would have been happy to see that love and unity had won and that we could all continue to embrace each other also in a life of territorial unity. But arrival at a crossroads demands a decision. I remember the story which is told in the book of Ruth, chapter 1, verses 16 and 17 (where Ruth says to Naomi):

"Don't urge me to leave you or to turn back from you. Where you go I will go, and where you stay I will stay. Your people will be my people and your God my God. Where you die I will die, and there I will be buried. May the Lord deal with me, be it ever so severely, if even death separates you and me." (The New International Version (NIV) of the Bible.)

We have cast our votes in the spirit of Ruth, a spirit filled with love and humility, not hatred and contempt for Ethiopia. May God, rich in His Grace, straighten that which man cannot straighten!

It is fully within you rights to ask:

But why do you write after having arrived at such a weighty decision, instead of writing before coming to your decision?

Our delay had nothing to do with an unwillingness to reveal our thoughts. We just felt that delay was in place in this case. We felt that we should abstain from mentioning our decision until the matter was 'sealed and delivered', as it were.

We have not been able to decide whether it would be appropriate for us to write to the leaders of our church about our present situation.[1] To you we could write without hesitation since you are a father both to our church and to us. We reasoned as follows:

Let us write to him even if the subject of our message can turn out to be burdensome for him. He is our father, after all!

It would be good if Qes Yadäsa could be informed about our situation as soon as possible. It would not be good if he were to get wind on this matter in roundabout ways. We suggest that you summarize the content of this letter for him, if you now feel that such a move would be appropriate. But we leave the decision to you.

The respect and love that we have for you remains unchanged.

Your children
Ezra and Gennet, Uppsala

Chapter 40

And here below is the reply that we received from Ato Emmanuel:

April 28, 1993, Addis Ababa

To my beloved children, friends Qes Ezra Gebremedhin and Gennet Awalom

Wishing that the peace of Our Saviour would abound for you, I send my greetings which are accompanied by my longings. I have received the letter written 17-4-93 and read it with care. I can understand, at least in part, the pain that your spirits and your consciences have experienced due to political decisions taken on Eritrea. The choice before you was indeed painful and you have explained in detail what it was that led you to the choice. In my view, you couldn't have done otherwise. This dilemma faced you not because you wanted it or had worked for it but because of the predicament created by those people who had been given a chance to lead the country. I don't believe that there is any Ethiopian or Eritrean who hates Ethiopia's and Eritrea's unity. But the steps taken from the beginning to bring about this unity have only created divisions, conflicts and killings, instead of bringing about unity. Because of this sate of things, a countless number of people have lost their lives and property has been destroyed. The inhabitants of Ethiopia and Eritrea were greatly embittered. The Eritreans launched a bitter struggle due to the cruelty and devastation to which they were subjected. Finally, they removed the leaders of destruction. Who can blame them if they, under these circumstances, say that they want self-government?

I am reminded of a woman who, rendered bitter by her husband, leaves him after many struggles. It is my wish that the present separation of these two peoples will be limited by time and not become permanent. Our geographical location, our history, the fact that we are basically one people and, above all, our economic benefits, oblige us to avoid being separated from each other permanently, even though the cruelties committed during the last thirty years and the losses in life that they have caused, have affected the spirit and thinking of today's generation. It is my hope and conviction that, in time, after the cooling down of all that has transpired and after forgiveness has taken its place, the power of the benefits and the friendship that result will create new love and unity between the two peoples and bring about an atmosphere of the kind that leads to the reconciliation of an estranged couple, not through coercion but out of free will, so that the two can be bound anew by shared benefits. Eritreans, both men and women, and especially the leader of Eritrea, who have been heard expressing their views during this week of referendum, have reflected the feelings and the type of thinking that I have mentioned above. It is gratifying to hear them express such feelings and thoughts and strengthen the hopes of many. May this be the will of our God!

Therefore, my dear friends: Let your spirits calm down. Both "Ethiopianness" and "Eritreanness" are yours. As you have already said, you can't forget Eritrea where your grandparents have lived and where they are buried. Who knows, both peoples may be bound together again in love and equality during your lifetime. I believe that a decisive factor in this matter is that all Ethiopians can announce a constitution based on the equality of all Ethiopians and establish a strong central government.[2]

According to your request, I have informed Qes Yadäsa, in private, about your situation and the decision that you have come to. He too, having realized that you had no other choice in the situation in which you found yourself, has stated that you should continue as usual. He has also agreed that it is not necessary to spread news on this matter. In the Oromo language this is called "*Habultu*."[3] It is like saying '*sine die*' in another language.[4] No one can take your church membership from you. And there are no causes for worry as far as the pastoral status of Qes Ezra is concerned. The church has made an administrative provision for the recognition of the pastoral status of those pastors who come from abroad for short periods of service, leave alone you who were born and brought up here. You should not worry about these matters.

May the merciful God watch over us, wherever we are! Woizero Eleni sends her greetings with her longings. Greet your children.

Yours, Emmanuel Abraham

Who Was Ato Emmanuel Abraham?

His Excellency Ato Emmanuel Abraham (1913–2016) was indeed one of the leading Ethiopian personalities of the twentieth century. I can only recommend that my readers look into his memoirs, *Reminiscences of My Life*, which came out in 2011. A section of the introduction to these memoirs, written on the very first page of the book, reads:

> He began his career as a teacher and headmaster in Eastern Ethiopia and entered public service in February 1939 at The Ethiopian Legation in London. Emperor Haile Sellassie I later appointed him to various diplomatic posts in London, New Delhi, Rome, and high level government positions in Addis Ababa, including among others Chief of Political Affairs in H.I.M's Private Cabinet; Minister of Posts, Telegraphs and Telephones; Minister of Communications; and finally, Minister of Mines ....

In 1963, Emmanuel Abraham was elected President of the Ethiopian Evangelical Church Mekane Yesus and led the church for the next 22 years.

He was, to the end of his days, a convinced and calm proponent of the view that Eritrea was, historically, part and parcel of Ethiopia. This was the position that he maintained throughout his years of diplomatic service. When he presented his credentials as Ethiopia's ambassador to Italy in Rome on June 19, 1952, he had told the President (Einaudi) that "Eritrea was an ancient province of Ethiopia" (*Reminiscences of My Life,* The Red Sea Press, Trenton NJ, 2011, p. 84; see also pages 71–72, 76–77). His letter to us does not reflect a change of his views on Eritrea's historical relationship to Ethiopia.

Let me add that my wife Gennet Awalom and I regarded him as a father, a relationship that we developed during our years of service within the Ethiopian Evangelical Church Mekane Yesus.

Notes

1 I am now thinking of The Ethiopian Evangelical Church Mekane Yesus. The president of the church at the time was Qes Yadäsa Daba.
2 On November 17, 1969, a University student by the name of Walleligne Mekonnen, at The Haile Sellassie I University in Addis Ababa, wrote a paper entitled: "On The Question of Nationalities in Ethiopia". In it he maintains: And what is this genuine national-state? It is a state in which all nationalities participate equally in state affairs, it is a state where every nationality is given equal opportunity to preserve and develop its language, its music and its history. It is a state where Amharas, Tigres, Oromos, Aderes [Harari], Somalis, Wollamos [Wolaytas], Gurages, etc. are treated equally. It is a state where no nation dominates another nation, be it economically or culturally.
His Excellency Ato Emmanuel was surely thinking along these lines when he wrote his words on his hopes for Eritrea's future relations with Ethiopia. For the text of Wallelign's article and for the latest commentary on it, see Yared Tibebu's, "*On The Question of Nationalities in Ethiopia." A Historical Review of Wallelign Mekonnen's Article Half A Century Later."* Zehabesha.com. November 20, 2019.
3 *Habultu* is, I understand, a word in Orommiffa. It means, roughly "Let it wait over the night!"
4 'Sine die' is a Latin expression: "a reference to business or proceedings that have been adjourned with no appointed date for resumption."

Year 2019
Chapter 41

Integration (I):
Sweden's Growing Challenge

Impressions from an Airport

I was at the arrival hall of Terminal 5 of Stockholm's Arlanda Airport, sometime about two years ago. Icelandic Airline's flight F-1306, on which I was expecting my wife from New York, via Reykjavik, was being awaited at 12:35 p.m. The bulletin board announced that the plane was already approaching for landing. As I waited, I watched passengers who had arrived on earlier flights, pushing their luggage-laden trolleys ahead of them. Some were alone. Others came in twos and threes, young and old, men and women, adults and children. But they all had something in common. The lifted head, the searching eyes, the hopeful gaze. These passengers were expecting to be received, welcomed, and hugged. The entire arrival hall was electrified by the unseen waves of expectation bringing together hearts arriving and hearts waiting.

I saw a youngish woman with oriental looks and a bouquet held high in her right hand. She gave a gentle sigh as she proceeded to welcome a cluster of boys. Tears ran down her cheeks as she hugged the young men and gave the bouquet to one of them. Were these children returning to Sweden from Iran or Lebanon or Turkey? Who knows? But one thing was clear. They were coming home. To Sweden!

I saw a teenager abandon his trolley as if he had been catapulted, and literally jump into the arms of a white man. An older boy and a woman, who could very well have been from Indonesia or Malaysia or China, came close after, more subdued but no less happy. They too were hugged and kissed by the white man. Perhaps a family, being reunited! These people were coming home. Here too, searching eyes met a waiting heart.

I said to myself, "Sweden, the country with open arms! Here are signs of integration at its best!" Or is this too optimistic a picture? Can one also speak of closed arms, eyes turned away and longing gazes left unmet?

Deportation of Afghani Youth

The editorial page of the Christian Swedish daily, *Dagen* (*The Day*) for November 21, 2018 carries an article entitled "The Important Message of the Protests." I shall refer to the first half of the article. The section under the first subtitle, "Deportations to Afghanistan a Shipwreck for Humaneness," reads as follows,

> When the bus left the place of custody in Märsta late on Monday evening, there were only about 26 persons who were to be deported to Afghanistan on board, not the 50 that many had feared would be deported. About 100 persons who had come to protest were still around, hoping that the decision on deportation would be withdrawn. Granted that things ended as they did, was their engagement worth a day and night of protest outside the place of custody? After all, the deportations were not as many as one had feared, and the protests don't seem to have had any effect on the implementation of the decision.
>
> The fact that the actions were limited to 26 and not to 50 persons is of no significance for the weight of the protest as such. Each refugee constituted a self-contained drama. Every individual is a whole universe which is also united to all of us ... They are young Afghans who deserve protection in the face of a civil war but who are nevertheless regarded as not qualified for such protection by The Immigration Centre and by the law-courts in Sweden.
>
> Sweden takes a tougher stand on the matter of recognizing reasons for the granting of protection, than do other countries. This is because Sweden maintains that there is a plausible possibility of living as a refugee in Afghanistan. This stand differs diametrically from the judgment of The UNHCR [The United Nations High Commission for Refugees].[1]

Sweden—Mounting Polarization

The two short narratives that I have reproduced above are perhaps not the best examples of the different sentiments, indeed the tensions, that now exist in Sweden with regard to views on receiving and accommodating refugees. The stories do however make it clear that Sweden has become a country with polarized views.

Chapter 41

On the evening of Friday, September 7, 2018, the political parties of Sweden met for their final verbal duels before the national elections on Sunday, September 9. In order of size, according to the latest polls, the parties were The Social Democrats, The Moderates, The Sweden Democrats, The Left, The Liberals, The Centre Party, The Environment Party, and The Christian Democrats. The debate, which was led by two experienced journalists, a man and a woman, took up a number of weighty issues. In terms of the emotional heat that it produced, the issue of the influx of refugees and immigrants stood to the fore. A closely related issue, that of "integration," was the subject of some very down-to-earth questions.

Two more prominent subjects, discussed with less heat but with much concern, were the question of overall health care and the issue of climate/environment. In Sweden there have been heated discussions on the subject of long, time-related *vårdköer* (literally "health care queues"). In spite of the high quality of Swedish health care, there have been widespread complaints about the time that it now takes to see a doctor or to receive urgent medical treatments. This subject was aired with a multitude of accusations and counter accusations among the parties in power and those in the opposition. The Sweden Democrats were not slow to point out that vast sums of money, devoted to the reception and settlement of refugees, should have been used for health care among Swedish citizens.

Discussions about issues of climate/environment and their global implications were fuelled this year by the fact that Sweden has had a summer with an unusually long period of drought and persistent and alarming forest fires. There were speakers who argued that Sweden should concentrate on tackling climate/environment problems locally, but also in poor Third-World countries, where pollution, deforestation, and the extermination of certain animal species are a far greater threat than they are in Sweden.

Much attention was devoted to the urgency of integration following the massive influx of refugees and immigrants in other categories, especially during the years leading to 2015. The Sweden Democrats, a party accused of being an ultra-conservative populist party, strongly opposed to a generous refugee policy, were particularly loud in their underlining of the severe failures in the integration of refugees into Swedish society.

The failure of refugees and their families to learn Swedish speedily and thoroughly and their inability to get into wage-earning jobs as fast as possible was emphasized not only by the Sweden Democrats but also by other parties within the so-called Alliance Constellation of Parties.

Some parties held forth the fact that refugees were not only burdens on the Swedish economy but also were resources that provided services, not least in the home-service branches of direct care of people. Ethiopians and Eritreans have been mentioned with appreciation in this connection, as are also some other categories of people from other countries in the Middle East and Africa.

The content of the political debates around the latest elections was analyzed critically by Inge Geremo, Senior Adviser at *Sveriges Lantbruksuniversitet* (SLU Global), Sweden's Agricultural University, in an article entitled "We Must See the Causes Behind the Refugee Crisis" in the Swedish daily *Dagen* on October 24, 2018. The article argues that the climate issue as well as the question of the challenge of cultivating a greater variety of crops that can withstand climate variations in sub-Saharan African countries should have been taken up in the Swedish election debates.

Concern over the inflow of refugees, expressed on the Swedish home front, have also been noted by non-Swedish journalists. In an article published on Sunday, September 9, 2018 from Stockholm under the title "Sweden: Far Right Gains Threaten Europe's Most Stable Political Order," a journalist for *The Guardian*, Jon Henley, writes:

> But like its Nordic neighbours before it, open, prosperous, liberal, tolerant Sweden is in uncharted waters, facing a right-wing populist insurgency …The rise of the populists, riding high on a raft of alternative political concerns – immigration, integration, identity, crime, welfare chauvinism – that cut across the traditional left-right divide, is forcing a wholesale realignment.

The realignment that Henley seems to be predicting has still to materialize. At least some of the leadership and members of the other Swedish political parties would agree with the reasoning that Sweden has perhaps received far too many refugees without a proper consideration of the consequences of such a move.

Racist organizations and individuals in Sweden are pouring fuel on these arguments. Jewish synagogues have been under attack in recent months both in Malmö and in Stockholm. There have been cases of arson against homes or centres where refugees live while their cases are being studied or while waiting for eventual placement. The sentiments behind such actions are rubbing off on Swedes in general, whose feelings against waves of refugees flooding their country are rising. The news section of the Swedish daily *Dagens Nyheter* for Sunday, October 21, 2018 has a couple of paragraphs under the title "Racism Against Employees at Pharmacies on The Increase." The text reads:

> According to a number of Pharmacy-chains, with which SVT (Swedish Television News) has talked, cases of employees who are subjected to racism by clients, constitute a growing problem. Clients demand, among

other things, that Pharmacy-employees take off their veils or that these clients be served by a Swede.

We are, unfortunately, witnessing an increase in such attitudes at our pharmacies. A number of co-workers have stated that this was the case. Camilla Ås, Chief of Public Relations at The Heart Pharmacy said to SVT, Sweden: "At times we have been forced to refuse service to clients whose bearing we judged to be threatening."

This article seems to be one of many examples of smaller protests slowly penetrating everyday life in Sweden.

What Is Integration?

What exactly is integration? We have some common sayings, in different languages, on what a person should do to live and survive in a given regional or national context. One such saying goes, "When in Rome, do as the Romans do!" We have the Amharic saying, *Indä agärou yinorou, indä wänzou yishagärou!* (እንደ ፡ አገሩ ፡ ይኖሩ ፡ እንደ ፡ ወንዙ ፡ ይሻገሩ ፡፡ – literally: "One lives as the country does, one crosses a river according to the [character] of the river [i.e., according to conditions demanded by the river]"). We also have the Tigrinja saying, ወይ ዝበሉኻ ግበረሎም ወይ ዓድም ግደፈሎም ፡፡ (literally: "Either do what they say or leave their country for them!")

These sayings have a sharp edge, an "either/or" character about them. They seem to imply that integration is a must. But surely integration must be more than forced imitation. In an article published on October 26, 2018, in the Swedish daily newspaper *Dagen*, under the title "*Vad är svenskhet i ett mångkulturellt samhälle?*" ("What Is Swedishness in a Multicultural Society?"), the author, Malina Abrahamsson, writes the following under the subtitle "From Oneness to Multiculture":

> This question has been current since Swedish politicians competed with each other in quoting the phrase 'Swedish values' most frequently at The Almedal Week [on the island of Gotland] in 2016.[2] The traits which were named were: Responsibility, equality and the will to be found having fulfilled that which is expected from the individual—in other words, not having been found to be a parasite.
>
> But are these exclusively Swedish values? And what has happened to those less flattering traits that are attributed to Nordic people?
>
> In the course of the latest decades, Sweden has developed from a unitary society to a multicultural one. Today, 20 percent of our population has its

background in other countries, and every year 100,000 people move to Sweden, many of them as refugees ....

Sheila Jerioth, who is from Kenya, says, "In Sweden I feel Kenyan but when I am in Kenya I am very Swedish.

Many basic values are the same, regardless of the part of the world from which one comes, but we have different ways of organizing our societies.

When I moved here from Kenya I felt that the differences were big, but now I see that younger generation Kenyans have a more Swedish way of behaving with regard to independence and equality."[3]

What we can say after considering the views expressed above is that integration is a many-sided concept and that it can be understood on different levels, depending on one's cultural background and on the kinds of encounter with others that one has gone through along life's journey. In the last analysis, integration too is a matter of dialogue—on many levels.

Anti-Black Racism and Discrimination in the Labour Market

In a press release published on November 16, 2018, Professor Irene Molina and Professor Mattias Gardell maintain that anti-black racism and discrimination shape the preconditions for the Swedish labour market. They write:

Afro-Swedes have an essentially lower gross-salary and disposable income than the rest of the Swedish population. They are over-represented in low-status professions. The number of days without employment increase among those Afro-Swedes who continue their studies after secondary school, and complete three years of post-secondary education, unlike the rest of the population among whom unemployment decreases with a higher level of education. A new study conducted at Uppsala University by the centre for Interdisciplinary Research on racism, on behalf of the County of Stockholm, has demonstrated this fact.[4]

The result is remarkable. The result of the study shows big differences between Afro-Swedes and the rest of the population within all the sectors examined: unemployment, gross salary, disposable income, access to low and high status, and the possibility of establishing careers and attaining positions of leadership commensurate with one's level of education.

The Divided Heart

"We want your land, not your hand!"

This statement is my parody of the action of a male Muslim, a member of one of the political parties in Sweden, who refused to shake hands with a female reporter, for religious reasons and who, consequently, announced that he was leaving politics. In a way, my parody is unfair because some people actually do avoid physical contact with members of the opposite sex for religious reasons, with the exception of persons in their immediate family. The formulation "We want your land, not your hand!" is an attempt to give a pedagogical twist to an attitude with implications for integration. Another way of formulating my statement would be: "I want the security and benefits that your country can give me but not the way you think in religious, moral, and cultural matters."

Many immigrants and refugees harbour similar attitudes or modes of reasoning.

Immigrants or refugees who come to Sweden want to be integrated into the society but strictly on their own terms. Citizens in the host countries can very well understand the desire of the newcomer to preserve his or her identity, to a certain extent. But they also expect some give-and-take in everyday life.

Language Services as Promoters of Integration

An expression heard often both among Swedish teachers and among newly arrived immigrants and refugees is "*Svenska för Invandrare*" (literally, "Swedish for immigrants"), abbreviated SFI. SFI is the national programme of instruction in Swedish for immigrants. The course is free of charge and anyone with a Swedish identity number or identity card is entitled to take part in the course.

The sponsor for this extensive educational undertaking, the *Folkuniversitetet* (The Folk University), has a long history and engages teachers with experience and dedication. The courses offered by SFI are tailor-made in ways that take the needs of individuals into consideration. In some places, courses are given online. Accomodations are made for persons with hearing impairment and similar handicaps.

Immigrants or refugees who arrive with records of post-secondary school or higher academic education have the possibility of launching into programmes for more speedy language education, which would usher them into "*Högskolespåret*" (the level of University Education). The *Folkuniversitet* also offers SFI on behalf of municipalities.

It is striking to read that studying SFI takes into account not only mastery of the language but also the acquisition of knowledge about Swedish society and its workaday world. This is one way of saying that SFI as a language promoter is also a promoter of integration into Swedish society.

Translation Bureaus

"*Vilket språk har du?*" she asked, in Swedish. "What language do you have?"

"Tigrinja," I answered. She nodded.

I had been called upon to help as an interpreter in both Tigrinja and Amharic, through *Uppsalatolkarna AB* (Uppsala Interpreters [Translators] Share Company). On this particular day we were at The *Sprintgymnasiet* (Sprint Secondary School) in Uppsala, the former *Bolandsgymnasiet* (The Bolands Secondary School), now devoted to young refugee students, mainly from Afghanistan and Eritrea. Elisabeth was the name of the person who addressed me. She was a teacher and needed to find out the level of knowledge that the new arrivals, who spoke different languages, had attained in different subjects, before arriving in Sweden.

The Tigrinja-speaking person for whom I was going to translate from Swedish was already in place. An elderly woman sat about three meters from me. When her client came, somewhat late, I learned that the person was from somewhere in French-speaking ("francophone") Africa. To my right sat two women, mother and daughter, whose language was Russian. You could add Arabic, Amharic, Orommiffa, Farsi, Ukrainian, Somali, and many other languages. It was as if waves of languages had reached the shores of Sweden from all the corners of the world. Languages accompanying flight! Flight due to conflict, persecution for religious or political reasons, risks to one's life, hunger and thirst, dreams of better lives!

Elisabeth was one of the dedicated Swedes in the integration service, although her function was specifically related to education. She is one of hundreds, indeed thousands, of Swedes of various professional categories, who give their time, patience, and energy to identify the national and family backgrounds, physical needs, psychological states, and educational backgrounds of tens of thousands of immigrant youth.

Among these often unsung heroes are teachers in a large variety of subjects, school nurses, doctors, lawyers, mentors, "sit-in" parents for youth who are still minors, and persons in other work categories. Conversations with the young refugees with the help of interpreters lead to decisions as to where the newcomers could best be placed to continue their education.

The translation bureau from which I get my assignments, *Uppsalatolkarna AB*, provides high-quality service in several languages. The provision of language services is its basic task. In this sense it has an enabling function among both refugees and Swedish authorities and institutions that request its services.

Semantix is the largest provider of interpreters in the Nordic countries. In 2015 it had to take the lion's share of providing interpreters for over 160,000 refugees who had come to Sweden to seek asylum. However, a good part of these urgent requirements for translation were met by other translation bureaus. During the autumn and winter, *Semantix* and other bureaus saw a bigger demand for interpreters than at any time in the past. The demands for interpreters in Dari, the language spoken in Afghanistan, had gone up by 300%, compared to demands the year before.

A very marked increase in the need for interpreters was recorded in such language families as *Arabic*, *Somali*, and *Tigrinja*. So much so that different translation bureaus needed to do their utmost to meet the challenges facing them in this regard. Shortages of translation services affected important functions of society as well as individuals who stood in need of interpreters for asylum-related issues, for medical care, and for other contacts with Swedish authorities.

Through their enabling functions as facilitators of communication among refugees and Swedish authorities and institutions, these mediators of interpretation have in fact contributed, indirectly, to sound and healthy integration into Swedish society.

Among the organizations that encourage "shared narratives," particularly in the form of literature and art, are The Swedish *Kulturrådet* (The Swedish Arts Council) and *Bibliotekstjänsten* (BTJ), The Library Service.

Kulturrådet is a public authority that operates under the Swedish Ministry of Culture. Among its specific aims is the promotion of the culture of the Sami people and other national, minority groups.

BTJ is a Swedish concern which makes available media products and infomation services for professional users, such as libraries, universities, and research units. Its supply of material consists of novels for adults, professional literature for adults, books for children and youth, printed material on music, compact discs for children, and fact-based films.

BTJ uses reviews also on non-Swedish literature to decide on the purchase of new books for libraries. One of its directives to reviewers reads:

> With regard to novels in languages other than Swedish, characterize the language and style. Indicate the level of comprehensibility of the book

and the type of knowledge that the book would require from a (potential) reader.

Such a directive has in mind readers among immigrants and refugees in Sweden. In this sense, BTJ can be said to be an enabler in the process of the integration of immigrants, refugees, and their families into Swedish society.

Creating a Fabric of Shared Narratives

One of the websites of The Church of Sweden on the issue of the treatment of immigrants and refugees reads:

> To strike root – to be integrated – means to create a fabric of shared narratives. People who have fled to Sweden carry memories and experiences; for example, from life in Syria, Somalia or Afghanistan, and the hardships connected with flight and the challenges that must be faced in settling in Sweden. These memories and hardships are an important part of the narrative about Sweden, just as significant and as important as if one had lived in Sweden through generations. The fabric of shared narratives takes shape when we listen to each other and allow the experiences of all others to be heard. Culture gives us important instruments for this task: literature, art, journalism, drama, etc.

People are more than their experiences. We have much that we share. We live in a time that is characterized by migrations. The way to fellowship and holding together is a matter of recognizing and accepting each other, of reciprocity and generosity.

These words constitute a sober and realistic challenge as far as integration is concerned, regardless of the places of origin of different categories of immigrants.

Immigrants from Continental Europe

Historically speaking, immigrants of Christian persuasions from continental Europe had a much easier time integrating into Swedish society than did immigrants from Asia, The Middle East, and Africa. Sweden's prowess as an industrial nation and its excellence in scholarship and scientific research rests, in no small measure, on the shoulders of generations of continental Europeans. To take a couple of examples, the different members of the families De la Gardie and De Geer, with their outstanding contributions to Swedish life in the fields of industry, scholarship, trade, military service, and diplomacy, are witnesses to this fact. The earliest representative of the De la Gardie family entered Sweden in 1565. The earliest representative of the

De Geer family became a Swedish citizen in 1627. The De la Gardie family traces its roots back to France while the De Geers are of Dutch origin. It was De Geer who became instrumental in the coming of the Walloons from the area around Liege in Belgium to Sweden. These were to make lasting contributions to Sweden's steel industry. The Walloons are further credited with the main role in the construction of the seaport of Gothenburg, now Sweden's second largest city. The benefits that have accrued to Sweden through centuries of Finnish immigration, especially into the richly forested northern parts of the country, are plentiful and lasting.

The fact remains that the number of immigrants from countries of the so-called Third World are now far higher in number than immigrants from continental Europe. This fact plays an important role in the whole matter of integration into Swedish society. A decisive factor in connection with the challenges of integration is, therefore, seeking and identifying potential points of contact, primarily with different categories of immigrants from non-continental Europe.

Shared narratives, listening to each other, literature, art, journalism, drama, accepting each other, reciprocity, and generosity—these are, for the Church of Sweden, the building blocks of a lasting integration. Shared narratives are best mediated by persons who are bridge builders, individuals who know two worlds, as it were, and have been formed by different traditions that can meet and permeate each other.

Comment on my Article

Here are some wise words from my friend Dr. Bereket Yebio:

> Integration is another theme that you reflect on. This issue is becoming increasingly important to focus on at this time of global mass-migration. Those of us who have gone through this process of integration need and can contribute by assisting new migrants, i.e. from Eritrea, to fully integrate in the new society through full participation while retaining and developing their cultural, religious or ethnic identity. There is no contradiction in becoming both Eritrean and Swedish. Integration helps to acquire new knowledge and experience. It also helps to develop beyond pre-occupation only with the past towards thinking globally and creatively. All need to learn to move from a conflict perspective towards united efforts to work for a world which is good and secure for all.

Notes

1   *"The Important Message of the Protests"* in Dagen (The Day), Stockholm, November 21, 2018.

2   Almedal Week, earlier called The Week of Politicians, is held every year in

Visby, Gotland, roughly the first week of July. Representatives of Sweden's political parties and other so-called "Interest Organizations" gather to discuss political and social issues. The sessions or seminars are open for all.

3 Malina Abrahamsson in *Vad är svenskhet i ett mångkulturellt samhälle?* (What is Swedishness in a Multicultural Society?), under the subtitle *From Oneness to Multiculture*, in Dagen, Stockholm, October 26, 2018.

4 News Release from the *Språkvetenskapliga fakulteten* (The Faculty of the Science of Languages), at Uppsala University, November 16, 2018.

Year 2019
Chapter 42

Integration (II):
Ethiopians and Eritreans Meet the Challenge

What can we say about the general inflow of refugees into Sweden after 1997 and about its possible impact on integration? I have not been able to conduct any study in depth on this subject and my answers can therefore be only tentative. The inflow of refugees has grown steadily until it reached an all-time peak in 2015. Refugees from war-torn Syria and its surroundings accounted for the greatest number of asylum seekers. In 2015 there were a total of about 160,000 asylum seekers in Sweden.

According to Sweden's Central Bureau of Statistics, there were a total of 35,142 immigrants born in Eritrea and living in Sweden as of 2015. Of these, 32,099 were citizens of Eritrea (18,742 men, 13,357 women). On December 31, 2015, there were 28,616 Eritrean residents in Sweden, born in Eritrea. There were, furthermore, 7,964 persons who were born in Sweden but had an Eritrean background or origin. According to the Swedish Statistical Central Bureau, there were a total of 45,593 Eritreans in Sweden as of December 2017. Of these, 39,081 had been born in Eritrea, while 6,512 had been born in Sweden. The inflow of Eritrean refugees in the year 2018 can hardly have decreased markedly. The total number of persons of Eritrean origin in Sweden must be somewhat higher than it was in 2017. Following Somalis, Eritreans constitute the largest group of Africans born outside Sweden.

According to Sweden's Central Bureau of Statistics, there were, as of 2016, a total 17,944 immigrants born in Ethiopia and living in Sweden. Of those, 6,225 are citizens of Ethiopia (3,319 men, 2,906 women). In 2016, there were 88 registered returnees ("remigrations") from Sweden to Ethiopia. The number of Ethiopians residing in Sweden as of December 31, 2017 was 24,900. Of these, 19,358 had been born in Ethiopia and 5,542 had been born in Sweden. A number of those who came to Sweden before 1993 were Eritreans but were registered as Ethiopians since Eritrea was a part of Ethiopia at the time.

A Quick Backward Glance

I remember that 21 years ago, I prepared a paper on the topic "Religious and Cultural Elements as Generators of Contact and Conflict among Swedes and Ethiopian and Eritrean Refugees" for presentation at a conference in Macerata, Italy. My main point was the identification of generators of contact and conflict. As a very general observation, I can say that the generators of contact that I pointed out in my article have continued to promote contact (and therefore integration) between Swedes and refugees or immigrants from Ethiopia and Eritrea. Among these generators of contact that are still valid (though, in some cases, to a lesser degree than before) are:

- A reservoir of Swedish missionary experiences from Eritrea and Ethiopia
- A reservoir of development-aid experiences from both countries after the Second World War
- The continuing activities of the *Svensk-Etiopiska Föreningen* (Swedish Ethiopian Association) and its organ *Tenaestelin*
- A meeting of Christian traditions
- Attractive features of refugee cultures like weddings and funerals (There is a clear rise in intermarriages between Ethiopians/Eritreans, and "white" Swedes. I have performed a number of such marriages.)
- A common respect for antiquity and history
-

Delays and Uncertainty in the Asylum-Seeking Process

Recently, I came upon a Swedish book entitled *Mellan hopp och förtvivlan. Erfarenheter och strategier i väntan på asyl* (*Between Hope and Despair. Experiences and Strategies while Waiting for Asylum*) by Rebecka Lennartsson. The subtitle of the book, which came out in 2007, reads: *An Ethnological Inquiry on the Situation of Seekers of Asylum with their own Houses in the Counties of Västmanland and Uppsala*. In the concluding section of the book the author writes:

To flee from one's homeland, demands decisiveness, strength and courage. The first period in Sweden is often characterized by a sense of relief. Soon however, this relief turns into frustration. Waiting begins to characterize the whole of one's life. Informants [i.e. contact persons assigned to asylum-seekers] describe the waiting period partly as 'empty time', marked by boredom, stagnation and painful memories with which one cannot consciously come to terms and partly by anxiety, confusion and nervousness. Many say that they don't dare to trust people. The majority of those who respond to pre-formulated interview questions say that they can't fill their time with something meaningful or with leisure-time activities which result in the development of the person. A feeling of helplessness is a persistently recurrent theme in stories about the daily lives of asylum-seekers. The kind of frustration which results from one's inability to be able to influence one's future and plan one's life is big.[1]

Short as it is, this paragraph gives us a comprehensive and many-sided picture of the challenges that face the asylum seeker in Sweden. It is interesting to note that waiting with uncertainty is the basic problem facing asylum seekers. The newcomer to Sweden is seldom exposed to hunger, thirst, and nakedness. Even medical care is available to the refugee, though probably to a limited extent! The body is taken care of. The mind and heart—i.e., the feelings and psyche—of the asylum seekers are the life spheres that are hit hard.

Helen Okbamikael's Case Study on Eritreans and the Migration-Process

Helen Okbamikael's college-level essay, "Den svenska humanismen i kläm. Fallstudie av den eritreanska migrationsprocessen" ("Swedish Humanism Caught in a Corner. A Case-Study of The Eritrean Migration-Process"), came out in essay form in the Spring Term of 2018, under the guidance of Yonhyok Choe, at Linnaeus University in Kalmar, Växjö. The study argues that Eritrean asylum seekers were highly inconvenienced by specific Swedish requirements. Helen's abstract of the essay reads:

> This essay aims to illustrate how a country like Sweden, that seems to be driven by humanism, can potentially act in a way that is completely different to its humanitarian image. This is illustrated by exploring the problematic features of the migration-process Eritreans face in Sweden today, a procedure that requires that they seek Eritrean embassies in order to obtain identity documents. This study is based on a text analysis of the international regulations that are being violated in the Eritrean case. The result has been analyzed and explained with the help of a framework based on Gidden's structuration theory. The research shows that there has

been a violation of human rights, of the Refugee Convention and of the UN resolution.[2]

Under the sub-title "Problemformulering" ("Formulation of Problem") in her paper, Helen writes:

> The case and the problem which is going to be dealt with in this essay arise from the confirmation of identity that The Swedish Migration Agency requires from Eritreans. This means that to be granted citizenship or family reunification in Sweden, the person in question needs either a passport from his/her homeland or a certificate accompanied by a photograph, issued by an Eritrean Embassy. The first alternative is practically impossible if one is to leave Eritrea, since the state seldom issues passports, given the fact that it is forbidden to leave the country. This leaves only an Eritrean embassy as an alternative.

> Internationally as well as in Stockholm, Eritrean embassies require that exiled Eritreans pay a two-percent tax and sign a so-called "Document of Regret" (Eritrean Embassy, 2018). The two-percent tax implies that the embassy requires payment from all incomes earned as of 1992 and forward. The Document of Regret, which is not available on the website of the embassy but has been mentioned by different sources, implies that one must apologize for having fled from National Service and be prepared to accept the punishment which is deemed appropriate. (Lifos, 2015, p. 21)[3]

Helen's study is available in Swedish and its publication at an academic institution in Sweden gives it the status of a source worthy of being referred to. Her study is primarily a critique of Swedish practice. Her arguments are to be taken seriously even though she has not *quoted* from the Document of Regret, allegedly formulated by Eritrean embassies, to prove her case. The problems that the essay takes up reflect some of the thorny issues with which Eritreans seeking asylum and integration in Sweden must grapple. After all, a turbulent entry into Swedish society must also imply a turbulent beginning in the process of integration.

Positive Developments

It should be pointed out that bilateral relations between Sweden and Eritrea as well as between Sweden and Ethiopia were not good during the two decades leading to 2018. The main cause of tension between Sweden and Eritrea had to do with the confinement, since September 2001 and without trial (according to Sweden), of the journalist Isaak Dawit, a Swedish citizen (according to Sweden) as well as an Eritrean citizen (according to Eritrea).

Chapter 42

The imprisonment of the two Swedish journalists, Martin Schibbye and Johan Persson, in Ethiopia in July of 2011 on charges of supporting terrorism in the Ogaden region was a major reason for strained relations between Ethiopia and Sweden. The two journalists were granted clemency in September of 2012.

The coming to power of Prime Minister Abiy Ahmed Ali in Ethiopia in 2018 and his successful rapprochement with President Isaias of Eritrea have contributed to the improvement of relations not only among nations on the Horn but also between Sweden and the two sister countries, Ethiopia and Eritrea.

Many of the refugees who had had to journey through the Sahara and Libya have been subjected to blackmail, imprisonment, beatings, rape, and other forms of mistreatment. Many of them come with unrealistically high expectations, and the simple fact of having to wait until their applications for asylum are processed creates turbulence in them. Such circumstances do not contribute to a smooth process of integration.

As a general observation, one can state that Ethiopian and Eritrean refugees have not been specifically targeted as burdens or risk factors in Swedish society. However, they too tend to be included in the more sweeping criticisms aimed at immigrants in more recent years.

Gratitude Among Elderly Eritreans and Ethiopians

Older Ethiopians and Eritreans living in Sweden are, in my opinion, among the most grateful witnesses to the generosity and care with which Swedish society has received immigrants and refugees. As a pastor, I have had many occasions to meet and talk to such people on a variety of subjects. Most of them came to Sweden to join their children or other close relatives after their labour-productive years were over. I have heard these older people say:

> These people [i.e., the Swedes] don't know us from Adam! We did not put any labour into the life and Economy of this country! We have not paid taxes. And yet they treat us as if we were deserving of pensions and other benefits! May God bless them! May God bless their earth [meaning "country"]!

Such expressions of gratitude do not imply that these older representatives of the Ethiopian and Eritrean refugee communities don't find Sweden's long and often dark and cold winters trying. It does not mean that they do not, at times, feel lonely and isolated. Their shaky knowledge of the Swedish language does create a barrier to communication in everyday contacts. Be they Christians or Muslims, these elderly Eritreans and Ethiopians often feel sadly confused in the face of Swedish lifestyles, faith in God being challenged by secularism and by moral standards deviating, according to these old Muslims or Orthodox and Evangelical faithful, from the will of The Creator.

The memory of the fact that Swedish missionaries had preached the Gospel in Eritrea and Ethiopia and taught people in these countries the tenets of the Christian Faith makes it very difficult for these older Ethiopian and Eritrean Christians to see a Sweden that they feel is losing its Christian past.

Integration Inwards and Integration Outwards

There are Ethiopian and Eritrean Orthodox Tewahdo congregations in Sweden. Their worship services are marked by vitality and youth are a conspicuous feature of their gatherings. I have the impression that the refugee experience, the feeling of being away from home, has created a longing and an eager engagement in efforts to plant one's home church and its rich ceremonial traditions on Swedish soil.

Such a development can contribute to integration into one's new, Swedish living space. It can provide a familiar and homelike platform for joint spiritual activities with one's own Ethiopian or Eritrean fellowmen. This is what I would call "Integration Inwards." This tendency is encouraged by our herd mentality. We are drawn to our likes on many levels: language, culture, festivals, food habits, humour, memories, etc. There is something positive and preservative about this herd mentality. But it is a tendency that does not favour a quick and effective integration into Swedish society.

Re-establishing and recreating one's old home milieu in one's new homeland can create distance between Orthodox Christians and Swedish Christian communities. It can affect what I call "Integration Outwards" negatively. This can result in parallel Christian communities that do not meet with each other in a meaningful manner. We thus have situations in which Ethiopian and Eritrean Orthodox Christians request Swedish congregations to give them access to places of worship and other kinds of assistance without showing a serious interest in what these Swedish Christian groups are and where they stand on matters of faith. There has, in short, been a lack of serious dialogue on the church level so far. Fortunately, I know that the leadership of the Church in Eritrea and here in Sweden now want a change in this regard. There are definite plans to set in motion the type of dialogue that can foster mutual understanding.

Some Examples of Successful Integration
My Ethiopian Cousin Fana Habteab

It was October 24, 2018, United Nations Day, and we were gathered at the *Fredens Hus* (The House of Peace) at Uppsala Castle. The time was 17:30. A small, colorful brochure with the title *Uppsalas Museum* (The Museum of Uppsala) describes *Fredens Hus* in the following words:

> At the House of Peace, you will find exhibitions on issues of human rights and challenges which encourage reflection, dialogue and action. You will learn about Dag Hammarskjold and Raoul Wallenberg, among others, all of whom have made important contributions in working for peace and human rights. Moreover, The House of Peace conducts educational programmes and produces material for a variety of audiences.

The female chairperson of the gathering reminded us that the UN was constituted on October 24, 1945. The audience at the day's gathering was cosmopolitan. Native Swedes, persons of Latin American backgrounds, Ethiopians, Eritreans, persons from other African countries, a person from the former Yugoslavia, one from Japan, and someone from the Middle East were among those who attended.

I had been invited by a female cousin on my mother's side, the active, 80-year-old Fana Habteab, the wife of Dr. Belatchew Asrat. Fana and three other persons were awarded The Uppsala Peace Prize for sacrificing their time and efforts to making the world a better place. The Peace Prize had been awarded in 2014 and 2016. It is given every other year.

On this occasion The Peace Prize of the United Nations Association of Uppsala, 2018, was awarded to the organization known as RISK (Riksföreningen stoppa kvinnlig könsstympning, or the National Association "Stop Female Genital Mutilation") and to Fana Habteab in the category called Human Rights, for their successful and extremely important work of enlightening people about and stopping female genital mutilation. The certificate of the award was signed by Mona Strindberg, chairperson of the association. Female genital mutilation is a problem that pops up here and there, mainly among immigrants and refugees in Sweden.

A woman by the name of Karin Sehlin received the Peace Prize for her contributions to the wellbeing of children who were new arrivals in Sweden. In 2017, she had written a book entitled *Ser du mig? Nyanlända barn och unga berättar.* (*Do You See Me? Newly Arrived Children and Youth Narrate*).

A group consisting of five women who answered to the name *Gottsunda Mammor* (Gottsunda Mothers) received the Uppsala Peace Prize for courageously giving their time and energy to youth in the often turbulent suburb of Uppsala known as Gottsunda. These women were described as bridge builders, encouragers, and rescuers of youth and families. One could see that they were persons of non-white backgrounds whose fluency in Swedish indicated a birth or upbringing in Sweden.

There were about 50 persons present for the ceremonious occasion in the pleasant assembly room with a high ceiling.

I would like to add that on December 7, 2006, my cousin Fana was given the *hedersbemärkelse* (Honourable Mention) for what was described as "tireless efforts on a very difficult question where the main aim was to protect children in conformity with human rights and the *UN Convention on the Rights of the Child* (CRC)." The recognition was given in memory of Karin and August Bangs and was signed by the chairperson, Beatrice Hofstadius.

Fana was, furthermore, awarded a diploma as The Year's Active Woman for 2018 by The National Union for Home and Society. The recognition for this diploma reads:

> Fana Habteab is a member at large and an elected member of the executive committee of Home and Society in Uppsala. She works with great engagement to prevent the lasting damage that can result in the lives of girls through genital mutilation. She is actively engaged in preventive measures both in Sweden and in other countries, particularly Ethiopia, her country of origin. She gives lectures and organizes seminars related to this subject, which is closely related to the concerns of Home and Society, not least in view of our involvement of many years in the Fistula Association.

The diploma was awarded on October 6, 2018 and was signed by the chairperson of Home and Society, Siw Warholm.

The evening whose activities I have described above testifies to encounters, challenges, efforts, confrontation, and mobilization in multicultural and multiracial contexts in present-day Swedish society. I have tried to illustrate the cosmopolitan character of the audience at the evening gathering. And what is striking is that a significant number of those who were recognized that evening had immigrant or refugee backgrounds. The creation of a culture of dialogue lies behind the success of the undertakings recognized that evening.

Architect Rahel Belatchew

It is now time for me to write some words about a daughter of my cousin Fana Habteab, whose engagement in issues related to female refugees and immigrants in Sweden was described in the preceding paragraphs. Rahel is a rising star in the field of architecture here in Sweden. She has done her climbing without too much noise, quietly, steadily, with a cold discipline, a stubborn kind of self-confidence, and a refusal to be defeated by obstacles and challenges.

One of the things she said to me was: "It is a matter of coming back, again and again. Not giving, up. Fighting on!"

She has been in Europe—more specifically, in France—away from her family, who live in Sweden. She has studied architecture in French, a language for which I have great respect. Rahel's skills and imaginative visions are being sought far and wide. Ethiopia has been summoning her. One of her plans is a church building for The Ethiopian Orthodox here in Sweden. She is a recognized jury member for top-level architectural competitions.

I read an article in Swedish, entitled *Belatchew and Svea-Buildings Win a Competition for Hagsättra Hub*. The first lines of the article read:

> Belatchew Architects and Svea-Residences have been selected as winners for the construction of a new landmark in the Hagsättra Centre with 130 flats for rent. The winning proposal goes under the name of H-Hub.

Belatchew Architects was established in 2006 by Rahel Belatchew. The headquarters of the office is in Stockholm, but its activities are international in scope. Belatchew Architects works with a broad spectrum of activities that cover private houses and flats as well as offices and buildings for communal purposes.

When Rahel turned fifty on January 13, 2019, the well-known Swedish daily, *Dagens Nyheter*, honoured her with an article. Here are some quotations from and remarks on the article that appeared in the Family Section on January 12, 2019:

> Things are going well for Architect Rahel Belatchew, the creator, among other projects, of *Tensta Tower* and the coming landmark *Discus* in central Nacka.

> In an interview in connection with her birthday, Rahel states that there were about 20 persons in her firm and that the firm needed to employ more people. She underlines the importance of perseverance in the work of an architect. She does admit that a building boom in recent years had contributed to her success but that the basic explanation for her success was plain hard work! She adds,

About fifteen years ago we, as architects, were almost marginalized. Right now architecture is at a premium. Municipalities that sell town-plots (for building purposes) demand architecture with quality. An example is Discus (which has already won two international architecture prizes), in Nacka, a neighbourhood with a 30-floor high residential block as a landmark drawn by Belatchew Architects.

As an architect, Rahel wants to be involved in all stages of a project. She is always on the lookout for new building opportunities in a somewhat sluggish construction industry. Among the fruits of Rahel's architectural efforts one can name Tensta Tower, a project granted recognition for its 18 floors with 243 flats. It won The Chamber of Commerce Prize for Town-milieus for 2018 and has been called the year's most daring, smartest, and most meaningful high-rise. As far as the future is concerned, Rahel envisions participation in foreign exhibitions, in localities like the studio museum of Carl Eldh and the Roca Gallery in London.[4]

I wanted to mention The *Tensta Tower* in particular because I know that Tensta is a neighbourhood with thousands of people of immigrant background. What is done for Tensta is bound to contribute to the success of integration in Tensta, and its vicinity!

An Eritrean Professor—Aman Russom

The children of Eritrean and Ethiopian immigrants or refugees are indeed making positive inroads into Swedish society. These are youth who have succeeded in the realm of integration into Swedish Society. In the latter part of the first week of October 16, 2018, an Eritrean in his early forties called to tell me the good news that he had been granted a professorship at The Royal Institute of Technology (*Kungliga Tekniska högskolan*) in Stockholm. I responded with great joy and added my fatherly blessings. After a couple of days, I wrote to the person in question, Aman Russom, and stated that I wanted to know more about the professorship that he had been granted. He wrote the following letter:

> You are such an inspiration and my heartfelt thanks to you and that was also why I decided to call and share the moment with you. I have become a Professor in 'Clinical micro fluidics': the subject is interdisciplinary within nanotechnology and biomedical engineering and my research line holds great promise to address some of the critical challenges in global heath, namely the need to develop affordable diagnostic tools for diagnosing neglected diseases at resource limited settings. Hence, it is my hope and vision that such a development would benefit countries in sub-Sahara Africa including our beloved Eritrea.

The respect and gratitude that Aman expresses in these words underlines the significance of the informal, traditional mentorship that is still alive among Ethiopians and Eritreans in the Diaspora. Respect for the aged is part of the upbringing of children in the traditions of both nations. This resource is a creator and sustainer of positive contact with people of all national backgrounds. It is also a tool for the solution of not a few conflicts among the young.

There is, however, more to say about the implications of his letter to me. Here is a son of immigrants or refugees who had come to Sweden, a group sometimes accused of being parasites that consume the hard-won financial and social resources of ageing Swedish people.

This young man is now engaged in *nanotechnology*, a new field of research. Here we have an area of knowledge that even native-born Swedes would find extremely challenging! Many Swedes can now begin to imagine that refugees too can contribute to Swedish life on such a level.

One cannot say that persons of immigrant background of Aman's capacity grow on trees in Sweden. But their numbers are increasing at a faster rate than many think. A source of gratitude and hope!

Lidia Habtemikael and Her Findings on Malaria in Eritrea

It was an evening in the month of September, 2019 here in Uppsala. The Eritrean parents of Lidia and Diana Habtemikael, Fitui Habtemikael and Saba Haile, had prepared a feast for a belated celebration in connection with the academic achievements of their two daughters. Though I arrived late, I was received with warmth. I am glad that I came to the feast.

I must jump over the details of the rich and happy feast. I did get in touch with the daughters after the feast and asked questions about their studies. Lidia told me that her younger sister, Diana, had acquired her college degree in Social Studies around Christmas time and was now, some weeks after the feast, back in Umeå to work for her Master's degree. A couple of weeks after the feast, Lidia sent me the paper she had written as part of her work for her M.Sc. In Pharmacy!

I doubt that the majority of the guests at the feast mentioned above knew about the subject of Lidia's research. She had done her academic work in both Sweden and Eritrea. She names José Pedro Gil (Department of Women's and Children's Health, International Maternal and Child Health) and Mulugeta Russom (Eritrean National Pharmacovigilance Centre, Ministry of Health, in Asmara, Eritrea) as supervisors.

Here is new knowledge about malaria being shared by Sweden and Eritrea, thanks to a bridge builder, a contributor of knowledge-based integration, a young female by the name of Lidia Habtemikael, and her Swedish and Eritrean research fellows. Talk of integration on a high, academic level between a poor East African nation and a rich Nordic nation! Lidia's research is a bridge-building project. And what did the bridge, the integration link, look like? What was its name? Here we go!

Extrapyramidal Side Effects (EPB)—Unusual Side Effects Resulting from Treatment for Malaria

Let me quote the "awesomely" technical title of this "bridge":

CYP2C8*3-Polymorphism and Extrapyramidal Adverse Events Associated with Antimalarial Artesunate/Amodiaquine Treatment in an Eritrean Population.

Wikipedia defines the term "Extrapyramidal" as follows:

The Extrapyramidal system regulates posture and skeletal muscle tone. Extrapyramidal symptoms (also called Extrapyramidal side effects) get their name because they are symptoms of disorders in this system.

I understand that CYP2C8 is a lever enzyme. And an enzyme, according to Longman's Dictionary, is:

A chemical substance produced by living cells in plants and animals that causes changes in other chemical substances without being changed itself.

In short, the paper that Lidia has written describes, to the best of my knowledge, a study in which the combination of a specific kind of medication against malaria (*Antimalarial Artesunate/ Amodiaquine Treatment*) and the action of a specific type of lever enzyme (CYP2C8*3) in the body can result in adverse side effects that go by the name of *Extrapyramidal* side effects. Some of these side effects are involuntary muscle movements, stiffness, and slurred speech.

It is also my layman's understanding that the research in which Lidia was involved has asked the question: Are these side effects the results of only a specific type of medication and the work of an enzyme on the medicine, or do they in fact go even further back to the genes of a specific population group?

Lidia writes:

Extrapyramidal side effects don't affect all. This raises the question as to whether patients who display these side effects have some genetic traits which make them especially sensitive to the medicine. To find such traits can be of significance for high-risk patients, since such patients should be offered alternative treatments for Malaria. There are two (compatible) hypotheses which stand out from the rest: the patients who have been affected [by side effects] are either unable to eliminate AQ [the medicine] well, or (and) they show an individual, non dose-dependent idiosyncratic reaction.

What I found most interesting among the points of departure was the suggestion that reactions to medication for malaria may be related to genes. I was also struck by the statement that "unlucky patients accumulate too much medication and are very sensitive to their effects."

At the very end of Lidia's paper there is a paragraph entitled Conclusion. She writes:

> The results of the presented study reveal that the low activity CYP2C8*3 allele [variant] is present in the investigated Eritrean population. However, larger genotyping studies, as well as pharmacokinetic and epidemiologic studies involving all nine ethnic groups are required to confirm the potential association of the minor allele with Extrapyramidal adverse events developed upon AS/AQ treatment for uncomplicated *P. falciparum* Malaria.

Do I understand everything in this paragraph? No, but I have a stubborn feeling that Lidia is telling us that the function of a certain type of enzyme (a protein in the body) in connection with a specific kind of medication for malaria, can possibly make Eritreans in the Sahel area more vulnerable to adverse side effects, and that genetic factors may play a role in this whole matter!

Read to find out more. And congratulate Lidia for being one of the trailblazers as far as academic research among Eritreans in Sweden is concerned.

Notes

1   Rebecka Lennartsson, p. 88.
2   H. Okbamikael, *Den svenska humanismen i kläm. Fallstudie av den eritreanska migrationsprocessen*. See Abstract in work mentioned above. 2018. college-level essay, "Den svenska humanismen i kläm. Fallstudie av den eritreanska migrationsprocessen" ("Swedish Humanism Caught in a Corner. A Case-Study of The Eritrean Migration-Process"), came out in essay form in the Spring Term of 2018, under the guidance of Yonhyok Choe, at Linnaeus University in Kalmar, Växjö.
3   H. Okbamikael, op.cit. P.1. Lifos is the designation for *Migrationsverkets databas för landinformation- och omvärldsanalys.* (The Database for Infor-

mation on countries and for the Analysis of the Surrounding World or Context). Whether Eritrean embassies regard the so-called "two-percent tax" as a 'tax' in the strict sense of the term has been debated.

4   See the book *Attitude As Style*. Rahel Belatchew, Architect. 2019. Edited by Thomas Lauri. Contributions by Daniel Golling, Nils Forsberg, Martin Rörby and Paul Finch. Published by Arvinius + Orfeus Publishers AB, Stockholm.

Year 2019
Chapter 43

Integration (III):
An Ethio-Swedish Family Makes Sweden Its Home

To strike root—to be integrated—means to create a fabric of shared narratives. That was what Ella Wolde Selassie did in 2014. She shared the narrative of her family. Ella is a former missionary of the *Evangeliska Fosterlands-Stiftelsen* (Swedish Evangelical Mission) to Ethiopia, married to Qes Taye Wolde Selassie, an Ethiopian pastor of the Evangelical Church Mekane Yesus. Ella gathered the whole of her family's history in a book entitled *Herdepojken och Bönhusflickan* (*The Shepherd Boy and the Girl from the Prayer House*) by Ella Wolde Selassie, wife of Qes (Pastor), now the late, Taye Wolde Selassie.

The term "Prayer House" is a translation of the Swedish word *bönhus* (literally, "prayer house"). The Swedish revival movement known as *Evangeliska Fosterlands Stiftelsen* (Evangelical Motherland Society), known internationally as Swedish Evangelical Mission, was established in 1856. It operated within the Church of Sweden but also enjoyed a good measure of independence in its work both in Sweden and abroad. In Sweden, this revival movement sponsored or arranged worship services or prayer meetings not only in church buildings owned by The Church of Sweden but also in simpler, smaller, home-like chapels known as prayer houses. Ella had evidently spent her childhood in the residential section of such a prayer house, most likely because her parents took care of the prayer house. She later became a missionary in Ethiopia. Her husband, Taye Wolde Sellassie, had spent a part of his childhood in Ethiopia as a shepherd boy!

In a review of the book for *Upsala Nya Tidning* (UNT, Uppsala's only daily) on July 10, 2014, Eva Hellberg writes:

> Her seeking for facts, letters from relatives, has now become a book of 370 pages. In the book, "The Shepherd Boy and the Girl from the Prayer House" she has documented a time gone by, with examples from culture, religion, life-style and traditions. Pictures, maps, and even a glossary are available to guide the reader. Ella Wolde Selassie says,

> It feels good that I am ready. I have reached my goal. I have written primarily for children and grandchildren, but also for others who are interested in reading our two life-narratives and see how times have changed in the course of a whole century.

Qes Taye, Ella's husband, left Ethiopia in May of 1977, on an invitation from Gamla Uppsala Parish, to serve as an exchange pastor for a year. His family followed suit in the summer of 1977. Ella writes:

> I and the children landed at Arlanda airport some days before Midsummer. Taye stood there with wide-open arms and welcomed us in the company of my brother Rune. We brought in our entire luggage without difficulty. I even had a thick, rolled-up Ethiopian mat [carpet]. The children were so happy that they clung to Taye. We headed towards the home of Rune where Taye had lived since his arrival some weeks earlier. ... We had much to narrate for each other.

> Next evening we took the train northwards. ... We had a whole summer ahead of us. We knew very little of what the year would imply but now that we had left Ethiopia there could be no obstacle that we wouldn't be able to overcome. When we arrived in Skellefteå on Thursday morning we met all those relatives who could take time to come and welcome us. ...

> Next day we woke up to a Midsummer Eve with a steady downpour. For us, who are used to rain [in Ethiopia] at this time of the year, rainfall didn't make any difference. But of course we would have preferred sunshine. In our hearts the sun shone all the time. Grandmother Anna and my other siblings with their children from Bureå came in the afternoon and we celebrated the day together. How could we dance around the Midsummer Pole while it rained cats and dogs all the time? We decorated the pole at the entrance of the barn, took it in and laid it on the floor. We then danced around it. For Taye, Ruth and Yohannes, everything was new but they danced and joined in the singing of songs like *Sju vackra flickor* (Seven beautiful girls), and *Björnen sover* (The bear is asleep). Soon the weather lightened up. The children and I went to bed. But Taye joined Gunilla

and Torsten who drove to the forest. Midsummer night was as bright as the day.

Up there in those latitudes the sun is hardly away for more than an hour during the day. Taye went around saying, "It is fantastic! It is fantastic"! To experience light at night! Their task in the forest was to gather birch-bark. They came home with big, long bits which would be stretched and dried. In the autumn Gunilla had attended a course in birch-handicraft. At the course they made some beautiful objects, among which was an Advent-star which we received as a gift the following Christmas. After many years Gunilla asked her children, who were adults now, which midsummer they remembered as the most pleasant. They answered, in unison: The one when we danced at the barn. Rain does not destroy everything. Instead it creates fellowship.[1]

To write in such a manner is indeed to create a fabric of shared narratives. Ella's narrative describes first encounters, first impressions, first discoveries, first joys, first hopes. It is a story of integration at its softest, at its most inviting. A necessary first step for an Ethio-Swedish family with fresh memories from turbulent Ethiopia. It is touching to read about Qes Taye, a dyed-in-the-wool Ethiopian, who says of his experiences in Sweden: "It is fantastic!"

But I remember meeting him in Uppsala many years later and greeting him with the question: *Indemin aläh?* (እንደምን አለህ), "How are you?" He gave me my oft-quoted reply: *Ikärakäralehu!* (እካረካራለሁ), literally, "I am debating or arguing!" [meaning: "I am fighting. I have not given up!"].

At the time when I greeted him, he was no longer enveloped in the soft and warm experiences of his first weeks in Sweden. Since then, he had had to make several adjustments. He had worked for a year as a visiting pastor in the parish of Old Uppsala, where he held talks on Ethiopia. He had also worked as a teacher of Amharic at the school in Nyby, also in Uppsala. He had learnt to ride a bicycle, as well as to ski. He said, among other things, that he saw that others liked eating fermented herring. That encouraged him to taste said fish dish.

When his one-year assignment at the Old Uppsala parish was over, Taye wondered what he was to do next. Returning to Ethiopia was not the most natural move to take at the time. Should he move to England and study Pastoral Counseling? But there was no scholarship that would help him to do that. He applied for a course in Swedish, which would then make it possible for him to take up some type of vocational training. He was accepted into the programme "Swedish for Immigrants." He was able to continue his subsidized studies for the vocation of a "turner" (a person who shapes wood or metal with a special tool). This gave him a chance to enrich his Swedish further. He finally got a full-time job at the company known as Sörlings, in the town of Märsta. He worked under the name of Wolde and was appreciated by many of his coworkers for his thoroughness. He retired in 1994.

My mind goes back to his words, *Ikärakäralehu!* (እካራካራለሁ) literally, "I am debating or arguing!" [meaning: "I am fighting. I have not given up!"]. These words too say something of the implications of integration into Swedish society, in spite of a demanding set of circumstances and contexts. Qes Taye, who passed away on July 13, 2017, was a successful "integrator"! Loved by Ethiopians and Swedes alike, he remembered his role as pastor and elder among Ethiopians and Eritreans.

Notes

1   Wolde Selassie 2014, 328–330.

Year 2005
Chapter 44

A Farewell to Cars!

It was a beautiful, sunny day in July of 2005. High summer in Sweden! I was waiting for bus Number 8, at the bus stop closest to our flat in the northern part of Uppsala. I watched cars speeding by. Some were driven by people who looked like Eritreans or Ethiopians or Somalis or Sudanese. As one of them passed, I felt a sting of regret, a jab of melancholy.

I can't drive a car here in Sweden. I don't have a Swedish driver's license. All of a sudden, I was faced with the real prospect of not being able to drive here in Sweden at all. Trying to secure a driver's license here is like working for a college degree. Almost! I have an old Ethiopian driver's license. The plain and somewhat embarrassing fact is that I have not, in spite of repeated efforts, passed the exams for a Swedish driver's license. Is this perhaps a farewell to cars?

It was in this connection that I thought of Ernest Hemingway's famous novel, *A Farewell to Arms*, which first appeared in the year 1929.

It occurred to me that there were many such farewells in life. This is so in sports. There was a day when Pelle, the legendary Brazilian football player, said "Farewell to Football!" There was a day when statesmen, army generals, athletes, and opera singers had to say "Farewell" to their respective professions.

There are certainly farewells of a more painful nature in the intimacies of family life. Perhaps due to damage, an accident that made it impossible for spouses to enjoy normal sexual relations! Where they in fact had to say: "Farewell to Sex!"

It is said of Emperor Haile Selassie I that he hung on to power too long, and that his sad end was probably a result of this fact. He was, according to this view, not prepared to say, "Farewell to Power!" early enough. Julius

Nyerere of Tanzania didn't make that mistake! He resigned from office in time, apparently willingly and readily. The difficult but noble secret of accepting hard facts! I am reminded of Paul Tournier's book *The Seasons of Life*,[1] a work that reminds us that life has its seasons and that these must be accepted and affirmed for what they are.

To accept a reduction of one's sphere of contacts and operations, without frantically struggling to hold on to one's past, is one of life's great challenges. It is the idea of finality, the idea of the irreversibility of an experience that tends to rule out hope and meaning in life. Churchill is said to have defined success as "going from failure to failure without loss of enthusiasm."[2] A jarring but fitting recipe for dealing with ageing and its implications!

Every farewell implies some kind of welcome. Every limitation opens the door to some kind of opportunity. Nyerere left the corridors of power but was welcomed into the select world of senior statesmen. Pelle left the limelight of football stadiums but became an honoured guest at special games and was consulted as a judge and counsellor.

For me, the experience at the bus stop mentioned above was a painful revelation. I discovered that my self-image was more dependent on what I could produce than on what I was as a person. My attitude seemed to suggest that a person's value is dependent on what he or she can produce. What hurt me and felt like an irreversible failure was the thought of not living up to a certain image, that of an owner and driver of a car.[3]

Aren't there more important things to grieve over for a man approaching seventy? In many African countries where there is war, hunger, sickness, persecution, there are millions of people who would gladly kiss the ground at the bus stop where I stood, a thousand times. For these utterly desperate people, the mere opportunity of stepping on Swedish soil would be a cause for jubilation, even if driver's licenses were to be forever banished from their lives! Indeed, our needs and sorrows are relative.

My thoughts go back to one of Eric Fromm's books, *To Have or To Be?* That is the crucial question. I also think of the two books in Swedish, *Den Tredje Åldern* (*The Third Age Bracket*) and *Tid att vara ensam* (*Time to Be Alone*) by Patricia Tudor Sandahl.[4]

We need visions, alarm-clocks to remind us, from time to time, of values that cannot be counted in terms of production and ownership.

Notes

1   Paul Thourner, The Seasons of Life. Westminster John Knox, 1963.
2   Quoted in Katrine Stewart's *A Book of Life*. 2001, Quiet Waters Publications, Bolivar MO, p.61.

3   I realise that those of you in the United States, Europe and other countries where the systems of public transportation are perhaps not highly developed, cannot do without your cars. I am thinking of Sweden where opportunities to use public buses, trains and bicycles are excellent.

4   E. Fromm, *To Have or To Be*. Bloomsbury Academic. 2013; Patricia Tudor Sandahl, *Den Tredje Åldern,* Bonniers Audio, 2007; Tid at vara ensam. Ljudbok 2014. Swedish.

Year 2010
Chapter 45

Eritrea's Nevertheless!

I visited my maternal uncle, Ato Woldeab Woldemariam, at his home in Asmara sometime in the first half of the 1990s. He was then already marked by his Parkinson's and his hand (or hands) shook. I knew that his days were numbered. He was not only a relative but also a father figure, a reminder of my parents, one of whom had already died. One day, while at his home, I felt a strong urge to ask him to bless me. I don't know exactly why. As I stood before him, he put his shaking hands on my head, bent over me and uttered a slow, well-formulated blessing.

I don't remember all that he said. But I have preserved some clear impressions. I know that he wanted me to stay true to Eritrea, the one overwhelming topic of his turbulent life. And on a day like May 24th, I feel that I must at least try to honour him, his fellow aspirers and contenders, and the generations of Eritreans who have become their spiritual heirs.

Should I Believe My Eyes?

I sat in front of our television set at home in Uppsala, Sweden, sometime in May of 2009. The pictures I saw left me dumbfounded. Carnage (slaughter) was the one word that came to my mind. Shreds of metal, tattered clothing, and mutilated limbs on military vehicles, on vegetation, on the ground. Here, an invisible hand had been at work. I couldn't see any soldiers in the photo. But someone had rolled tanks, bodies, and trees into a bizarre graveyard. A couple of days later I saw TV pictures from an official reception. A victory was being celebrated in the presence of well-dressed men of state and army commanders. And what was the occasion? The crushing of a highly motivated movement! Indeed, the bringing to an end of an almost forty-year-old struggle for self-determination.

Louise Arbour, the head of the International Crisis Group which has called for an internal review of the U.N.'s conduct during Sri Lanka's bloody 2009 civil war, has drawn our attention to the charge that the Tamil Tigers were one of the world's most brutal insurgent movements, held by some to be responsible for massive war crimes, forcing hundreds of thousands of civilians to serve as human shields, and murdering those who sought to flee to safety. I am not in a position to comment on such devastating accusations. I shall not try to idolize or defend the Tamil Tigers. I do however want to draw attention to the frightful end that their struggle met and to say that Eritrea would have probably met a similar fate, had Mengistu Haile-Mariam and his allies had their way.[1]

Nevertheless, Eritrea didn't.

I had seen the losers, the Tamil Tigers, on other pictures and TV presentations, both before and after the scenes I have described above. My eyes beheld thousands of men, women, and children. Once they were reputed as heroic and tenacious. Now they had been reduced to a worn-out, hungry, and broken multitude. A former colleague of mine, a Professor of History of Religion at the University of Uppsala, told me that about 280,000 refugees from said conflict now lived under conditions that reminded one of concentration camps. He should know. For years he has had close contacts with the leadership of the organization I have in mind.[2]

In his blog for July 29, 2009, Selvarasa Pathmanathan (PK), "heir" to LTTE's (Liberation Tigers of Tamil Eelam) late leader, Veluppillai Pirapakaran, writes:

> There were principally two reasons as to why benefits did not come our way through the open diplomatic doors.
>
> 1. On the basis of geopolitical interests in the regions of South Asia and the Indian Ocean, Super powers such as India, US and China opted to safeguard their interests by keeping Sri Lanka as a single territorial entity. This gave way to an international position that was against our goal of Tamil Eelam.
>
> 2. The entire world had come to a common opinion that the armed struggle in the island should somehow come to an end. As a result it became impractical to gain international support for an armed struggle.

One could very well argue that Eritrea and tens (probably hundreds) of thousands of Eritreans could have met the same fate, had Colonel Mengistu Haile-Mariam and his allies had their way. And, for almost the *same* reasons for which the struggle of LTTE ended in a crushing defeat!

Nevertheless, Eritrea didn't meet the same fate.

Hotel Rwanda

I wrote the following words (here reproduced with some editorial additions) at my home in Uppsala on the evening of August 8, 2009:

> It is 23.06 and I have just finished watching the film Hotel Rwanda. I am both shaken and moved. A conflagration, a holocaust, frenzy, inhumanity! Hatred cultivated, consciously, religiously, through generations. Cruelty refined. Death made a daily routine. The machete made an instrument of virtue among Hutus on their murderous rampage among completely helpless Tutsi.
>
> The Hutu too had once been hurt, I am told, by the preferential treatment shown to the Tutsi by a colonial power called Belgium. And now the Hutu were taking vengeance. This is roughly the way the background of the conflict has been explained to us who make up the rank and file among the observers of this tragedy.
>
> Of course all films tend to accentuate both virtues and vices. But the Hutu, Paul Rusesabagina, manager of Sabena de Mille Collins Hôtel in Kigali, and his wife Tatiana, of Tutsi blood, remain imprinted on my mind. Their courageous acts of mercy and bridge-building among Hutu and Tutsi, among black and white, are deeply impressive. The songs (one of which had the recurring words 'Rwanda, Rwanda'), still echo in my ears and heart. At the end of the film, as the television screen kept rolling out the long list of actors, co-actors, scene people, and other coworkers in the production of the film, I sat in my chair, sunken in sorrow and immovable.

Eritrea's tribal and religious conflicts were not as pronounced as those of Rwanda. But there were the makings of trouble. And I asked myself: "What if the rumblings of religious and regional conflicts in Eritrea in the late 1940s had ended where the Hutu-Tutsi conflict did in 1994?"

Nevertheless, they didn't.

Stephen H. Longrigg's Words on Eritrea's Future

I was at Carolina Rediviva, the main library of Uppsala University, on the afternoon of February 26, 2010, to claim a book that I had ordered. The book was Stephen Longrigg's *A Short History of Eritrea*, which came out in 1945. It was the first time that I had had a copy of the book in my hands. In my eagerness, I went straight to the preface and started reading.

Longrigg spoke warmly and appreciatively about the people of Eritrea but eventually uttered the following words:

> Rich or great, Eritrea will never become; it may, indeed, disappear as a political unit completely from the map. But few who have lived and worked there will view it otherwise than with sympathy, or fail to wish its people well.[3]

Indeed, Eritrea has had close brushes with frightening fate since Longrigg penned these words.

Nevertheless, Eritrea is still on the map. And Longrigg was not the only non-Eritrean to express his appreciation of the *people* of this land. Eritrea may indeed not become rich, to go back to Longrigg's words. Nevertheless, the way things are, it may not, it just may not, remain stuck in poverty!

Am I encouraging flight from reality?

I can imagine my reader asking:

> Why these backward glances and attempts at flimsy assurances? Why dwell on the past when we have enough pains and puzzles in the present? Are you trying to disarm and pacify angry Eritreans who know the sources of the present day sufferings of their families, friends and religious institutions? Shouldn't you rather join in the loud and irresistible chorus of critics, instead of preaching gratitude for dangers averted in the past?

Friend, believe me, I am not trying to silence you. I don't want to silence anyone who feels led, by an honest and enlightened conscience, to speak and act on matters that have to do with Eritrea. Love of one's people can't mean avoiding questions and challenges. One doesn't have to be malicious or treasonous to say so. My point in narrating the anecdotes recorded above is to remind us that a backward glance at the history of a people can awaken a sense of gratitude and provide us with a sense of proportion in the tackling of problems. The past can be a teacher and stabilizer for those who are willing to listen and take counsel.

Reexamining one's convictions is a rare virtue. A lot of the reasoning in the recent flood of articles on Eritrean websites has been urging us to do so. But surely a surgeon's knife should tackle sick tissue, and not cut indiscriminately into organs, veins, and arteries in a body. After all, the story of the body is far older than the stories of the sicknesses that attack it. The body has, in fact, age-old ways of healing itself. And people, communities are like living bodies. Who is to say that they don't have historical, cultural, religious resources that can be used to heal the ailments of nations?

Outraged crusaders, many with absolutely honourable causes, run the risk of causing collateral (related) damage to objects that should be left in peace. Our tendencies to praise and take to task can take on epidemic proportions. Surely, all of us know that rumours have wings. We should watch out for the subtle temptation of pouring contempt on Eritrea's history and people while attacking issues which we regard as evil. Again, this is not to question or reject criticism based on solid facts. And we have been confronted by some highly disturbing questions in the way things have been conducted in high places in Eritrea in recent days!

Can One Speak of a Mystery of Survival?

There is, in my opinion, a remarkable element of what I would call the "Nevertheless," the "In spite of" in Eritrea's past. A "mystery" of survival when all seems to be lost! Am I preaching superstition? No! I am calling to mind what our forefathers used to call "counting one's blessings"—recalling favours and letups in one's past with gratitude. I am thinking of rare times of *rahwa* (ራሁዋ), breathing space, in Eritrea's past! This doesn't mean that Eritrea is always going to be granted ways of escape from its tight spots. The wise learn or should learn from their woes, errors, and slips. Every emergence from a crisis implies, or should imply, a going forward with one more warning, one more summons to watchfulness and radical change, and one less chance. That is life's hard reality. We can't squander our chances and opportunities with impunity.

"Luck" is not always as unpredictable as we may think. No wonder Arnold Palmer, a golf professional of world fame, once said, "The more I practice, the luckier I get."[4] Survival takes work, on all levels of life, and all the time—work that means, first and foremost, self-examination and a sober picture of oneself and one's surroundings![5]

Having said so, I want to affirm once again that I feel that Eritrea's happy circumstances in the past, those events in her history that border on the unexplainable, can also serve its people as sources of hope, wisdom, and inspiration. The Tamils of LTTE and the Rwandans were not as fortunate.

Not all of our forebears were saints, regardless of how fervently we may lift up their names and exploits. Not all were kind and just. Not all were always courageous. Not all were always loyal. Not all were always happy. But they have all left us a heritage, villages and towns, languages, faiths, cultures, and customs to which we can come and where we have the right to be, whether other Eritreans like our presence or not. Let us face the fact that Eritrea will continue to be a country of both "wheat and tares," to use a biblical analogy. Virtues and vices will alternate in its life in high and low places. We need neither glorify nor demonize Eritrea.

Who can deny that Eritrea's journey towards independence, with all its dark aspects, was the fruit of the efforts of all Eritreans, the children, grandchildren, and great grandchildren of witnesses of old? All are a part of the "Nevertheless" of Eritrea's history, of the "In spite of" of its dark moments. This is the sort of thing that our parents and grandparents would have said about Eritrea. Let us not allow bitterness, disappointment, and a sense of having been betrayed alienate us from home and hearth. Act we must, if and when we have to. But despair, hatred and pessimism haven't helped anyone, anywhere. They only darken heart and mind. Only the creative mind and tender heart can bring about healing, even though solid change always takes time. May God grant wisdom, love, faith, and hope!

(Note: This article is dedicated to Naigzy Gebremedhin, both brother and friend, a man with a heart for Eritrea and a friend of all, on the occasion of his 75th birthday, on August 11, 2009.)

May 2010
Ezra Gebremedhin

Notes

1. What Zekre Lebona writes under the title *Revisiting the Orthodoxy "Against All Odds"* on asmarino.com on Thursday, 23 July 2009 is illustrative of this truth. "Encircled from all sides, they and some of their forcibly taken civilians were cornered in a small sliver of lagoon for several months. What makes their defeat unique, however, was not the cause they espoused, but among many reasons the circumstances of their guerrilla war in the small island nation, which denied them any sort of haven or a chance to retreat and fight another day or *starategikawi mezelak* (strategic retreat) as the EPLF loves to call it. Nature was so generous to some, like the Chinese communists in the Long March. Mao at one time bragged about it." One can add, "Nature was also generous to Eritreans".

2. Professor Peter Schalk has written several scholarly articles on the LTTE. In the Swedish collection of essays entitled *Riter och ritteorier? Religionshistoriska diskussioner och teoretiska ansatser* (Rites and Theories of Rites. Discussions Related to History of Religion and Attempts at Theoretical Points of Departure), Peter Schalk has an article entitled: "Konsten att dö. Om den ritualiserade fridöden bland ilavar på ön Ilam" (The Art of Dying. On Ritualized Voluntary Death among the Ilavs on the Island of Eelam), pp. 157–215, edited by Michael Stausberg, Olof Sundqvist and Anna Lydia Svalastog and published by Nya Doxa 2002, Nora, Sweden.

3. S. Longrigg, in Preface to *A Short History of Eritrea* (Oxford, UK: Clarendon

Press, 1945).

4   Quoted from Michael Dennis Browne's article, "10 Truths about Writing (and One Untruth)" p. 9, in the periodical entitled *Bearings for the Life of Faith* (Winter/Spring) 2009.

5   Professor Tekeste Negash, who had read this chapter, wrote: "You have a chapter called "Eritrea Nevertheless". Countries come and go but people remain. A country is where a person can live in peace. A country that does not ensure and guarantee the rights of people to live their lives is no country to die for and I think that is why hundreds of thousands of people have left Eritrea and never to return! Sadly enough! I suggest that you reflect a little bit more on the title." I am not unaware of his concerns and I hope readers realize that I am not writing about Eritrea as a fairyland of justice and fair play! But there is something to the title: "Eritrea's Nevertheless"!

Year 2020
Epilogue

I have come to the end of my book, to the tying up of my reflections on Eritrea, Ethiopia and Sweden. I am writing these words in Uppsala, Sweden, late on the evening of April 4, 2020. Our world is in the grip of a pandemic called COVID-19, the ravages of an invisible invader by the name of Corona Virus. This modern-day pest is spreading like wildfire, without visible flames. The powerful feel powerless. The wise are scratching their heads in puzzlement. The rich see their businesses crumbling, their wallets "leaking." Fear and uncertainty are in the air. Death has become an everyday reality.

የኅዳር ፡ በሽታ — My mind went back to the beginning of this book, yes to the cover-photo with my mother, Aster Woldemariam, and her friend Sema'itu Awalom, taken in Asmara in 1922. What would they say if they were among us today? At least my mother, who associated closely with well-informed Swedish missionaries, would presumably say something like the following:

> The pandemic through which you are going now is no stranger to us. Sema'itu and I went through it all, almost exactly one hundred years ago. It was then that a forerunner of the pest which has hit you now, and which had the name *The Spanish Flu* [known as *Yehidar Beshita* – The November Sickness in Ethiopi]hit not only Europe and Asia but also poor Africa. Yes, also poor Eritrea and Ethiopia! The 1918 influenza pandemic lasted from January 1918 to December 1920. It is believed to have infected about 500 million people around the world. Probably close to 100 million people died from the flu.

Let one of the female Swedish mentors of my mother, Rosa Holmer, tell us about what my mother went through in connection with the pandemic known as The Spanish Flu. Here are Rosa's words, taken from the Swedish periodical, *Budbäraren* (*The Messenger*), the organ of the Swedish Evangelical Mission, in No. 50,1931:

> She [meaning Aster] came to the school at Adi Ugri at the age of twelve, a happy, lively girl who felt at home right away at the home for girls. She involved herself industriously in the domestic duties ....
>
> After some time we went home [to Sweden] to rest. ... When we came back to Africa and were stationed in Asmara for a certain period, Aster came to us and offered to help me. A severe nerve-fever swept across the country and the epidemic spread in Asmara and its surroundings. Many were snatched away by death and children were left helpless in the empty homes. The sick people lay there, alone and dying, while fear of infection paralyzed relatives. Bodies lay on Asmara's square, unattended, until the stench of death forced people to bury them.
>
> A rich Muslim donated shrouds (sheets for burial) for the many poor who died and were buried daily. During this period, Aster was an extraordinary source of help: good, strong and faithful. We went out daily to the sick, from home to home, and helped them as best we could. Whole families lay in their homes, sick and out of their senses, due to the depth of their misery. Everywhere there was need and death. Finally Aster too fell ill but recovered after some weeks. How grateful we were to God! We had gathered a great number of orphans and Aster helped them selflessly and with tenderness. ...

My mother, and surely her friend Sema'itu, were involved in a selfless fight against a pandemic in Eritrea already a hundred years ago. And they would add: "Your pandemic too will pass!"

In this sense too, this book is a call to mutual concern, to selfless service, to harmony among men and women around us, in Sweden, in Ethiopia, and in Eritrea, the countries to which this book is dedicated.